The Wealth of Nations
REPRESENTATIVE SELECTIONS

Adam Smith

Edited, with an Introduction, by
Bruce Mazlish

DOVER PUBLICATIONS, INC.
Mineola, New York

Bibliographical Note

The Wealth of Nations: Representative Selections, first published in 2002, is an unabridged republication of the work originally published in 1961 by The Bobbs-Merrill Company, Inc., New York. It comprises an abridgment of the fourth edition, which was, in turn, a reprint of the third—the last one that Smith himself edited. (For further bibliographical details, see page xxv herein.) The original work was first published in 1776 under the title *An Inquiry into the Nature and Causes of The Wealth of Nations.*

Library of Congress Cataloging-in-Publication Data

Smith, Adam, 1723–1790.
    [Inquiry into the nature and causes of the wealth of nations. Selections]
    The wealth of nations : representative selections / Adam Smith ; edited, with an introduction by Bruce Mazlish.
       p. cm.
    Originally published: An inquiry into the nature and causes of the wealth of nations. New York : Bobbs-Merrill, 1961.
    Includes bibliographical references and index.
    ISBN 0-486-42513-4 (pbk.)
    1. Economics. I. Mazlish, Bruce, 1923– II. Title.

HB161 .S6522 2002
330'.01—dc21

                                                         2002031334

Manufactured in the United States of America
Dover Publications, Inc., 31 East 2nd Street, Mineola, N.Y. 11501

CONTENTS
· · · · · · · · · · · · · · · ·

THE WEALTH OF NATIONS

BOOK ONE

OF THE CAUSES OF IMPROVEMENT IN THE PRODUCTIVE POWERS OF LABOR, AND OF THE ORDER ACCORDING TO WHICH ITS PRODUCE IS NATURALLY DISTRIB-UTED AMONG THE DIFFERENT RANKS OF PEOPLE

BOOK TWO

OF THE NATURE, ACCUMULATION, AND EMPLOYMENT OF STOCK

BOOK THREE

OF THE DIFFERENT PROGRESS OF OPULENCE IN DIFFERENT NATIONS

BOOK FOUR

OF SYSTEMS OF POLITICAL ECONOMY

BOOK FIVE

OF THE REVENUE OF THE SOVEREIGN OR COMMONWEALTH

EDITOR'S INTRODUCTION

On the eve of the American Revolution, to be precise, on the ninth of March, 1776, a revolution occurred in the realm of thought: economics emerged as a science. The cause of the revolution was the publication of Adam Smith's *The Wealth of Nations*. Of this work, one eminent contemporary economist has aptly remarked that it is "the most successful, not only of all books on economics, but, with the possible exception of Darwin's *Origin of Species*, of all scientific books that have appeared to this day." [1]

The claims of the *Wealth of Nations* on our interest, however, are broader even than those of a great scientific work on economics, though that has been its main fame. Smith was a philosopher before he was an economist (indeed, as we shall show, he became an economist because he was a philosopher), and his work is a philosophic, as well as a scientific, treatise. As such, it belongs as much to the general study of ideas as it does to the history of economics, and it is at least as important for students of humanities as it is for students of economics.

It is this belief which has guided the selection presented here from the complete text of the *Wealth of Nations*. While, it is hoped, adequate material has been taken from the economic parts of Smith's work, the emphasis has been on choosing materials which would illustrate the larger aspects of the Scottish thinker: a historian, a sociologist, and a moralist; a theorist on imperialism; a practical advisor to governments—in the broadest sense, a brilliant political scientist and philosopher of history.

The man for whom these rather awesome claims are made was overtly a simple man who led an outwardly uneventful life. Smith was born in the little town of Kirkcaldy, Scotland,

[1] Joseph Schumpeter, *History of Economic Analysis* (Oxford, 1954), p. 181.

in 1723. His father, who died a few months before the child was delivered, held the Controllership of Customs at Kirkcaldy; his mother was the daughter of a local proprietor. Thus, Smith's immediate social background was the Scottish civil service—respectable but modest, related to business activity but from an aloof, critical situation.

Smith, who took his early schooling in his home town, was a delicate child, given even then to the periods of absent-mindedness which characterized his later life. At the age of fourteen, he was sent to the University of Glasgow, where he showed himself especially fond of mathematics. At Glasgow, he also came under the influence of Francis Hutcheson, Professor of Moral Philosophy, to whose chair he was to succeed. Going on to Oxford, at the age of seventeen, Smith studied mainly literature: Greek, Latin, Italian, French, and English. Although he stayed there for six years, he did not take religious orders, as his mother had hoped, and he did not approve of the education offered him, as he amply showed in his chapter on education in the *Wealth of Nations*.

Returning to Edinburgh, after a short period of erratic employment, Smith gave lectures on English literature and, in 1750-51, a series of lectures on political economics. Appointed in 1751 to the Professorship of Logic at Glasgow, his old university, Smith unexpectedly also was called upon to substitute for the Professor of Moral Philosophy. This post he took over permanently the next year. The Chair of Logic, which he now relinquished, had included rhetoric and belles-lettres; his new chair in Moral Philosophy embraced ethics, natural theology, jurisprudence, and politics; and it was under the latter two rubrics that Smith, following the example of his former teacher, Hutcheson, delivered his material on political economics. As John Millar, one of Smith's students, tells us, "In the last of his lectures he examined those political regulations which are founded, not upon the principle of 'justice' but that of 'expediency,' and which are calculated to increase the riches, the power, and the property of a state . . . . " [2]

2 John Rae, *Life of Adam Smith* (London, 1895), p. 55.

Smith remained a Professor of Philosophy at Glasgow until 1764; during all his early productive life, therefore, he was an academician—a professional intellectual. His interests were wide, and he dabbled in belles-lettres as well as in a grandiose plan of writing a "history of the liberal sciences and elegant arts." For example, Smith reviewed Dr. Johnson's *Dictionary* and Rousseau's *Discourse on the Origin and Foundation of the Inequality of Mankind* for the *Edinburgh Review*, and he wrote six essays of his planned "History," which were printed posthumously as *Essays on Philosophical Subjects by the late Adam Smith . . .* (1st ed. 1795).

The work which brought him his initial fame, however, was one involving his own academic specialty: moral philosophy. *The Theory of Moral Sentiments*—to which, incidentally, he appended a *Discourse on the Origin of Languages* in the third edition—was published in 1759, and its reading amply demonstrates that Smith was aware constantly of the ethical, as well as economic, nature of man; indeed, it seems evident that in writing the *Wealth of Nations* Smith assumed on the part of his reader an acquaintance with the earlier work.

More and more, however, Smith's interests turned—it seems partly due to the stimulus of his friend, David Hume, who was engaged in speculations on economic subjects—to an exposition of the principles underlying the aspect of man's life which was based on "expediency" rather than on "justice." By 1763, his students were taking notes on material that was later published (although not until 1896) under the title, *Lectures on Justice, Police, Revenue and Arms*. And just before retiring from his professorship in 1764, Smith appears to have composed an early draft of the *Wealth of Nations* (called a *Treatise on Public Opulence*). In these tentative efforts, he already employed as important elements in his thought such concepts as self-interest, free trade, and the division of labor.

The systematic and comprehensive aspect of his work, however, owed much to his trip to the Continent in 1764. In that year he accepted the offer to go abroad as a private tutor for the Duke of Buccleuch. After resigning his professorship at

Glasgow, Smith traveled with his pupil from 1764-1766 on the Continent, mostly in France. Here, Smith met the luminaries of the Enlightenment—men like Voltaire, D'Alembert, Holbach, Helvétius—and mixed in conversation with the founders of a new school of economics—the Physiocrats, men like Quesnay, Mirabeau (the elder), and Turgot (who, although not a member of the school, was affiliated with it). Here, too, he began to compose his full-scale *Inquiry into the Nature and Causes of the Wealth of Nations.*

Upon his return to Scotland, Smith retired to his home in Kirkcaldy, where he lived with his mother, the only woman who appears to have been important in his life. Financially secure—the reward for his tutorship had been a salary of £300 a year as well as an annual pension for life of the same amount—Smith worked in semiseclusion for the next ten years, completing his work on economics. The *Wealth of Nations* appeared in 1776, in the midst of the gathering clouds over the American colonies. It was a great success, partly because of its economics and partly because of its comments on the international scene.

After the publication of the *Wealth of Nations,* Smith seems to have dallied with the notion of writing a major work on jurisprudence, which would place his economic efforts in a more general moral and philosophic system. In all probability, however, he realized that he had already done this, though in a somewhat haphazard manner, in the great book of 1776. In any case, in 1778, he accepted the post of Commissioner of Customs in Kirkcaldy at £600 a year and occupied himself with that and with a circle of friends in Edinburgh, which included Black, the chemist, and Hutton, the geologist. Every now and then, he would edit a new version of the *Wealth of Nations* (he added to it substantially in the third edition, 1784). At his death on July 17, 1790, he had sixteen volumes of unpublished manuscripts burned before his own eyes. Posterity already had in the *Wealth of Nations* the valuable part of his work: a science of economics, a treatise on political science, and a philosophy of history.

From the details of Smith's life emerge a number of key facts—or problems:

1. Smith was not a member of the business class nor a member of the ruling English political strata; he was an academician and then a civil servant, a Scotsman who saw the inefficiency of the English bureaucracy and the corruption of the politicians.

2. His work was rooted in the atmosphere of the Scottish Enlightenment, i.e., in the natural-law philosophy of the schools and the moral tradition of Hutcheson, first imbibed by Smith at Glasgow.[3] Indeed, Smith's thought was permeated with the images and ideas of the so-called age of enlightenment, to which he himself contributed so importantly, and his feelings about society, state, and church were colored by the same currents of opinion which affected such contemporaries as Hume, Gibbon, and Voltaire.

3. Smith gradually turned from morality per se to that part of it which is based on the ethics of expediency rather than on beneficence; most of his work was done before he went to France, but the influence of the Physiocrats helped, especially in specific points such as bringing to his attention the concept of the production and distribution of wealth as an *annual* affair, and, in general, by causing him to look for broad, rational principles underlying the mere appearances of economic phenomena.

4. He always conceived his work in economics as being part of a larger concern with society and its historical progress. The rational principles underlying the "science" of economics were not reached by deduction from an a priori system but were deposited by the stream of history; as early as 1751, Smith was dealing with economics as "the slow progress of opulence." It is a synthesis, therefore, of economic principles in the broad framework of a philosophy of history that Smith attempts to present us in the *Wealth of Nations*.

---

[3] See Gladys Bryson, *Man and Society: The Scottish Inquiry of the Eighteenth Century* (Princeton, 1945).

It would be audacious in this Introduction to attempt a large-scale interpretation of Smith's work. Our only purpose here is to provide an *introduction* to the work, to indicate important areas for attention and to sketch some of the main themes present in the *Wealth of Nations,* in order that the reader may better pursue his own inquiry into the thought of Adam Smith.[4] We can accomplish this best, perhaps, by looking at Smith in the various roles he assumed. We shall consider these roles separately, but we must remember that in Smith they were never disjointed but part of one synthesizing personality.

Smith as Economist

Smith's reputation has been primarily that of an economist. His economic thought, like that of all thinkers—revolutionary or otherwise—was built on the labor of others, and his new comprehensive "science" of economics was largely a synthesis of two elements: (1) "political arithmetic," which dealt with such practical problems as credit, banking, and balance of trade; and (2) rationalistic systems based on natural law, such as Physiocracy.

The first—political arithmetic—was the work of men like Sir William Petty, and involved a good deal of valuable research in statistics. The second—Physiocracy (i.e., government by nature) —involved an attempt at a systematic analysis of wealth and its "circulation" in society; of it, Smith said, "This system . . . with all its imperfections is, perhaps, the nearest approximation to the truth that has yet been published upon the subject of political economy." [5]

[4] Cf. J. Bronowski and Bruce Mazlish, *The Western Intellectual Tradition* (New York, 1960), Chap. 19, "Adam Smith."

[5] On "political arithmetic" see any good treatment of the history of economic theory, such as Gide and Rist's *History of Economic Doctrines* (Boston, n.d.), or Erich Roll's *History of Economic Thought* (New York, 1940). On the Physiocrats, see Georges Weulersse, *Le mouvement physiocratique en France,* 2 vols. (Paris, 1910), as well as his *Les Physiocrats* (Paris, 1931); and, in English, Henry Higgs, *Physiocrats* (London, 1897).

As part of his synthesis of political arithmetic and Physiocracy, of course, Smith has to his credit many specific contributions to economic theory. They are, however, at once too many to enumerate and too much the province of specialists in the subject for the general reader to trespass upon them with security; nevertheless, they should be regarded, even if distantly. Most of this material—on the price of commodities, wages of labor, profits of stock, rent of land, etc.—appears in Books One and Two, and makes up what is frequently—though perhaps unfortunately—called "Smith's system." There are, however, three elements of this part of Smith's work which must be carefully remarked upon, even by the general student: (1) the labor theory of value; (2) the division of labor; and (3) the general doctrine of laissez faire, which involves, economically, the free circulation of commodities, and, politically, noninterference by government.

1. The opening words of the *Wealth of Nations* talk about "the annual labor of every nation," and Smith contends that it is the produce of this labor which constitutes a nation's opulence. By espousing this view, Smith set himself against the prevalent notion, advanced by the mercantilist thinkers of his time, that the wealth of a nation consists in the amount of money which it possesses.[6] Although he reserved the full exposure of the mercantilist fallacy—of what he called this "popular notion"—to Book Four, Smith stated his own positive assumptions about labor clearly in the very beginning of his work. Thus, he did not have to devote too much of his attention to a discussion of the balance of trade and of the best way of obtaining supplies of bullion; instead, he could apply his energies to an analysis of the improvements possible in the productive powers of labor as well as of the consequences which flow from this improvement. Therefore, in place of a relatively static supply of wealth merely being exchanged by trade, Smith thought in terms of an increasing opulence—

[6] For an overall treatment of Mercantilism, see the stimulating work by Eli Heckscher, *Mercantilism*, tr. by Mendel Schapiro, 2 vols. (London, 1935).

increasing because of changes in labor output—circulating throughout society.

2. Having set forth the view that a nation's real wealth resides in its labor, Smith next takes up the question of what constitutes and contributes to a nation's supply of labor. In his view, the main factor to which the improvement of the productive powers of mankind must be attributed is the division of labor. The famous example he offers as proof is the pin industry; and he gives a wonderful *analysis* (in an almost Cartesian sense) of its operations based on the division of labor.

With the advent of division of labor, Smith declares, there is an end to man's self-sufficiency. The logical result is the introduction of barter, as a necessary institution. Fortunately, the institution of barter is rooted in a "propensity" of human nature. Barter, however, raises problems of exchange, and Smith leads us through discussions of the means of exchange—money—and of the real and nominal prices of commodities.

It is at this point that he returns to his emphasis on labor per se, and introduces the famous labor theory of value. His reasoning is as follows. The nominal price of a commodity is its money price. Its real price, however, is its price in labor. (And here we must bypass the whole discussion of why Smith insists on a "real" price; he is, after all, a contemporary of the same Enlightenment which produced Immanuel Kant and his *Ding an sich*.) Now, at this important junction, Smith wavers between two views: Is real price equal to the labor necessary to produce the article or is it equal to the labor which the article can exchange for? A Picasso painting might take eighty hours to produce but purchase eight-thousand hours of other men's work. Needless to say, Smith was not naïve about such factors as scarcity, talent, and so forth which entered into price, but his unfortunate looseness of phrase and his ambiguity in the matter persisted and plagued the thought of many later economists, especially Karl Marx.

One other problem—this, of a semiphilosophical nature—

emerged from Smith's work on labor and price. Was man, too, to be treated as a commodity with a price attached? Is labor primarily an activity or a commodity? As an economist, Smith was able to say, "It is in this manner that the demand for men, *like that for any other commodity* [my italics], necessarily regulates the production of men . . . ." As a philosopher, he lamented the condition of man—the commodity—and admitted the deplorable fact that in the progress of division of labor, the worker "generally becomes as stupid and ignorant as it is possible for a human creature to become." Obviously, there is ample material in Smith for a discussion of the nature of man in a commercial society.

3. Smith forced himself to accept the "necessary" ancillary conditions of economic progress. He allowed himself to believe that the improvement of the worker's standard of living compensated for the degradation of his character; and he accepted the fact that "expediency," rather than benevolence, reigned supreme in the economic world. He had already done this in his *Theory of Moral Sentiments,* where he said:

> Regard to our own private happiness and interest, too, appear upon many occasions very laudable principles of action. The habits of economy, industry, discretion, attention, and application of thought, are generally supposed to be cultivated from self-interested motives, and at the same time are apprehended to be very praiseworthy qualities which deserve the esteem and approbation of everybody;

and he reiterated his acceptance in the very famous phrase of the *Wealth of Nations:*

> It is not from the benevolence of the butcher, the brewer or the baker that we expect our dinner, but from their regard of their own interest. We address ourselves not to their humanity, but to their self-love, and never talk to them of our necessities, but of their advantage.

From this appeal to individual personal advantage, Smith moved almost imperceptibly to his doctrine of laissez faire. In answer to the question as to whether the individual's self-love should be given free rein, Smith shows how a policy of free circulation of commodities, fostered by a government "hands-off" approach, leads to the greatest benefit of the greatest number.[7] Laissez faire works because of the "law" of supply and demand, which automatically regulates the economic life of society when it is not interfered with by the bungling extension of government power—an extension constantly advocated by the Mercantilists. The reason it works—and here, in part, the Physiocratic influence on Smith shows itself—is because nature—the structure of things—has authorized this "law." Close examination of this part of Smith's theory will show that it is an impressive piece of analysis mixed with metaphysical assumptions.

Smith as Philosopher and Philosopher of History

At the point mentioned above, the moral philosopher in Smith joined hands with the economist. The individual's self-love had to be shown, not only as economically justified, but as truly being, on a higher level, moral and selfless. Expediency had to be made into benevolence: and a new theodicy given to the world by economics. Smith could do this because he held an overwhelming faith in Providence, that "great Conductor of the universe." It was the Deist in Smith which could effect the famous justification of free, self-interested activity, and lead him to say: "He [the self-interested individual] intends only his own gain, and he is in this, as in many other cases, led by an invisible hand to promote an end which was no part of his original intention" (p. 166). Thus, the gentle,

---

[7] Smith was not opposed to any and all governmental intervention; indeed, government was to provide the necessary juridical controls—the boundary conditions—within which free enterprise might safely exist. In fact, Smith went beyond even this proviso and accepted the British navigation acts, increased governmental regulation of the East India Company, and other seeming violations of his general theory of laissez faire. On this important point—a notorious cliché about Smith and the Classical Economists—cf. Lionel Robbins, *The Theory of Economic Policy in English Classical Political Economy* (London, 1952).

self-effacing, selfless Adam Smith transmuted what had traditionally been regarded as evil into good.[8]

In the course of this transmutation, Smith also metamorphosed himself from a moral philosopher into a philosopher of history. His theory of the "invisible hand" anticipated in some ways the development by Hegel of the notion of Spirit realizing itself in history, and the thought of Karl Marx.[9] Indeed, I should like to suggest here that Smith reached, although only gropingly and without using the technical term, the notion of the "dialectic," and, what is more, the dialectic working itself out in economic terms. He came to this notion because he was interested in the "progress toward opulence." And, in the "progress toward opulence," he discerned an "invisible hand" which led men to promote an end they had not intended. It is the magnificently prophetic, but neglected, Book Three which contains Smith's theory.[10] In this Book, for example, he explains the dialectic transition from feudalism to capitalism, and concludes that:

> A revolution of the greatest importance to the public happiness was in this manner brought about by two different orders of people who had not the least intention to serve the public. To gratify the most childish vanity was the sole motive of the great proprietors. The merchants and artificers, much less ridiculous, acted merely from a view to their own interest, and in pursuit of their own peddler principle of turning a penny wherever a penny was to be got. Neither of them had either knowledge or foresight of that great revolution which the folly of the one, and the industry of the other, was gradually bringing about. (See pp. 152-53.)

[8] A predecessor, in this part of Smith's work, was Bernard de Mandeville, who, in his *Fable of the Bees,* talked of "Private Vices Made Public Benefits." On the general shift of moral and economic values, see R. H. Tawney, *Religion and the Rise of Capitalism* (New York, 1947).

[9] Cf. Robert C. Tucker, "The Cunning of Reason in Hegel and Marx," *The Review of Politics* (July, 1956).

[10] Schumpeter, *op. cit.,* p. 187, remarks: "This Third Book did not attract the attention it seems to merit. In its somewhat dry and uninspired wisdom, it might have made an excellent starting point of a historical sociology of economic life that was never written."

Later on, in Book Five, Smith set forth a theory as to the past stages of society. He singles out the "first period of society, that of hunters," and the "second period of society, that of shepherds," which precede the later periods of agriculture and commerce, and gives a fairly extensive disquisition on the necessary institutions and arrangements of these periods. Throughout, his eye is always on the historical aspect. Like his fellow thinkers of the Enlightenment, Turgot and Condorcet, Smith was interested in the changing nature of society, and in the order and "laws" by which change takes place. Thus, in his treatment of economics, Smith is aware of "stages of development" (indeed, it is this which makes him today so relevant to discussions about underdeveloped countries and stages of economic and social growth, about "progress toward opulence").

Smith, however, was not a mere "theorist" of history equipped with a priori assumptions and no empirical data. He was solidly grounded in the historical knowledge of his time and prepared to use that knowledge directly in all his work. It is true that Smith did not, like his friend Hume, who wrote an imposing *History of England*, construct a full-scale historical work; perhaps he did not because he used the materials for a *philosophy* of history. He did, however, sketch, for example, a history of astronomy; and he filled the *Wealth of Nations* with historical interludes. To indicate the subjects he covered: he traced the historical origin of freedom, the history of Rome, the origin of city independence, the rise of the third estate, and the changes in war and militias. He investigated the origin of money and gave an extensive disquisition on the history of price movements; and he devoted a long chapter to the history of colonies (which has special pertinence to our time of colonial revolts).

The important thing to remark about all this, however, is not so much the particular historical subjects which Smith treated; it is rather to notice, and to stress, the fact that he brought to all his work a *historical attitude*. What constantly concerned him was the historical dimension, the factor of change. And it is this which, coupled with an attempt to explain what happened in man's social past and why, is the distinguishing mark of the historically minded thinker.

Smith as Sociologist and Political Scientist

The dividing line is thin between Smith the historian and philosopher of history and Smith the sociologist and political scientist. For example, in his interpretation of history, progress toward opulence is accompanied by change in the socio-political structure. Thus, Smith states that "civil government supposes a certain subordination. But as the necessity of civil government gradually grows up with the acquisition of valuable property, so the principal causes which naturally introduce subordination gradually grow up with the growth of that valuable property."

Throughout, Smith's thought is permeated with images of rank, class, place, power, and with all these in a complex interrelationship. In the *Theory*, he has a chapter, "The Origin of Ambition and of the Distinction of Rank"; in the *Wealth*, the description of Book One talks of "The Different Ranks of the People." His section on the "Expense of Justice" is really an analysis of "subordination" and "superiority" as the forces holding civil society together. Already, in the *Theory*, he had declared that "Upon this disposition of mankind to go along with all the passions of the rich and the powerful is grounded the distinction of ranks and the order of society"; in his analysis of the causes of the American Revolution in the *Wealth of Nations*, he added that "Upon the power which the greater part of the leading men, the natural aristocracy of every country, have of preserving or defending their respective importance, depends the stability and duration of every system of free government. . . . The leading men of America, like those of all other countries, desire to preserve their own importance."

Aware as he was of the competition for place and power, of rank and class, Smith did not fall into the error of seeing history as the history of class struggle. He was too much alive to the individual and his role. It is true that, while avoiding the Physiocratic division into barren and productive labor, he talked of a division into "Productive and Unproductive Labor"; [11] but he meant this as a matter purely of economic analysis, and not of social exploitation. Instead of class conflict, therefore, Smith emphasized class co-operation, and his entire work on division of labor and the "invisible hand" assumed an ultimate balance and coincidence of interests.

Nevertheless, Smith's keen sense of realism made him aware of the immediate fact that men *did* conflict and compete with each other. What he wanted, therefore, was free competition, not the elimination of competition, and he wanted this because apparent disharmony meant eventual real harmony. This was true in the political as well as the economic sphere, and Smith took the liberal position that free conflict of ideas and interests made for the good of the commonwealth. He was not blind to the iniquities of corrupt politicians, and he had extremely harsh words for the merchants and manufacturers who threatened the general good by their monopolistic tendencies, but he believed the corrective to these conditions was enlightenment as to the real interests of *all* parties in the state. It was this enlightenment which he intended his *Wealth of Nations* to offer.

Smith as Policy Advisor

In his innermost thought, Smith considered political economy "as a branch of the science of a statesman or legislator." For this reason his philosophy of history and his sociology, rooted though they were in economics, never became a deterministic economic interpretation of history and society. Economic possibilities, he believed, are controlled by laws and institutions; and these, after all, are the work of men (and it is here that Smith's sociology comes into fullest play). Thus, he could say of China that it had "long ago acquired that full

11 Cf. Book Two, Chap. III, p. 111.

complement of riches which is consistent with the nature of its laws and institutions. But this complement may be much inferior to what, with other laws and institutions, the nature of its soil, climate, and situation might admit of."

Now we can see the real importance of Smith's work. He wished, through his achievement in political economy—his inquiry into the nature and causes of the wealth of nations—to enlighten men so that they might create better laws and institutions. In this, he may have shared the naïve optimism of his period. But it was a noble aspiration and expressed a rather lofty faith in man's power to control the blind forces of the material world.

Smith's belief that he could affect opinion did have, even in his own time, strong practical consequences. He was the "brain-truster" of the English movement toward more intelligent fiscal policy and toward greater free trade. Thus, in the budget of 1777, Lord North is reputed to have imposed two new taxes based on an idea from the *Wealth of Nations;* and in a Parliamentary debate of 1792, William Pitt alluded to the constant tendency of capital to increase "whenever it is not obstructed by some public calamity, or by some mistaken or mischievous policy," and went on to eulogize "an author of our time, now, unfortunately, no more (I mean the author of a celebrated treatise on the wealth of nations), whose extensive knowledge of detail and philosophical research will, I believe, furnish the best solution to every question concerned with the history of commerce or with the system of political economy." [12]

So, too, Smith's views on the colonies, although initially ignored, were proved right by the events of the American Revolution and became eventually an important element in British colonial policy. What he had to say on the East India Company was heeded. His comments on war and the financial basis of military operations had their effect. Matters of public finance, of tariffs and bounties, all felt the impress of the quiet

[12] Quoted in R. B. Haldane, *Life of Adam Smith* (London, 1887), pp. 74-75.

Scotsman's mind. In England, he corresponded directly with those in power: Pitt, Lord Shelburne, Sir John Sinclair, William Eden. In other countries, he reached the ear of statesmen and legislators through the translation of his great work. By the turn of the century, in addition to nine English editions in Britain and others in Ireland and the United States, there were Danish, Dutch, French, German, Italian and Spanish editions of his work, as well as a Russian edition by 1802-06.[13] Smith's title, the *Wealth of Nations,* was accurate in its use of the plural, "nations," for he influenced not only his own country but the world.

Smith's work is fundamentally all of a piece. It is the broad, synoptic view of a polyhistor which Smith offers us. And his book should be treated as such. The way to do this is by taking Smith seriously in all his roles: economist, philosopher, historian, sociologist, political scientist, and advisor to statesmen.

In the course of his work, Smith laid down the lineaments of a science of economics, but he also attempted to sketch the features of a possible philosophy of history and a science of society. His peculiar talent was that he could do specific, specialized work—in economics—at the same time that he was making an attempt to integrate all the important elements of man's life in society into one coherent body of theory. The latter task he left incomplete and in a merely suggestive stage, and, as such, it remains to us, largely as a challenge. The selections from the *Wealth of Nations* offered here are made in the hope of presenting, along with Smith's achievement in economics, the nature of his challenge in the larger field.

BRUCE MAZLISH

[13] Schumpeter, *op. cit.,* p. 193. That Smith's influence was real is supported by his biographer, John Rae, who states, for example, that "Stein shaped his policy on it" (*op. cit.,* p. 360).

NOTE ON THE TEXT

The present text is an abridgment of the fourth edition, which is a reprint of the third, the last one Smith himself edited. The extent of abridgment is indicated in the Table of Contents. In the text, in each case, the omissions are summarized briefly by the present editor.

The editors' footnotes are bracketed to distinguish them from those of Smith. Professor Mazlish has incorporated, abridging where advisable, many of the notes of Edwin Cannan, who was the editor of the 1904 edition, which has, through its elaborate critical apparatus, become the standard edition of this work. The present editor and the publishers wish to express their indebtedness to Cannan's scholarship. The notes of the editors are identified by "C" and "M" respectively.

Spelling has been modernized in accordance with present-day American usage, and Smith's elaborate punctuation has in general been altered only where necessary for clarity.

SELECTED BIBLIOGRAPHY

WORKS BY ADAM SMITH

Essays on Philosophical Subjects. London: 1795.

An Inquiry into the Nature and Causes of the Wealth of Nations. 1st ed. 2 vols. London: 1775–1776.

Lectures on Justice, Police, Revenue and Arms, ed. Edwin Cannan. Oxford: 1896.

The Theory of Moral Sentiments. 1st ed. London: 1759.

Adam Smith's Moral and Political Philosophy, ed. Herbert W. Schneider. New York: 1948.

"A Treatise on Public Opulence" in *Adam Smith as Student and Professor.* Glasgow: 1937.

The Works of Adam Smith, LL. D. 5 vols. London: 1811.

COLLATERAL READING

Adam Smith, 1776–1926. Chicago: 1928. Commemorative lectures.

BONAR, JAMES. *A Catalogue of the Library of Adam Smith.* London: 1894.

BRYSON, GLADYS. *Man and Society: The Scottish Inquiry of the Eighteenth Century.* Princeton: 1945.

CROPSEY, JOSEPH. *Polity and Economy: An Interpretation of the Principles of Adam Smith.* The Hague: 1957.

FARRAR, J. A. *Adam Smith.* London: 1881.

FAY, C. R. *Adam Smith and the Scotland of His Day.* Cambridge: 1956.

FRANKLIN, BURT and CORDASCO, FRANCESCO. *Adam Smith: A Bibliographical Checklist.* New York: 1950.

HALDANE, R. B. *Life of Adam Smith.* London: 1887.

MORROW, GLENN R. *The Ethical and Economic Theories of Adam Smith: A Study in the Social Philosophy of the Eighteenth Century.* New York: 1923.

RAE, JOHN. *Life of Adam Smith.* London: 1895.

ROBBINS, LIONEL. *The Theory of Economic Policy in English Classical Political Economy*. London: 1952.

SALOMON, ALBERT. "Adam Smith as Sociologist," *Social Research*, XII (1945), 22–42.

SCHUMPETER, JOSEPH. *History of Economic Analysis*. New York: 1954.

SCOTT, WILLIAM ROBERT. "Studies Relating to Adam Smith During the Last Fifty Years," ed. Alec L. Macfie, Proceedings of the British Academy, XXVI (1940).

SMALL, ALBION W. *Adam Smith and Modern Sociology*. Chicago: 1907.

An Inquiry
into the Nature and Causes of
The Wealth of Nations

INTRODUCTION AND PLAN
OF THE WORK

The annual [1] labor of every nation is the fund which originally supplies it with all the necessaries and conveniencies of life [2] which it annually consumes, and which consist always either in the immediate produce of that labor, or in what is purchased with that produce from other nations.

According therefore, as this produce, or what is purchased with it, bears a greater or smaller proportion to the number of those who are to consume it, the nation will be better or worse supplied with all the necessaries and conveniencies for which it has occasion.[3]

But this proportion must in every nation be regulated by two different circumstances: first, by the skill, dexterity, and judgment with which its labor is generally applied; and, secondly, by the proportion between the number of those who are employed in useful labor, and that of those who are not so employed.[4] Whatever be the soil, climate, or extent of territory of any particular nation, the abundance or scantiness of

[1] [This word, with "annually" just below, at once marks the transition from the older British economists' ordinary practice of regarding the wealth of a nation as an accumulated fund. Following the physiocrats, Smith sees that the important thing is how much can be produced in a given time.—C.]

[2] [Cp. with this phrase Locke, *Some Considerations of the Consequences of the Lowering of Interest and Raising the Value of Money*, ed. of 1696, p. 66, "the intrinsic natural worth of anything consists in its fitness to supply the necessities or serve the conveniencies of human life."—C.]

[3] [The implication that the nation's welfare is to be reckoned by the average welfare of its members, not by the aggregate, is to be noticed.—C.]

[4] [This second circumstance may be stretched so as to include the duration and intensity of the labor of those who are usefully employed, but another important circumstance, the quantity and quality of the accumulated instruments of production, is altogether omitted.—C.]

its annual supply must, in that particular situation, depend upon those two circumstances.

The abundance or scantiness of this supply, too, seems to depend more upon the former of those two circumstances than upon the latter. Among the savage nations of hunters and fishers, every individual who is able to work is more or less employed in useful labor, and endeavors to provide, as well as he can, the necessaries and conveniencies of life, for himself, or such of his family or tribe as are either too old, or too young, or too infirm to go hunting and fishing. Such nations, however, are so miserably poor that from mere want they are frequently reduced, or at least think themselves reduced, to the necessity sometimes of directly destroying, and sometimes of abandoning, their infants, their old people, and those afflicted with lingering diseases, to perish with hunger, or to be devoured by wild beasts. Among civilized and thriving nations, on the contrary, though a great number of people do not labor at all—many of whom consume the produce of ten times, frequently of a hundred times, more labor than the greater part of those who work—yet the produce of the whole labor of the society is so great that all are often abundantly supplied; and a workman, even of the lowest and poorest order, if he is frugal and industrious, may enjoy a greater share of the necessaries and conveniencies of life than it is possible for any savage to acquire.

The causes [5] of this improvement in the productive powers of labor, and the order according to which its produce is naturally distributed among the different ranks and conditions of men in the society, make the subject of the First Book of this Inquiry.

Whatever be the actual state of the skill, dexterity, and judgment with which labor is applied in any nation, the abundance or scantiness of its annual supply must depend, during the continuance of that state upon the proportion between the number of those who are annually employed in useful labor, and that of those who are not so employed. The num-

[5] [Only one cause, the division of labor, is actually treated.—C.]

ber of useful and productive [6] laborers, it will hereafter appear, is everywhere in proportion to the quantity of capital stock which is employed in setting them to work, and to the particular way in which it is so employed. The Second Book, therefore, treats of the nature of capital stock, of the manner in which it is gradually accumulated, and of the different quantities of labor which it puts into motion, according to the different ways in which it is employed.

Nations tolerably well advanced as to skill, dexterity, and judgment in the application of labor have followed very different plans in the general conduct or direction of it; and those plans have not all been equally favorable to the greatness of its produce. The policy of some nations has given extraordinary encouragement to the industry of the country; that of others to the industry of towns. Scarcely any nation has dealt equally and impartially with every sort of industry. Since the downfall of the Roman Empire, the policy of Europe has been more favorable to arts, manufactures, and commerce—the industry of towns—than to agriculture—the industry of the country. The circumstances which seem to have introduced and established this policy are explained in the Third Book.

Though those different plans were, perhaps, first introduced by the private interests and prejudices of particular orders of men, without any regard to, or foresight of, their consequences upon the general welfare of the society; yet they have given occasion to very different theories of political economy, of which some magnify the importance of that industry which is carried on in towns, others of that which is carried on in the country. Those theories have had a considerable influence, not only upon the opinions of men of learning, but upon the public conduct of princes and sovereign states. I have endeavored, in the Fourth Book, to explain, as fully and distinctly as I can, those different theories, and the principal effects which they have produced in different ages and nations.

---

[6] [This word slips in here as an apparently unimportant synonym of "useful," but subsequently ousts "useful" altogether, and is explained in such a way that unproductive labor may be useful. (See p. 113.)—C.]

To explain in what has consisted the revenue of the great body of the people, or what has been the nature of those funds, which, in different ages and nations, have supplied their annual consumption, is the object of these first four Books. The Fifth and last Book treats of the revenue of the sovereign, or commonwealth. In this Book I have endeavored to show: first, what are the necessary expenses of the sovereign, or commonwealth; which of those expenses ought to be defrayed by the general contribution of the whole society; and which of them by that of some particular part only, or of some particular members of it; secondly, what are the different methods in which the whole society may be made to contribute towards defraying the expenses incumbent on the whole society, and what are the principal advantages and inconveniencies of each of those methods; and, thirdly and lastly, what are the reasons and causes which have induced almost all modern governments to mortgage some part of this revenue, or to contract debts, and what have been the effects of those debts upon the real wealth, the annual produce of the land and labor of the society.[7]

7 [Read in conjunction with the first two paragraphs, this sentence makes it clear that the wealth of a nation is to be reckoned by its *per capita* income. But this view is often temporarily departed from in the course of the work.—C.]

BOOK ONE

OF THE CAUSES OF IMPROVEMENT IN THE
PRODUCTIVE POWERS OF LABOR, AND OF
THE ORDER ACCORDING TO WHICH ITS PRO-
DUCE IS NATURALLY DISTRIBUTED AMONG
THE DIFFERENT RANKS OF THE PEOPLE

CHAPTER I

OF THE DIVISION OF LABOR

The greatest improvement in the productive powers of labor and the greater part of the skill, dexterity, and judgment with which it is anywhere directed or applied seem to have been the effects of the division of labor.

The effects of the division of labor, in the general business of society, will be more easily understood by considering in what manner it operates in some particular manufactures. It is commonly supposed to be carried furthest in some very trifling ones; not perhaps that it really is carried further in them than in others of more importance, but in those trifling manufactures which are destined to supply the small wants of but a small number of people, the whole number of workmen must necessarily be small; and those employed in every different branch of the work can often be collected into the same workhouse, and placed at once under the view of the spectator. In those great manufactures, on the contrary, which are destined to supply the great wants of the great body of the people, every different branch of the work employs so great a number of workmen that it is impossible to collect them all into the same workhouse.[1] We can seldom see more, at one time, than those employed in one single branch. Though in such manufactures, therefore, the work may really be divided into a much greater number of parts than in those of a more trifling nature, the division is not nearly so obvious, and has accordingly been much less observed.

To take an example, therefore, from a very trifling manufacture, but one in which the division of labor has been very

---

[1] [It is quite obvious that Smith did not anticipate the use of large-scale factories for the purpose of mass production.—M.].

often taken notice of, the trade of the pin-maker; a workman not educated to this business (which the division of labor has rendered a distinct trade), nor acquainted with the use of the machinery employed in it (to the invention of which the same division of labor has probably given occasion) could scarcely, perhaps, with his utmost industry, make one pin in a day, and certainly could not make twenty. But in the way in which this business is now carried on, not only the whole work is a peculiar trade, but it is divided into a number of branches, of which the greater part are likewise peculiar trades. One man draws out the wire, another straightens it, a third cuts it, a fourth points it, a fifth grinds it at the top for receiving the head; to make the head requires two or three distinct operations; to put it on is a peculiar business, to whiten the pins is another; it is even a trade by itself to put them into the paper; and the important business of making a pin is, in this manner, divided into about eighteen distinct operations, which in some manufactories are all performed by distinct hands, though in others the same man will sometimes perform two or three of them.[2] I have seen a small manufactory of this kind where ten men only were employed, and where some of them consequently performed two or three distinct operations. But though they were very poor, and therefore but indifferently accommodated with the necessary machinery, they could, when they exerted themselves, make among them about twelve pounds of pins in a day. There are in a pound upwards of four thousand pins of a middling size. Those ten persons, therefore, could make among them upwards of forty-eight thousand pins in a day. Each person, therefore, making a tenth part of forty-eight thousand pins, might be considered as

2 [In Adam Smith's Lectures, p. 164, the business is, as here, divided into eighteen operations. This number is doubtless taken from the Encyclopédie, tom. v. (published in 1755), s.v. Epingle. The article is ascribed to M. Delaire, "qui décrivait la fabrication de l'épingle dans les ateliers même des ouvriers," p. 807. In some factories the division was carried further. E. Chambers, Cyclopædia, vol. ii., 2nd ed., 1738, and 4th ed., 1741, s.v. Pin. makes the number of separate operations twenty-five.--C.]

making four thousand eight hundred pins in a day. But if they had all wrought separately and independently, and without any of them having been educated to this peculiar business, they certainly could not each of them have made twenty, perhaps not one pin in a day; that is, certainly, not the two hundred and fortieth, perhaps not the four thousand eight hundredth, part of what they are at present capable of performing, in consequence of a proper division and combination of their different operations.[3]

In every other art and manufacture,[4] the effects of the division of labor are similar to what they are in this very trifling one; though, in many of them, the labor can neither be so much subdivided, nor reduced to so great a simplicity of operation. The division of labor, however, so far as it can be introduced, occasions, in every art, a proportionable increase of the productive powers of labor. The separation of different trades and employments from one another seems to have taken place in consequence of this advantage. This separation, too, is generally carried furthest in those countries which enjoy the highest degree of industry and improvement; what is the work of one man in a rude state of society being generally that of several in an improved one. In every improved society, the farmer is generally nothing but a farmer; the manufacturer, nothing but a manufacturer. The labor, too, which is necessary to produce any one complete manufacture is almost always divided among a great number of hands. How many different trades are employed in each branch of the linen and woolen manufactures, from the growers of the flax and the wool to the bleachers and smoothers of the linen, or to the dyers and dressers of the cloth! The nature of agriculture, indeed, does

---

[3] [It is interesting to compare Smith's "proper division and combination" with Descartes' rules for correct thinking (especially rule two) in the *Discourse on Method.*—M.]

[4] [The term "art" or "arts" was used frequently in the eighteenth century to refer to technical skills. It was often used in conjunction with the term "manufactures," as in the "Society of Arts and Manufactures," founded in England in 1754.—M.]

not admit of so many subdivisions of labor, nor of so complete a separation of one business from another, as manufactures. It is impossible to separate so entirely the business of the grazier from that of the corn farmer, as the trade of the carpenter is commonly separated from that of the smith. The spinner is almost always a distinct person from the weaver; but the plowman, the harrower, the sower of the seed, and the reaper of the corn are often the same. The occasions for those different sorts of labor returning with the different seasons of the year, it is impossible that one man should be constantly employed in any one of them. This impossibility of making so complete and entire a separation of all the different branches of labor employed in agriculture is perhaps the reason why the improvement of the productive powers of labor in this art does not always keep pace with their improvement in manufactures. The most opulent nations, indeed, generally excel all their neighbors in agriculture as well as in manufactures; but they are commonly more distinguished by their superiority in the latter than in the former. Their lands are, in general, better cultivated, and, having more labor and expense bestowed upon them, produce more in proportion to the extent and natural fertility of the ground. But this superiority of produce is seldom much more than in proportion to the superiority of labor and expense. In agriculture, the labor of the rich country is not always much more productive than that of the poor; or, at least, it is never so much more productive, as it commonly is in manufactures. The corn of the rich country, therefore, will not always, in the same degree of goodness, come cheaper to market than that of the poor. The corn of Poland, in the same degree of goodness, is as cheap as that of France, notwithstanding the superior opulence and improvement of the latter country. The corn of France is, in the corn provinces, fully as good and in most years nearly about the same price with the corn of England, though in opulence and improvement, France is perhaps inferior to England. The cornlands of England, however, are better cultivated than those of France, and the cornlands of France are said to be much better cultivated than those of Poland. But, though the poor country, notwithstanding the inferiority of its cultivation, can, in some measure, rival the rich in the cheapness and goodness of its corn, it can pretend to no such competition in its manufactures, at least if those manufactures suit the soil, climate, and situation of the rich country. The silks of France are better and cheaper than those of England, because the silk manufacture, at least under the present high duties upon the importation of raw silk, does not so well suit the climate of England as that of France. But the hardware and the coarse woolens of England are beyond all comparison superior to those of France, and much cheaper, too, in the same degree of goodness. In Poland there are said to be scarcely any manufactures of any kind, a few of those coarser household manufactures excepted, without which no country can well subsist.

This great increase of the quantity of work, which, in consequence of the division of labor, the same number of people are capable of performing, is owing to three different circumstances: first, to the increase of dexterity in every particular workman; secondly, to the saving of the time which is commonly lost in passing from one species of work to another; and lastly, to the invention of a great number of machines which facilitate and abridge labor, and enable one man to do the work of many.[5]

First, the improvement of the dexterity of the workman necessarily increases the quantity of the work he can perform; and the division of labor, by reducing every man's business to some one simple operation, and by making this operation the sole employment of his life, necessarily increases very much the dexterity of the workman. A common smith, who, though accustomed to handling the hammer, has never been used to make nails, if upon some particular occasion he is obliged to attempt it, will scarcely, I am assured, be able to make above

[5] [All three advantages mentioned in the text above are included in the French *Encyclopédie*, (1751) I, p. 717, *s.v.* Art. It is worth noting that neither Smith nor the *Encyclopédie* stresses the role of the machine.—M.]

two or three hundred nails in a day, and those, too, very bad
ones. A smith who has been accustomed to make nails, but
whose sole or principal business has not been that of a nailer,
can seldom with his utmost diligence make more than eight
hundred or a thousand nails in a day. I have seen several boys
under twenty years of age who had never exercised any other
trade but that of making nails, and who, when they exerted
themselves, could make, each of them, upwards of two
thousand three hundred nails in a day. The making of a nail,
however, is by no means one of the simplest operations. The
same person blows the bellows, stirs or mends the fire as there
is occasion, heats the iron, and forges every part of the nail.
 In forging the head, too, he is obliged to change his tools. The
different operations into which the making of a pin, or of a
 metal button, is subdivided are all of them much more simple,
and the dexterity of the person, of whose life it has been the
sole business to perform them, is usually much greater. The
rapidity with which some of the operations of those manufactures are performed exceeds what the human hand could,
by those who had never seen them, be supposed capable of
acquiring.

Secondly, the advantage which is gained by saving the time
commonly lost in passing from one sort of work to another is
much greater than we should at first view be apt to imagine it.
 It is impossible to pass very quickly from one kind of work to
another that is carried on in a different place and with quite
different tools. A country weaver, who cultivates a small farm,
must lose a good deal of time in passing from his loom to the
field and from the field to his loom. When the two trades can
be carried on in the same workhouse, the loss of time is, no
doubt, much less. It is even in this case, however, very considerable. A man commonly saunters a little in turning his
hand from one sort of employment to another. When he first
begins the new work, he is seldom very keen and hearty; his
mind, as they say, does not go to it, and for some time he
rather trifles than applies to good purpose. The habit of
sauntering and of indolent careless application, which is

naturally, or rather necessarily, acquired by every country workman who is obliged to change his work and his tools every half hour, and to apply his hand in twenty different ways almost every day of his life, renders him almost always slothful and lazy, and incapable of any vigorous application even on the most pressing occasions. Independent, therefore, of his deficiency in point of dexterity, this cause alone must always reduce considerably the quantity of work which he is capable of performing.

Thirdly, and lastly, everybody must be sensible how much labor is facilitated and abridged by the application of proper machinery. It is unnecessary to give any example. I shall only observe, therefore, that the invention of all those machines by which labor is so much facilitated and abridged seems to have been originally owing to the division of labor. Men are much more likely to discover easier and readier methods of attaining any object when the whole attention of their minds is directed toward that single object, than when it is dissipated among a great variety of things. But in consequence of the division of labor, the whole of every man's attention comes naturally to be directed toward some one very simple object. It is naturally to be expected, therefore, that some one or other of those who are employed in each particular branch of labor should soon find out easier and readier methods of performing their own particular work, wherever the nature of it admits of such improvement. A great part of the machines made use of in those manufactures in which labor is most subdivided were originally the inventions of common workmen, who, being each of them employed in some very simple operation, naturally turned their thoughts toward finding out easier and readier methods of performing it. Whoever has been much accustomed to visit such manufactures must frequently have been shown very pretty machines, which were the inventions of such workmen, in order to facilitate and quicken their own particular part of the work. In the first fire engines,[6]

6 [I.e., steam engines.—M.]

a boy was constantly employed to open and shut alternately the communication between the boiler and the cylinder, according as the piston either ascended or descended. One of those boys, who loved to play with his companions, observed that by tying a string from the handle of the valve which opened this communication to another part of the machine, the valve would open and shut without his assistance, and leave him at liberty to divert himself with his playfellows. One of the greatest improvements that has been made upon this machine, since it was first invented, was in this manner the discovery of a boy who wanted to save his own labor.[7]

All the improvements in machinery, however, have by no means been the inventions of those who had occasion to use the machines. Many improvements have been made by the ingenuity of the makers of the machines, when to make them became the business of a peculiar trade; and some by that of those who are called philosophers or men of speculation, whose trade it is not to do anything, but to observe everything; and who, upon that account, are often capable of combining together the powers of the most distant and dissimilar objects.[8] In the progress of society, philosophy or speculation

[7] [This pretty story is largely, at any rate, mythical. It appears to have grown out of a misreading (not necessarily by Smith) of J. T. Desaguliers, *Course of Experimental Philosophy*, vol. ii., 1744, p. 533. From pp. 469, 471, it appears that hand labor was originally used before the "buoy" was devised.—C.]

[8] [In *Lectures*, p. 167, the invention of the plough is conjecturally attributed to a farmer and that of the handmill to a slave, while the invention of the waterwheel and the steam engine is credited to philosophers. Mandeville is very much less favorable to the claims of the philosophers: "They are very seldom the same sort of people, those that invent arts and improvements in them and those that inquire into the reason of things: this latter is most commonly practised by such as are idle and indolent, that are fond of retirement, hate business and take delight in speculation, whereas none succeed oftener in the first than active, stirring and laborious men, such as will put their hand to the plough, try experiments and give all their attention to what they are about."—*Fable of the Bees*, pt. ii. (1729), dial. iii., p. 151. He goes on to give as examples the improvements in soap boiling, grain dyeing, etc.—C.]

becomes, like every other employment, the principal or sole
trade and occupation of a particular class of citizens. Like
every other employment, too, it is subdivided into a great
number of different branches, each of which affords occupation to a peculiar tribe or class of philosophers; and this sub-
division of employment in philosophy, as well as in every
other business, improves dexterity and saves time. Each individual becomes more expert in his own peculiar branch,
more work is done upon the whole, and the quantity of science is considerably increased by it.

It is the great multiplication of the productions of all the
different arts, in consequence of the division of labor, which
occasions, in a well-governed society, that universal opulence
which extends itself to the lowest ranks of the people. Every
workman has a great quantity of his own work to dispose of
beyond what he himself has occasion for; and every other
workman being exactly in the same situation, he is enabled
to exchange a great quantity of his own goods for a great
quantity, or, what comes to the same thing, for the price of a
great quantity of theirs. He supplies them abundantly with
what they have occasion for, and they accommodate him as
amply with what he has occasion for, and a general plenty
diffuses itself through all the different ranks of the society.

Observe the accommodation of the most common artificer or
day laborer in a civilized and thriving country, and you will
perceive that the number of people of whose industry a part,
though but a small part, has been employed in procuring
him this accommodation exceeds all computation. The woolen
coat, for example, which covers the day laborer, as coarse and
rough as it may appear, is the produce of the joint labor of a
great multitude of workmen. The shepherd, the sorter of the
wool, the wool comber or carder, the dyer, the scribbler, the
spinner, the weaver, the fuller, the dresser, with many others,
must all join their different arts in order to complete even
this homely production. How many merchants and carriers,
besides, must have been employed in transporting the materials from some of those workmen to others who often live

in a very distant part of the country! How much commerce
and navigation in particular, how many shipbuilders, sailors,
sailmakers, ropemakers, must have been employed in order to
bring together the different drugs made use of by the dyer,
which often come from the remotest corners of the world!
What a variety of labor too is necessary in order to produce
the tools of the meanest of those workmen! To say nothing of
such complicated machines as the ship of the sailor, the mill
of the fuller, or even the loom of the weaver, let us consider
only what a variety of labor is requisite in order to form that
very simple machine, the shears with which the shepherd clips
the wool. The miner, the builder of the furnace for smelting
the ore, the feller of the timber, the burner of the charcoal to
be made use of in the smelting house, the brickmaker, the
bricklayer, the workmen who attend the furnace, the mill-
wright, the forger, the smith, must all of them join their
different arts in order to produce them. Were we to examine,
in the same manner, all the different parts of his dress and
household furniture, the coarse linen shirt which he wears
next his skin, the shoes which cover his feet, the bed which he
lies on, and all the different parts which compose it, the
kitchen grate at which he prepares his victuals, the coals which
he makes use of for that purpose, dug from the bowels of the
earth, and brought to him perhaps by a long sea and a long
land carriage, all the other utensils of his kitchen, all the
furniture of his table, the knives and forks, the earthen or
pewter plates upon which he serves up and divides his victuals,
the different hands employed in preparing his bread and his
beer, the glass window which lets in the heat and the light,
and keeps out the wind and the rain, with all the knowledge
and art requisite for preparing that beautiful and happy invention without which these northern parts of the world
could scarcely have afforded a very comfortable habitation, together with the tools of all the different workmen employed in
producing those different conveniences; if we examine, I say,
all these things, and consider what a variety of labor is employed about each of them, we shall be sensible that without

the assistance and co-operation of many thousands, the very meanest person in a civilized country could not be provided, even according to what we very falsely imagine as the easy and simple manner in which he is commonly accommodated. Compared, indeed, with the more extravagant luxury of the great, his accommodation must no doubt appear extremely simple and easy; and yet it may be true, perhaps, that the accommodation of a European prince does not always so much exceed that of an industrious and frugal peasant, as the accommodation of the latter exceeds that of many an African king, the absolute master of the lives and liberties of ten thousand naked savages.[9]

CHAPTER II

OF THE PRINCIPLE WHICH GIVES OCCASION TO THE DIVISION OF LABOR

This division of labor, from which so many advantages are derived, is not originally the effect of any human wisdom which foresees and intends that general opulence to which it gives occasion. It is the necessary, though very slow and gradual, consequence of a certain propensity in human nature which has in view no such extensive utility: the propensity to truck, barter, and exchange one thing for another.

Whether this propensity be one of those original principles in human nature, of which no further account can be given;

[9] [This paragraph was probably taken bodily from the MS. of the author's lectures. It appears to be founded on Mun, *England's Treasure by Forraign Trade*, chap. iii., at end; Locke, *Civil Government*, § 43; Mandeville, *Fable of the Bees*, pt. i., Remark P, 2nd ed., 1723, p. 182, and perhaps Harris, *Essay upon Money and Coins*, pt. i., § 12. See *Lectures*, pp. 161-162 and notes.—C.]

or whether, as seems more probable, it be the necessary consequence of the faculties of reason and speech, it belongs not to
our present subject to inquire. It is common to all men, and to
be found in no other race of animals, which seem to know
neither this nor any other species of contracts. Two grey-
hounds, in running down the same hare, have sometimes the
appearance of acting in some sort of concert. Each turns her
toward his companion, or endeavors to intercept her when his
companion turns her toward himself. This, however, is not
the effect of any contract, but of the accidental concurrence of
their passions in the same object at that particular time. Nobody ever saw a dog make a fair and deliberate exchange of
one bone for another with another dog. Nobody ever saw one
animal by its gestures and natural cries signify to another, this
is mine, that yours; I am willing to give this for that. When
an animal wants to obtain something either of a man or of
another animal, it has no other means of persuasion but to
gain the favor of those whose service it requires. A puppy
fawns upon its dam, and a spaniel endeavors by a thousand
attractions to engage the attention of its master who is at
dinner, when it wants to be fed by him. Man sometimes uses
the same arts with his brethren, and when he has no other
means of engaging them to act according to his inclinations,
endeavors by every servile and fawning attention to obtain
their good will. He has not time, however, to do this upon
every occasion. In civilized society he stands at all times in
need of the co-operation and assistance of great multitudes,
while his whole life is scarcely sufficient to gain the friendship
of a few persons. In almost every other race of animals each
individual, when it is grown up to maturity, is entirely independent, and in its natural state has occasion for the assistance
of no other living creature. But man has almost constant occasion for the help of his brethren, and it is in vain for him to
expect it from their benevolence only. He will be more likely
to prevail if he can interest their self-love in his favor, and
show them that it is for their own advantage to do for him
what he requires of them. Whoever offers to another a bargain

of any kind proposes to do this. Give me that which I want, and you shall have this which you want, is the meaning of every such offer; and it is in this manner that we obtain from one another the far greater part of those good offices which we stand in need of. It is not from the benevolence of the butcher, the brewer, or the baker that we expect our dinner, but from their regard to their own interest. We address ourselves not to their humanity, but to their self-love, and never talk to them of our own necessities, but of their advantages. Nobody but a beggar chooses to depend chiefly upon the benevolence of his fellow citizens. Even a beggar does not depend upon it entirely. The charity of well-disposed people, indeed, supplies him with the whole fund of his subsistence. But though this principle ultimately provides him with all the necessities of life for which he has occasion, it neither does nor can provide him with them as he has occasion for them. The greater part of his occasional wants are supplied in the same manner as those of other people, by treaty, by barter, and by purchase. With the money which one man gives him he purchases food. The old clothes which another bestows upon him he exchanges for other old clothes which suit him better, or for lodging, or for food, or for money, with which he can buy either food, clothes, or lodging as he has occasion.[1]

As it is by treaty, by barter, and by purchase that we obtain from one another the greater part of those mutual good offices which we stand in need of, so it is this same trucking disposition which originally gives occasion to the division of labor. In a tribe of hunters or shepherds a particular person makes bows and arrows, for example, with more readiness and dexterity than any other. He frequently exchanges them for cattle or for venison with his companions; and he finds at last that he can in this manner get more cattle and venison than if he himself went to the field to catch them. From a regard to his own interest, therefore, the making of bows and arrows grows to be his chief business, and he becomes a sort of

[1] [The paragraph is repeated from *Lectures*, p. 169. It is founded on Mandeville, *Fable of the Bees*, pt. ii. (1729), dial. vi., pp. 421, 422.—C.]

armorer. Another excels in making the frames and covers of their little huts or movable houses. He is accustomed to be of use in this way to his neighbors, who reward him in the same manner with cattle and with venison, till at last he finds it his interest to dedicate himself entirely to this employment and to become a sort of house carpenter. In the same manner a third becomes a smith or a brazier; a fourth, a tanner or dresser of hides or skins, the principal part of the clothing of savages. And thus the certainty of being able to exchange all that surplus part of the produce of his own labor, which is over and above his own consumption, for such parts of the produce of other men's labor as he may have occasion for, encourages every man to apply himself to a particular occupation, and to cultivate and bring to perfection whatever talent or genius he may possess for that particular species of business.

The difference of natural talents in different men is, in reality, much less than we are aware of; and the very different genius which appears to distinguish men of different professions, when grown up to maturity, is not upon many occasions so much the cause as the effect of the division of labor.[2] The difference between the most dissimilar characters, between a philosopher and a common street porter, for example, seems to arise not so much from nature, as from habit, custom, and education. When they came into the world, and for the first six or eight years of their existence, they were, perhaps, very much alike, and neither their parents nor playfellows could perceive any remarkable difference. About that age, or soon after, they come to be employed in very different occupations. The difference of talents comes then to be taken notice of, and widens by degrees, till at last the vanity of the philosopher is willing to acknowledge scarcely any resemblance. But without the disposition to truck, barter, and exchange, every man

2 [This is apparently directed against Harris, *Money and Coins,* pt. i., § 11, and is in accordance with the view of Hume, who asks readers to "consider how nearly equal all men are in their bodily force, and even in their mental powers and faculties, ere cultivated by education."—"Of the Original Contract," in *Essays, Moral and Political,* 1748, p. 291.—C.]

must have procured to himself every necessity and convenience of life which he wanted. All must have had the same duties to perform and the same work to do and there could have been no such difference of employment as could alone give occasion to any great difference of talents.

As it is this disposition which forms that difference of talents, so remarkable among men of different professions, so it is this same disposition which renders that difference useful. Many tribes of animals acknowledged to be all of the same species derive from nature a much more remarkable distinction of genius than what, antecedent to custom and education, appears to take place among men. By nature a philosopher is not in genius and disposition half so different from a street porter, as a mastiff is from a greyhound, or a greyhound from a spaniel, or this last from a shepherd's dog. Those different tribes of animals, however, though all of the same species, are of scarcely any use to one another. The strength of the mastiff is not in the least supported either by the swiftness of the greyhound, or by the sagacity of the spaniel, or by the docility of the shepherd's dog. The effects of those different geniuses and talents, for want of the power or disposition to barter and exchange, cannot be brought into a common stock, and do not in the least contribute to the better accommodation and convenience of the species. Each animal is still obliged to support and defend itself, separately and independently, and derives no sort of advantage from that variety of talents with which nature has distinguished its fellows. Among men, on the contrary, the most dissimilar geniuses are of use to one another; the different produces of their respective talents, by the general disposition to truck, barter and exchange, being brought as it were into a common stock, where every man may purchase whatever part of the produce of other men's talents he has occasion for.

CHAPTER III

THAT THE DIVISION OF LABOR IS LIMITED
BY THE EXTENT OF THE MARKET

As it is the power of exchanging that gives occasion to the division of labor, so the extent of this division must always be limited by the extent of that power, or, in other words, by the extent of the market. When the market is very small, no person can have any encouragement to dedicate himself entirely to one employment for want of the power to exchange all that surplus part of the produce of his own labor, which is over and above his own consumption, for such parts of the produce of other men's labor as he has occasion for.

There are some sorts of industry, even of the lowest kind, which can be carried on nowhere but in a great town. A porter, for example, can find employment and subsistence in no other place. A village is much too narrow a sphere for him; even an ordinary market town is scarcely large enough to afford him constant occupation. In the lone houses and very small villages which are scattered about in so deserted a country as the Highlands of Scotland every farmer must be butcher, baker, and brewer for his own family. In such situations we can scarcely expect to find even a smith, a carpenter, or a mason within less than twenty miles of another of the same trade. The scattered families that live at eight or ten miles distance from the nearest of them must learn to perform themselves a great number of little pieces of work, for which, in more populous countries, they would call in the assistance of those workmen. Country workmen are almost everywhere obliged to apply themselves to all the different branches of industry that have so much affinity to one another as to be employed about the same sort of materials. A country carpenter deals in every sort of work that is made of wood; a country smith, in every sort of work that is made of iron. The former is not only a carpenter, but a joiner, a cabinetmaker, and even a carver in wood, as well as a wheelwright, a plowwright, a cart and wagonmaker. The employments of the latter are still more various. It is impossible there should be such a trade as even that of a nailer in the remote and inland parts of the Highlands of Scotland. Such a workman at the rate of a thousand nails a day, and three hundred working days in the year, will make three hundred thousand nails in the year. But in such a situation it would be impossible to dispose of one thousand, that is, of one day's work in the year.

As by means of water carriage a more extensive market is opened to every sort of industry than what land carriage alone can afford it, so it is upon the seacoast, and along the banks of navigable rivers that industry of every kind naturally begins to subdivide and improve itself; and it is frequently not till a long time after that those improvements extend themselves to the inland parts of the country. A broad-wheeled wagon, attended by two men and drawn by eight horses, in about six weeks' time carries and brings back between London and Edinburgh nearly four ton weight of goods. In about the same time a ship navigated by six or eight men, and sailing between the ports of London and Leith, frequently carries and brings back two hundred ton weight of goods. Six or eight men, therefore, by the help of water carriage can carry and bring back in the same time the same quantity of goods between London and Edinburgh, as fifty broad-wheeled wagons, attended by a hundred men and drawn by four hundred horses. Upon two hundred tons of goods, therefore, carried by the cheapest land carriage from London to Edinburgh, there must be charged the maintenance of a hundred men for three weeks, and both the maintenance and, what is nearly equal to the maintenance, the wear and tear of four hundred horses, as well as of fifty great wagons. Whereas, upon the same quantity of goods carried by water, there is to be charged only the maintenance of six or eight men, and the wear and tear of a ship of two hundred tons burden, together with the value of the superior risk, or the difference of the insurance between land and water carriage. Were there no other communication between those two places, therefore, but by land carriage, as no goods could be transported from the one to the other, except such whose price was very considerable in proportion to their weight, they could carry on but a small part of that commerce which at present subsists between them, and consequently could give but a small part of that encouragement which they at present mutually afford to each other's industry. There could be little or no commerce of any kind between the distant parts of the world. What goods could bear the expense of land carriage between London and Calcutta?[1] Or if there were any so precious as to be able to support this expense, with what safety could they be transported through the territories of so many barbarous nations? Those two cities, however, at present carry on a very considerable commerce with each other, and by mutually affording a market, give a good deal of encouragement to each other's industry.

Since such, therefore, are the advantages of water carriage, it is natural that the first improvements of art and industry should be made where this convenience opens the whole world for a market to the produce of every sort of labor, and that they should always be much later in extending themselves into the inland parts of the country. The inland parts of the country can for a long time have no other market for the greater part of their goods but the country which lies round about them and separates them from the seacoast and the great navigable rivers. The extent of their market, therefore, must for a long time be in proportion to the riches and populousness of that country, and consequently their improvement

1 [W. Playfair, in his edition of *The Wealth of Nations* (1805), p. 30, says that, equalizing the out and home voyages, goods were carried from London to Calcutta by sea at the same price as from London to Leeds by land. Smith, of course, was writing at the beginning of an industrial revolution which, as we now know, expanded the market by the invention of the railroad—which used a "land carriage"—around 1825.—M.]

must always be posterior to the improvement of that country. In our North American colonies the plantations have constantly followed either the seacoast or the banks of navigable rivers, and have scarcely anywhere extended themselves to any considerable distance from both.

The nations that, according to the best authenticated history, appear to have been first civilized were those that dwelt round the coast of the Mediterranean Sea. That sea, by far the greatest inlet that is known in the world, having no tides, nor consequently any waves, except such as are caused by the wind only, was by the smoothness of its surface, as well as by the multitude of its islands and the proximity of its neighboring shores, extremely favorable to the infant navigation of the world; when, from their ignorance of the compass, men were afraid to quit the view of the coast, and from the imperfection of the art of shipbuilding, to abandon themselves to the boisterous waves of the ocean. To pass beyond the pillars of Hercules, that is, to sail out of the Straits of Gibraltar was, in the ancient world, long considered as a most wonderful and dangerous exploit of navigation. It was late before even the Phoenicians and Carthaginians, the most skillful navigators and shipbuilders of those old times, attempted it; and they were for a long time the only nations that did attempt it.

Of all the countries on the coast of the Mediterranean Sea, Egypt seems to have been the first in which either agriculture or manufactures were cultivated and improved to any considerable degree. Upper Egypt extends itself nowhere above a few miles from the Nile, and in Lower Egypt that great river breaks itself into many different canals, which, with the assistance of a little art, seem to have afforded a communication by water carriage not only between all the great towns, but between all the considerable villages, and even to many farmhouses in the country—nearly in the same manner as the Rhine and the Maas do in Holland at present. The extent and easiness of this inland navigation was probably one of the principal causes of the early improvement of Egypt.

The improvements in agriculture and manufactures seem

likewise to have been of very great antiquity in the provinces of Bengal in the East Indies and in some of the eastern provinces of China, though the great extent of this antiquity is not authenticated by any histories of whose authority we, in this part of the world, are well assured. In Bengal the Ganges and several other great rivers form a great number of navigable canals in the same manner as the Nile does in Egypt. In the eastern provinces of China too, several great rivers form, by their different branches, a multitude of canals, and by communicating with one another afford an inland navigation much more extensive than that either of the Nile or the Ganges, or perhaps than both of them put together. It is remarkable that neither the ancient Egyptians, nor the Indians, nor the Chinese, encouraged foreign commerce, but seem all to have derived their great opulence from this inland navigation.

All the inland parts of Africa, and all that part of Asia which lies any considerable way north of the Black and Caspian seas, the ancient Scythia, the modern Tartary and Siberia, seem in all ages of the world to have been in the same barbarous and uncivilized state in which we find them at present. The sea of Tartary is the frozen ocean which admits of no navigation, and though some of the greatest rivers in the world run through that country, they are at too great a distance from one another to carry commerce and communication through the greater part of it. There are in Africa none of those great inlets, such as the Baltic and Adriatic Seas in Europe, the Mediterranean and Black Seas in both Europe and Asia, and the Gulfs of Arabia, Persia, India, Bengal, and Siam, in Asia, to carry maritime commerce into the interior parts of that great continent; and the great rivers of Africa are at too great a distance from one another to give occasion to any considerable inland navigation. The commerce, besides, which any nation can carry on by means of a river which does not break itself into any great number of branches or canals, and which runs into another territory before it reaches the sea, can never be very considerable; because it is always in the power of the nations who possess that other territory to ob-struct the communication between the upper country and the sea. The navigation of the Danube is of very little use to the different states of Bavaria, Austria, and Hungary, in comparison of what it would be if any of them possessed the whole of its course till it falls into the Black Sea.

CHAPTER IV

OF THE ORIGIN AND USE OF MONEY

When the division of labor has been once thoroughly established, it is but a very small part of a man's wants which the produce of his own labor can supply. He supplies the far greater part of them by exchanging that surplus part of the produce of his own labor, which is over and above his own consumption, for such parts of the produce of other men's labor as he has occasion for. Every man thus lives by exchanging, or becomes in some measure a merchant, and the society itself grows to be what is properly a commercial society.

But when the division of labor first began to take place, this power of exchanging must frequently have been very much clogged and embarrassed in its operations. One man, we shall suppose, has more of a certain commodity than he himself has occasion for, while another has less. The former consequently would be glad to dispose of, and the latter to purchase, a part of this superfluity. But if this latter should chance to have nothing that the former stands in need of, no exchange can be made between them. The butcher has more meat in his shop than he himself can consume, and the brewer and the baker would each of them be willing to purchase a part of it. But they have nothing to offer in exchange, except the different productions of their respective trades, and the butcher is already provided with all the bread and beer which he has immediate occasion for. No exchange can, in this case, be made between them. He cannot be their merchant, nor they his customers; and they are all of them thus mutually less serviceable to one another. In order to avoid the inconvenience of such situations, every prudent man in every period of society, after the first establishment of the division of labor, must naturally have endeavored to manage his affairs in such a manner, as to have at all times by him, besides the peculiar produce of his own industry, a certain quantity of some one commodity or other, such as he imagined few people would be likely to refuse in exchange for the produce of their industry.

Many different commodities, it is probable, were successively both thought of and employed for this purpose. In the rude ages of society, cattle are said to have been the common instrument of commerce; and, though they must have been a most inconvenient one, yet in old times we find things were frequently valued according to the number of cattle which had been given in exchange for them. The armor of Diomedes, says Homer, cost only nine oxen; but that of Glaucus cost a hundred oxen. Salt is said to be the common instrument of commerce and exchanges in Abyssinia; a species of shells in some parts of the coast of India; dried cod at Newfoundland; tobacco in Virginia; sugar in some of our West Indian colonies; hides or dressed leather in some other countries; and there is at this day a village in Scotland where it is not uncommon, I am told, for a workman to carry nails instead of money to the baker's shop or the alehouse.

In all countries, however, men seem at last to have been determined by irresistible reasons to give the preference, for this employment, to metals above every other commodity. Metals can not only be kept with as little loss as any other commodity, scarcely anything being less perishable than they are, but they can likewise, without any loss, be divided into any

number of parts, as by fusion those parts can easily be re-
united again—a quality which no other equally durable commodities possess, and which more than any other quality
renders them fit to be the instruments of commerce and circulation. The man who wanted to buy salt, for example, and
had nothing but cattle to give in exchange for it, must have
been obliged to buy salt to the value of a whole ox, or a whole
sheep, at a time. He could seldom buy less than this, because
what he was to give for it could seldom be divided without
loss; and if he had a mind to buy more, he must, for the same
reasons, have been obliged to buy double or triple the quantity, the value, to wit, of two or three oxen, or of two or three
sheep. If, on the contrary, instead of sheep or oxen, he had
metals to give in exchange for it, he could easily proportion
the quantity of the metal to the precise quantity of the commodity which he had immediate occasion for.

Different metals have been made use of by different nations
for this purpose. Iron was the common instrument of commerce among the ancient Spartans; copper among the ancient
Romans; and gold and silver among all rich and commercial
nations.

Those metals seem originally to have been made use of for
this purpose in rude bars, without any stamp or coinage. Thus
we are told by Pliny,[1] upon the authority of Timaeus, an
ancient historian, that, till the time of Servius Tullius, the
Romans had no coined money, but made use of unstamped
bars of copper to purchase whatever they had occasion for.
These rude bars, therefore, performed at this time the function of money.

The use of metals in this rude state was attended with two
very considerable inconveniences: first, with the trouble of
weighing; and, secondly, with that of assaying them. In the
precious metals, where a small difference in the quantity makes
a great difference in the value, even the business of weighing,

[1] Plin, Hist. Nat. lib. 33. cap. 3. ["Servius rex primus signavit aes. Antea
rudi usos Romæ Timæus tradit."—C.]

with proper exactness, requires at least very accurate weights and scales. The weighing of gold in particular is an operation of some nicety. In the coarser metals, indeed, where a small error would be of little consequence, less accuracy would, no doubt, be necessary. Yet we should find it excessively troublesome, if every time a poor man had occasion either to buy or sell a farthing's worth of goods, he was obliged to weigh the farthing. The operation of assaying is still more difficult, still more tedious, and, unless a part of the metal is fairly melted in the crucible, with proper dissolvents, any conclusion that can be drawn from it is extremely uncertain. Before the institution of coined money, however, unless they went through this tedious and difficult operation, people must always have been liable to the grossest frauds and impositions, and instead of a pound weight of pure silver, or pure copper, might receive in exchange for their goods an adulterated composition of the coarsest and cheapest materials, which had, however, in their outward appearance, been made to resemble those metals. To prevent such abuses, to facilitate exchanges, and thereby to encourage all sorts of industry and commerce, it had been found necessary, in all countries that have made any considerable advances toward improvement, to affix a public stamp upon certain quantities of such particular metals, as were in those countries commonly made use of to purchase goods. Hence the origin of coined money and of those public offices called mints, institutions exactly of the same nature with those of the alnagers and stampmasters of woolen and linen cloth. All of them are equally meant to ascertain, by means of a public stamp, the quantity and uniform goodness of those different commodities when brought to market.

The first public stamps of this kind that were affixed to the current metals seem in many cases to have been intended to ascertain what it was both most difficult and most important to ascertain, the goodness or fineness of the metal, and to have resembled the sterling mark which is at present affixed to plate and bars of silver, or the Spanish mark which is sometimes affixed to ingots of gold, and which, being struck only upon one side of the piece and not covering the whole surface, ascertains the fineness, but not the weight of the metal. Abraham weighs to Ephron the four hundred shekels of silver which he had agreed to pay for the field of Machpelah.[2] They are said however to be the current money of the merchant, and yet are received by weight and not by [tally], in the same manner as ingots of gold and bars of silver are at present. The revenues of the ancient Saxon kings of England are said to have been paid not in money but in kind, that is, in victuals and provisions of all sorts. William the Conqueror introduced the custom of paying them in money. This money, however, was, for a long time, received at the exchequer by weight and not by tale.

The inconvenience and difficulty of weighing those metals with exactness gave occasion to the institution of coins, of which the stamp, covering entirely both sides of the piece and sometimes the edges too, was supposed to ascertain not only the fineness, but the weight of the metal. Such coins, therefore, were received by tale as at present, without the trouble of weighing.[3]

The denominations of those coins seem originally to have expressed the weight or quantity of metal contained in them. In the time of Servius Tullius, who first coined money at Rome, the Roman *as* or *pondo* contained a Roman pound of good copper. It was divided in the same manner as our Troyes pound, into twelve ounces, each of which contained a real ounce of good copper. The English pound sterling in the time of Edward I contained a pound, Tower weight, of silver of a known fineness. The Tower pound seems to have been something more than the Roman pound, and something less than the Troyes pound. This last was not introduced into the

[2] [Genesis xxiii. 16.—C.]

[3] [The following is no longer of contemporary interest, but it does show Smith's grasp of the actual detail of his subject. One interesting point is his indictment of the royal habit of debasing the coinage.—M.]

mint of England till the 18th of Henry VIII. The French
livre contained in the time of Charlemagne a pound, Troyes
weight, of silver of a known fineness. The fair of Troyes in
Champagne was at that time frequented by all the nations of
Europe, and the weights and measures of so famous a market
were generally known and esteemed. The Scots money pound
contained, from the time of Alexander the First to that of
Robert Bruce, a pound of silver of the same weight and fineness with the English pound sterling. English, French, and
Scots pennies, too, contained all of them originally a real
pennyweight of silver, the twentieth part of an ounce, and
the two-hundred-and-fortieth part of a pound. The shilling
too seems originally to have been the denomination of a
weight. *When wheat is at twelve shillings the quarter,* says an
ancient statute of Henry III, *then wastel bread of a farthing
shall weigh eleven shillings and four pence.* The proportion,
however, between the shilling and either the penny on the
one hand, or the pound on the other, seems not to have been
so constant and uniform as that between the penny and the
pound. During the first race of the kings of France, the French
sou or shilling appears upon different occasions to have contained five, twelve, twenty, and forty pennies. Among the
ancient Saxons a shilling appears at one time to have contained only five pennies, and it is not improbable that it may
have been as variable among them as among their neighbors,
the ancient Franks. From the time of Charlemagne among the
French, and from that of William the Conqueror among the
English, the proportion between the pound, the shilling, and
the penny seems to have been uniformly the same as at present, though the value of each has been very different. For in
every country of the world, I believe, the avarice and injustice
of princes and sovereign states, abusing the confidence of their
subjects, have by degrees diminished the real quantity of
metal which had been originally contained in their coins. The
Roman As, in the latter ages of the Republic, was reduced to
the twenty-fourth part of its original value, and, instead of

weighing a pound, came to weigh only half an ounce.[4] The English pound and penny contain at present about a third only, the Scots pound and penny about a thirty-sixth, and the French pound and penny about a sixty-sixth part of their original value. By means of those operations the princes and sovereign states which performed them were enabled, in appearance, to pay their debts and to fulfill their engagements with a smaller quantity of silver than would otherwise have been requisite. It was indeed in appearance only, for their creditors were really defrauded of a part of what was due to them. All other debtors in the state were allowed the same privilege, and might pay with the same nominal sum of the new and debased coin whatever they had borrowed in the old. Such operations, therefore, have always proved favorable to the debtor, and ruinous to the creditor, and have sometimes produced a greater and more universal revolution in the fortunes of private persons than could have been occasioned by a very great public calamity.

It is in this manner that money has become in all civilized nations the universal instrument of commerce, by the intervention of which goods of all kinds are bought and sold, or exchanged for one another.

What are the rules which men naturally observe in exchanging them either for money or for one another, I shall now proceed to examine. These rules determine what may be called the relative or exchangeable value of goods.

The word VALUE, it is to be observed, has two different meanings, and sometimes expresses the utility of some particular object, and sometimes the power of purchasing other goods which the possession of that object conveys. The one may be called "value in use"; the other, "value in exchange." The things which have the greatest value in use have frequently little or no value in exchange; and on the contrary, those which have the greatest value in exchange have fre-

---

[4] [Pliny, *Hist. Nat.*, lib. xxxiii., cap. iii.; see also pp. 287f.–C.]

quently little or no value in use. Nothing is more useful than water, but it will purchase scarcely anything; scarcely anything can be had in exchange for it. A diamond, on the contrary, has scarcely any value in use; but a very great quantity of other goods may frequently be had in exchange for it.

In order to investigate the principles which regulate the exchangeable value of commodities, I shall endeavor to show:

First, what is the real measure of this exchangeable value; or, wherein consists the real price of all commodities.

Secondly, what are the different parts of which this real price is composed or made up.

And, lastly, what are the different circumstances which sometimes raise some or all of these different parts of price above, and sometimes sink them below, their natural or ordinary rate; or, what are the causes which sometimes hinder the market price, that is, the actual price of commodities, from coinciding exactly with what may be called their natural price.

I shall endeavor to explain, as fully and distinctly as I can, those three subjects in the three following chapters, for which I must very earnestly entreat both the patience and attention of the reader: his patience in order to examine a detail which may perhaps in some places appear unnecessarily tedious; and his attention in order to understand what may, perhaps, after the fullest explication which I am capable of giving of it, appear still in some degree obscure. I am always willing to run some hazard of being tedious in order to be sure that I am perspicuous; and after taking the utmost pains that I can to be perspicuous, some obscurity may still appear to remain upon a subject in its own nature extremely abstracted.

CHAPTER V

OF THE REAL AND NOMINAL PRICE OF COMMODITIES, OR OF THEIR PRICE IN LABOR, AND THEIR PRICE IN MONEY

Every man is rich or poor according to the degree in which he can afford to enjoy the necessities, conveniences, and amusements of human life. But after the division of labor has once thoroughly taken place, it is but a very small part of these with which a man's own labor can supply him. The far greater part of them he must derive from the labor of other people, and he must be rich or poor according to the quantity of that labor which he can command, or which he can afford to purchase. The value of any commodity, therefore, to the person who possesses it, and who means not to use or consume it himself, but to exchange it for other commodities, is equal to the quantity of labor which it enables him to purchase or command. Labor, therefore, is the real measure of the exchangeable value of all commodities.

The real price of everything, what everything really costs to the man who wants to acquire it, is the toil and trouble of acquiring it. What everything is really worth to the man who has acquired it, and who wants to dispose of it or exchange it for something else, is the toil and trouble which it can save to himself, and which it can impose upon other people. What is bought with money or with goods is purchased by labor,[1] as much as what we acquire by the toil of our own body. That money or those goods indeed save us this toil. They contain the value of a certain quantity of labor which we exchange for what is supposed at the time to contain the value of an

---

[1] ["Everything in the world is purchased by labour."—Hume, "Of Commerce," in *Political Discourses*, 1752, p. 12.—C.]

equal quantity. Labor was the first price, the original pur-
chase-money that was paid for all things. It was not by gold or
silver, but by labor, that all the wealth of the world was
originally purchased; and its value, to those who possess it,
and who want to exchange it for some new productions, is
precisely equal to the quantity of labor which it can enable
them to purchase or command.

Wealth, as Mr. Hobbes says, is power.[2] But the person who
either acquires, or succeeds to a great fortune, does not necessarily acquire or succeed to any political power, either civil or
military. His fortune may, perhaps, afford him the means of
acquiring both, but the mere possession of that fortune does
not necessarily convey to him either. The power which that
possession immediately and directly conveys to him is the
power of purchasing—a certain command over all the labor or
over all the produce of labor which is then in the market. His
fortune is greater or less, precisely in proportion to the extent
of this power, or to the quantity either of other men's labor,
or, what is the same thing, of the produce of other men's labor,
which it enables him to purchase or command. The exchangeable value of everything must always be precisely equal to the
extent of this power which it conveys to its owner.

But though labor be the real measure of the exchangeable
value of all commodities, it is not that by which their value is
commonly estimated. It is often difficult to ascertain the proportion between two different quantities of labor. The time
spent in two different sorts of work will not always alone determine this proportion. The different degrees of hardship en-
dured, and of ingenuity exercised, must likewise be taken into
account. There may be more labor in an hour's hard work
than in two hours' easy business; or in an hour's application
to a trade which it cost ten years' labor to learn, than in a
month's industry at an ordinary and obvious employment. But
it is not easy to find any accurate measure either of hardship

[2] ["Also riches joined with liberality is Power, because it procureth
friends and servants: without liberality not so, because in this case they
defend not but expose men to envy as a prey."—*Leviathan*, I., x.—C.]

or ingenuity. In exchanging indeed the different productions of different sorts of labor for one another, some allowance is commonly made for both. It is adjusted, however, not by any accurate measure, but by the higgling and bargaining of the market, according to that sort of rough equality which, though not exact, is sufficient for carrying on the business of common life.[3]

Every commodity, besides, is more frequently exchanged for, and thereby compared with, other commodities than with labor. It is more natural, therefore, to estimate its exchangeable value by the quantity of some other commodity than by that of the labor which it can purchase. The greater part of people too understand better what is meant by a quantity of a particular commodity, than by a quantity of labor. The one is a plain, palpable object; the other an abstract notion, which, though it can be made sufficiently intelligible, is not altogether so natural and obvious.

But when barter ceases, and money has become the common instrument of commerce, every particular commodity is more frequently exchanged for money than for any other commodity. The butcher seldom carries his beef or his mutton to the baker, or the brewer, in order to exchange them for bread or for beer; but he carries them to the market, where he exchanges them for money, and afterwards exchanges that money for bread and for beer. The quantity of money which he gets for them regulates too the quantity of bread and beer which he can afterwards purchase. It is more natural and obvious to him, therefore, to estimate their value by the quantity of money, the commodity for which he immediately exchanges them, than by that of bread and beer, the commodities for which he can exchange them only by the intervention of another commodity; and rather to say that his butcher's meat is worth threepence or fourpence a pound, than that it is worth three or four pounds of bread, or three or four quarts of small beer. Hence it comes to pass that the exchangeable

[3] [The absence of any reference to the lengthy discussion of this subject in Chap. X is curious.—C.]

value of every commodity is more frequently estimated by the
quantity of money, than by the quantity either of labor or of
any other commodity which can be had in exchange for it.

Gold and silver, however, like every other commodity, vary
in their value, are sometimes cheaper and sometimes dearer,
sometimes of easier and sometimes of more difficult purchase.
The quantity of labor which any particular quantity of them
can purchase or command, or the quantity of other goods
which it will exchange for, depends always upon the fertility
or barrenness of the mines which happen to be known about
the time when such exchanges are made. The discovery of the
abundant mines of America reduced, in the sixteenth century,
the value of gold and silver in Europe to about a third of
what it had been before. As it cost less labor to bring those
metals from the mine to the market, so when they were
brought thither they could purchase or command less labor;
and this revolution in their value, though perhaps the greatest, is by no means the only one of which history gives some
account. But as a measure of quantity, such as the natural
foot, fathom, or handful, which is continually varying in its
own quantity, can never be an accurate measure of the quantity of other things; so a commodity, which is itself continually
varying in its own value, can never be an accurate measure
of the value of other commodities. Equal quantities of labor,
at all times and places, may be said to be of equal value to the
laborer. In his ordinary state of health, strength, and spirits,
in the ordinary degree of his skill and dexterity, he must always lay down the same portion of his ease, his liberty, and
his happiness. The price which he pays must always be the
same, whatever may be the quantity of goods which he receives in return for it. Of these, indeed, it may sometimes
purchase a greater and sometimes a smaller quantity; but it
is their value which varies, not that of the labor which purchases them. At all times and places that is dear which it is
difficult to come at, or which it costs much labor to acquire;
and that cheap which is to be had easily, or with very little
labor. Labor alone, therefore, never varying in its own value,

is alone the ultimate and real standard by which the value of all commodities can at all times and places be estimated and compared. It is their real price; money is their nominal price only.

But though equal quantities of labor are always of equal value to the laborer, yet to the person who employs him they appear sometimes to be of greater and sometimes of smaller value. He purchases them sometimes with a greater and sometimes with a smaller quantity of goods, and to him the price of labor seems to vary like that of all other things. It appears to him dear in the one case, and cheap in the other. In reality, however, it is the goods which are cheap in the one case, and dear in the other.

In this popular sense, therefore, labor, like commodities, may be said to have a real and a nominal price. Its real price may be said to consist in the quantity of the necessaries and conveniences of life which are given for it; its nominal price, in the quantity of money. The laborer is rich or poor, is well or ill rewarded, in proportion to the real, not to the nominal price of his labor.

The distinction between the real and the nominal price of commodities and labor is not a matter of mere speculation, but may sometimes be of considerable use in practice. The same real price is always of the same value; but on account of the variations in the value of gold and silver, the same nominal price is sometimes of very different values. When a landed estate, therefore, is sold with a reservation of a perpetual rent, if it is intended that this rent should always be of the same value, it is of importance to the family in whose favor it is reserved that it should not consist in a particular sum of money. Its value would in this case be liable to variations of two different kinds: first, to those which arise from the different quantities of gold and silver which are contained at different times in coin of the same denomination; and, secondly, to those which arise from the different values of equal quantities of gold and silver at different times.

Princes and sovereign states have frequently fancied that

they had a temporary interest to diminish the quantity of pure metal contained in their coins; but they seldom have fancied that they had any to augment it. The quantity of metal contained in the coins, I believe of all nations, has, accordingly, been almost continually diminishing, and hardly ever augmenting. Such variations therefore tend almost always to diminish the value of a money rent.

The discovery of the mines of America diminished the value of gold and silver in Europe. This diminution, it is commonly supposed, though I apprehend without any certain proof, is still going on gradually, and is likely to continue to do so for a long time. Upon this supposition, therefore, such variations are more likely to diminish than to augment the value of a money rent, even though it should be stipulated to be paid, not in such a quantity of coined money of such a denomination (in so many pounds sterling, for example), but in so many ounces either of pure silver, or of silver of a certain standard.

The rents which have been reserved in corn [4] have preserved their value much better than those which have been reserved in money, even where the denomination of the coin has not been altered. By the 18th of Elizabeth it was enacted that a third of the rent of all college leases should be reserved in corn, to be paid either in kind or according to the current prices at the nearest public market. The money arising from this corn rent, though originally but a third of the whole, is in the present times, according to Doctor Blackstone, commonly nearly double of what arises from the other two-thirds. The old money rents of colleges must, according to this account, have sunk almost to a fourth part of their ancient value; or are worth little more than a fourth part of the corn which they were formerly worth. But since the reign of Philip and Mary the denomination of the English coin has undergone little or no alteration, and the same number of pounds, shillings and pence have contained very nearly the same quan-

---

[4] [The word "corn" is not used by Smith in the sense of Indian corn, or maize, but in the sense of a cereal crop; in England, this was generally wheat.—M.]

tity of pure silver. This degradation, therefore, in the value of the money rents of colleges has arisen altogether from the degradation in the value of silver.

When the degradation in the value of silver is combined with the diminution of the quantity of it contained in the coin of the same denomination, the loss is frequently still greater. In Scotland, where the denomination of the coin has undergone much greater alterations than it ever did in England, and in France, where it has undergone still greater than it ever did in Scotland, some ancient rents, originally of considerable value, have in this manner been reduced almost to nothing.

Equal quantities of labor will at distant times be purchased more nearly with equal quantities of corn, the subsistence of the laborer, than with equal quantities of gold and silver, or perhaps of any other commodity. Equal quantities of corn, therefore, will, at distant times, be more nearly of the same real value or enable the possessor to purchase or command more nearly the same quantity of the labor of other people. They will do this, I say, more nearly than equal quantities of almost any other commodity; for even equal quantities of corn will not do it exactly. The subsistence of the laborer, or the real price of labor, as I shall endeavor to show hereafter, is very different upon different occasions; more liberal in a society advancing to opulence than in one that is standing still, and in one that is standing still than in one that is going backwards. Every other commodity, however, will at any particular time purchase a greater or smaller quantity of labor in proportion to the quantity of subsistence which it can purchase at that time. A rent, therefore, reserved in corn is liable only to the variations in the quantity of labor which a certain quantity of corn can purchase. But a rent reserved in any other commodity is liable, not only to the variations in the quantity of labor which any particular quantity of corn can purchase, but to the variations in the quantity of corn which can be purchased by any particular quantity of that commodity.

Though the real value of a corn rent, it is to be observed
however, varies much less from century to century than that
of a money rent, it varies much more from year to year. The
money price of labor, as I shall endeavor to show hereafter,[5]
does not fluctuate from year to year with the money price of
corn, but seems to be everywhere accommodated, not to the
temporary or occasional, but to the average or ordinary price
of that necessity of life. The average or ordinary price of corn
again is regulated, as I shall likewise endeavor to show hereafter,[6] by the value of silver, by the richness or barrenness of
the mines which supply the market with that metal, or by the
quantity of labor which must be employed, and consequently
of corn which must be consumed, in order to bring any particular quantity of silver from the mine to the market. But
the value of silver, though it sometimes varies greatly from
century to century, seldom varies much from year to year, but
frequently continues the same, or very nearly the same, for
half a century or a century together. The ordinary or average
money price of corn, therefore, may, during so long a period,
continue the same or very nearly the same too, and along
with it the money price of labor, provided, at least, the society continues, in other respects, in the same or nearly in
the same condition. In the meantime the temporary and occasional price of corn may frequently be double one year of
what it had been the year before, or fluctuate, for example,
from five-and-twenty to fifty shillings the quarter. But when
corn is at the latter price, not only the nominal but the real
value of a corn rent will be double of what it is when at the
former, or will command double the quantity either of labor
or of the greater part of other commodities; the money price
of labor, and along with it that of most other things, continuing the same during all these fluctuations.

Labor, therefore, it appears, evidently is the only universal,
as well as the only accurate, measure of value, or the only
standard by which we can compare the values of different com-

[5] [See pp. 74, 84ff.]
[6] [See Book I, Chapter XI (not included in this edition).]

modities at all times and at all places. We cannot estimate, it is allowed, the real value of different commodities from century to century by the quantities of silver which were given for them. We cannot estimate it from year to year by the quantities of corn. By the quantities of labor we can, with the greatest accuracy, estimate it both from century to century and from year to year. From century to century, corn is a better measure than silver, because from century to century, equal quantities of corn will command the same quantity of labor more nearly than equal quantities of silver. From year to year, on the contrary, silver is a better measure than corn because equal quantities of it will more nearly command the same quantity of labor.[7]

But though in establishing perpetual rents, or even in letting very long leases, it may be of use to distinguish between real and nominal price; it is of none in buying and selling, the more common and ordinary transactions of human life.

At the same time and place the real and the nominal price of all commodities are exactly in proportion to one another. The more or less money you get for any commodity, in the London market, for example, the more or less labor it will at that time and place enable you to purchase or command. At the same time and place, therefore, money is the exact measure of the real exchangeable value of all commodities. It is so, however, at the same time and place only.

Though at distant places, there is no regular proportion between the real and the money price of commodities, yet the merchant who carries goods from the one to the other has nothing to consider but their money price, or the difference between the quantity of silver for which he buys them, and that for which he is likely to sell them. Half an ounce of silver at Canton in China may command a greater quantity both of labor and of the necessities and conveniences of life, than an ounce at London. A commodity, therefore, which sells for half an ounce of silver at Canton may there be really dearer, of

[7] [Cf., Locke, *Some Considerations of the Consequences of the Lowering of Interest and Raising the Value of Money*, ed. of 1696, pp. 74, 75.—C.]

more real importance to the man who possesses it there, than a commodity which sells for an ounce at London is to the man who possesses it at London. If a London merchant, however, can buy at Canton for half an ounce of silver a commodity which he can afterwards sell at London for an ounce, he gains a hundred per cent by the bargain, just as much as if an ounce of silver was at London exactly of the same value as at Canton. It is of no importance to him that half an ounce of silver at Canton would have given him the command of more labor and of a greater quantity of the necessities and conveniences of life than an ounce can do at London. An ounce at London will always give him the command of double the quantity of all these, which half an ounce could have done there, and this is precisely what he wants.

As it is the nominal or money price of goods, therefore, which finally determines the prudence or imprudence of all purchases and sales, and thereby regulates almost the whole business of common life in which price is concerned, we cannot wonder that it should have been so much more attended to than the real price.

In such a work as this, however, it may sometimes be of use to compare the different real values of a particular commodity at different times and places, or the different degrees of power over the labor of other people which it may, upon different occasions, have given to those who possessed it. We must in this case compare, not so much the different quantities of silver for which it was commonly sold, as the different quantities of labor which those different quantities of silver could have purchased. But the current prices of labor at distant times and places can scarcely ever be known with any degree of exactness. Those of corn, though they have in few places been regularly recorded, are in general better known and have been more frequently taken notice of by historians and other writers. We must generally, therefore, content ourselves with them, not as being always exactly in the same proportion as the current prices of labor, but as being the nearest approximation which can commonly be had to that proportion. I shall hereafter have occasion to make several comparisons of this kind.[8]

In the progress of industry, commercial nations have found it convenient to coin several different metals into money: gold for larger payments, silver for purchases of moderate value, and copper, or some other coarse metal, for those of still smaller consideration. They have always, however, considered one of those metals as more peculiarly the measure of value than any of the other two; and this preference seems generally to have been given to the metal which they happened first to make use of as the instrument of commerce. Having once begun to use it as their standard, which they must have done when they had no other money, they have generally continued to do so even when the necessity was not the same.

The Romans are said to have had nothing but copper money till within five years before the first Punic war,[9] when they first began to coin silver. Copper, therefore, appears to have continued always the measure of value in that republic. At Rome all accounts appear to have been kept, and the value of all estates to have been computed, either in *Asses* or in *Sestertii*. The *As* was always the denomination of a copper coin. The word *Sestertius* signifies two *Asses* and a half. Though the *Sestertius,* therefore, was originally a silver coin, its value was estimated in copper. At Rome, one who owed a great deal of money, was said to have a great deal of other people's copper.[10]

The northern nations who established themselves upon the ruins of the Roman Empire seem to have had silver money from the first beginning of their settlements, and not to have known either gold or copper coins for several ages thereafter. There were silver coins in England in the time of the Saxons, but there was little gold coined till the time of Edward III nor any copper till that of James I of Great Britain. In England, therefore, and for the same reason, I believe, in all other

[8] [Chap. xi. *passim.*—C. (not included in this edition.—M.)]
[9] Pliny, lib. xxxiii. c. 3.
[10] [*Habere aes alienum.*—C.]

modern nations of Europe, all accounts are kept, and the value of all goods and of all estates is generally computed in silver, and when we mean to express the amount of a person's fortune, we seldom mention the number of guineas, but the number of pounds sterling which we suppose would be given for it.

Originally, in all countries, I believe, a legal tender of payment could be made only in the coin of that metal which was peculiarly considered as the standard or measure of value. In England, gold was not considered as a legal tender for a long time after it was coined into money. The proportion between the values of gold and silver money was not fixed by any public law or proclamation, but was left to be settled by the market. If a debtor offered payment in gold, the creditor might either reject such payment altogether, or accept of it at such a valuation of the gold as he and his debtor could agree upon. Copper is not at present a legal tender, except in the change of the smaller silver coins. In this state of things the distinction between the metal which was the standard, and that which was not the standard, was something more than a nominal distinction.

In process of time, and as people became gradually more familiar with the use of the different metals in coin and consequently better acquainted with the proportion between their respective values, it has in most countries, I believe, been found convenient to ascertain this proportion, and to declare by a public law that a guinea, for example, of such a weight and fineness, should exchange for one-and-twenty shillings, or be a legal tender for a debt of that amount. In this state of things, and during the continuance of any one regulated proportion of this kind, the distinction between the metal which is the standard, and that which is not the standard, becomes little more than a nominal distinction.

In consequence of any change, however, in this regulated proportion, this distinction becomes, or at least seems to become, something more than nominal again. If the regulated value of a guinea, for example, was either reduced to twenty or raised to two-and-twenty shillings, all accounts being kept and almost all obligations for debt being expressed in silver money, the greater part of payments could in either case be made with the same quantity of silver money as before, but would require very different quantities of gold money, a greater in the one case, and a smaller in the other. Silver would appear to be more invariable in its value than gold. Silver would appear to measure the value of gold, and gold would not appear to measure the value of silver. The value of gold would seem to depend upon the quantity of silver which it would exchange for, and the value of silver would not seem to depend upon the quantity of gold which it would exchange for. This difference, however, would be altogether owing to the custom of keeping accounts and of expressing the amount of all great and small sums rather in silver than in gold money. One of Mr. Drummond's notes for five-and-twenty or fifty guineas would, after an alteration of this kind, be still payable with five-and-twenty or fifty guineas in the same manner as before. It would, after such an alteration, be payable with the same quantity of gold as before, but with very different quantities of silver. In the payment of such a note, gold would appear to be more invariable in its value than silver. Gold would appear to measure the value of silver, and silver would not appear to measure the value of gold. If the custom of keeping accounts, and of expressing promissory notes and other obligations for money in this manner, should ever become general, gold, and not silver, would be considered as the metal which was peculiarly the standard or measure of value.[11]

---

[11] [Once again, what might be a fatiguing absorption on Smith's part in the history of coinage takes on a more interesting light if we bear in mind that the questions of inflation and devaluation of the currency are still fundamental questions in the economic life of modern nations. A few pages, however, suffice to give the gist of Smith's approach, and we have, therefore, deleted about five pages of this chapter.—M.]

CHAPTER VI

OF THE COMPONENT PARTS OF THE PRICE OF COMMODITIES

In that early and rude state of society which precedes both the accumulation of stock and the appropriation of land, the proportion between the quantities of labor necessary for acquiring different objects seems to be the only circumstance which can afford any rule for exchanging them for one another. If among a nation of hunters, for example, it usually costs twice the labor to kill a beaver which it does to kill a deer, one beaver should naturally exchange for or be worth two deer. It is natural that what is usually the produce of two days' or two hours' labor should be worth double of what is usually the produce of one day's or one hour's labor.

If the one species of labor should be more severe than the other, some allowance will naturally be made for this superior hardship; and the produce of one hour's labor in the one way may frequently exchange for that of two hours' labor in the other.

Or if the one species of labor requires an uncommon degree of dexterity and ingenuity, the esteem which men have for such talents will naturally give a value to their produce superior to what would be due to the time employed about it. Such talents can seldom be acquired but in consequence of long application, and the superior value of their produce may frequently be no more than a reasonable compensation for the time and labor which must be spent in acquiring them. In the advanced state of society, allowances of this kind, for superior hardship and superior skill, are commonly made in the wages of labor; and something of the same kind must probably have taken place in its earliest and rudest period.

In this state of things, the whole produce of labor belongs to the laborer; and the quantity of labor commonly employed in acquiring or producing any commodity is the only circumstance which can regulate the quantity of labor which it ought commonly to purchase, command, or exchange for.

As soon as stock has accumulated in the hands of particular persons, some of them will naturally employ it in setting to work industrious people, whom they will supply with materials and subsistence, in order to make a profit by the sale of their work, or by what their labor adds to the value of the materials. In exchanging the complete manufacture either for money, for labor, or for other goods, over and above what may be sufficient to pay the price of the materials and the wages of the workmen, something must be given for the profits of the undertaker of the work who hazards his stock in this adventure. The value which the workmen add to the materials, therefore, resolves itself in this case into two parts, of which the one pays their wages, the other the profits of their employer upon the whole stock of materials and wages which he advanced. He could have no interest to employ them unless he expected from the sale of their work something more than what was sufficient to replace his stock to him; and he could have no interest to employ a great stock rather than a small one unless his profits were to bear some proportion to the extent of his stock.

The profits of stock, it may perhaps be thought, are only a different name for the wages of a particular sort of labor, the labor of inspection and direction. They are, however, altogether different, are regulated by quite sufficient principles, and bear no proportion to the quantity, the hardship, or the ingenuity of this supposed labor of inspection and direction. They are regulated altogether by the value of the stock employed, and are greater or smaller in proportion to the extent of this stock. Let us suppose, for example, that in some particular place, where the common annual profits of manufacturing stock are ten per cent, there are two different manufactures in each of which twenty workmen are employed at the rate of fifteen pounds a year each, or at the expense of three hundred a year in each manufactory. Let us suppose, too, that the coarse materials annually wrought up in the one cost only seven hundred pounds, while the finer materials in the other cost seven thousand. The capital annually employed [1] in the one will in this case amount only to one thousand pounds, whereas that employed in the other will amount to seven thousand three hundred pounds. At the rate of ten per cent, therefore, the undertaker of the one will expect a yearly profit of about one hundred pounds only, while that of the other will expect about seven hundred and thirty pounds. But though their profits are so very different, their labor of inspection and direction may be either altogether or very nearly the same. In many great works, almost the whole labor of this kind is committed to some principal clerk. His wages properly express the value of this labor of inspection and direction. Though in settling them some regard is had commonly, not only to his labor and skill, but to the trust which is reposed in him, yet they never bear any regular proportion to the capital of which he oversees the management; and the owner of this capital, though he is thus discharged of almost all labor, still expects that his profits should bear a regular proportion to his capital. In the price of commodities, therefore, the profits of stock constitute a component part altogether different from the wages of labor, and regulated by quite different principles.

In this state of things, the whole produce of labor does not always belong to the laborer. He must in most cases share it with the owner of the stock which employs him. Neither is the quantity of labor commonly employed in acquiring or producing any commodity the only circumstance which can regulate the quantity which it ought commonly to purchase, command, or exchange for. An additional quantity, it is evident, must be due for the profits of the stock which advanced the wages and furnished the materials of that labor.

As soon as the land of any country has all become private

---

[1] ["The capital annually employed" is the working expenses for twelve months, not the capital in the usual modern sense.—C.]

property, the landlords, like all other men, love to reap where they never sowed, and demand a rent even for its natural produce. The wood of the forest, the grass of the field, and all the natural fruits of the earth, which, when land was in common, cost the laborer only the trouble of gathering them, come, even to him, to have an additional price fixed upon them. He must give up to the landlord a portion of what his labor either collects or produces. This portion, or, what comes to the same thing, the price of this portion, constitutes the rent of land, and in the price of the greater part of commodities makes a third component part.

The real value of all the different component parts of price, it must be observed, is measured by the quantity of labor which they can, each of them, purchase or command. Labor measures the value not only of that part of price which resolves itself into labor, but of that which resolves itself into rent, and of that which resolves itself into profit.

In every society the price of every commodity finally resolves itself into some one or other, or all of those three parts; and in every improved society, all the three enter more or less, as component parts, into the price of the far greater part of commodities.

In the price of corn, for example, one part pays the rent of the landlord, another pays the wages or maintenance of the laborers and laboring cattle employed in producing it, and the third pays the profit of the farmer. These three parts seem either immediately or ultimately to make up the whole price of corn. A fourth part, it may perhaps be thought, is necessary for replacing the stock of the farmer, or for compensating the wear and tear of his laboring cattle, and other instruments of husbandry. But it must be considered that the price of any instrument of husbandry, such as a laboring horse, is itself made up of the same three parts: the rent of the land upon which he is reared, the labor of tending and rearing him, and the profits of the farmer who advances both the rent of this land and the wages of this labor. Though the price of the corn, therefore, may pay the price as well as the maintenance of the horse, the whole price still resolves itself either immediately or ultimately into the same three parts of rent, labor, and profit.

In the price of flour or meal, we must add to the price of the corn the profits of the miller and the wages of his servants; in the price of bread, the profits of the baker and the wages of his servants; and in the price of both, the labor of transporting the corn from the house of the farmer to that of the miller, and from that of the miller to that of the baker, together with the profits of those who advance the wages of that labor.

The price of flax resolves itself into the same three parts as that of corn. In the price of linen we must add to this price the wages of the flax-dresser, of the spinner, of the weaver, of the bleacher, etc., together with the profits of their respective employers.

As any particular commodity comes to be more manufactured, that part of the price which resolves itself into wages and profit comes to be greater in proportion to that which resolves itself into rent. In the progress of the manufacture, not only the number of profits increase, but every subsequent profit is greater than the foregoing, because the capital from which it is derived must always be greater. The capital which employs the weavers, for example, must be greater than that which employs the spinners, because it not only replaces that capital with its profits, but pays, besides, the wages of the weavers; and the profits must always bear some proportion to the capital.[2]

In the most improved societies, however, there are always a few commodities of which the price resolves itself into two parts only, the wages of labor, and the profits of stock; and a still smaller number in which it consists altogether in the

[2] [The fact that the later manufacturer has to replace what is here called the capital, i.e., the periodical expenditure of the earlier manufacturer, does not necessarily require him to have a greater capital to deal with the same produce. It need not be greater if he requires less machinery and buildings and a smaller stock of materials.—C.]

wages of labor. In the price of seafish, for example, one part pays the labor of the fishermen, and the other the profits of the capital employed in the fishery. Rent, very seldom makes any part of it, though it does sometimes, as I shall show hereafter. It is otherwise, at least through the greater part of Europe, in river fisheries. A salmon fishery pays a rent, and rent, though it cannot well be called the rent of land, makes a part of the price of a salmon as well as wages and profit. In some parts of Scotland a few poor people make a trade of gathering, along the seashore, those little variegated stones commonly known by the name of Scotch Pebbles. The price which is paid to them by the stonecutter is altogether the wages of their labor; neither rent nor profit make any part of it.

But the whole price of any commodity must still finally resolve itself into some one or other, or all of those three parts; as whatever part of it remains after paying the rent of the land and the price of the whole labor employed in raising, manufacturing, and bringing it to market, must necessarily be profit to somebody.[3]

As the price or exchangeable value of every particular commodity, taken separately, resolves itself into some one or other, or all of those three parts; so that of all the commodities which compose the whole annual produce of the labor of every country, taken complexly, must resolve itself into the same three parts, and be parcelled out among different inhabitants of the country either as the wages of their labor, the profits of their stock, or the rent of their land.[4] The whole of what is annually either collected or produced by the labor of every society, or what comes to the same thing, the whole price of it, is in this manner originally distributed among some of its different members. Wages, profit, and rent are the

[3] [Only true if "commodity" be understood to include solely goods which constitute income.—C.]

[4] [The "whole annual produce" must be taken to mean the income and not the whole mass of goods produced, including those which perish or are used up in the creation of others.—C.]

three original sources of all revenue as well as of all exchangeable value. All other revenue is ultimately derived from some one or other of these.

Whoever derives his revenue from a fund which is his own must draw it either from his labor, from his stock, or from his land. The revenue derived from labor is called wages. That derived from stock, by the person who manages or employs it, is called profit. That derived from it by the person who does not employ it himself, but lends it to another, is called the interest or the use of money. It is the compensation which the borrower pays to the lender for the profit which he has an opportunity of making by the use of the money. Part of that profit naturally belongs to the borrower, who runs the risk and takes the trouble of employing it; and part to the lender, who affords him the opportunity of making this profit. The interest of money is always a derivative revenue, which, if it is not paid from the profit which is made by the use of the money, must be paid from some other source of revenue, unless perhaps the borrower is a spendthrift, who contracts a second debt in order to pay the interest of the first. The revenue which proceeds altogether from land is called rent, and belongs to the landlord. The revenue of the farmer is derived partly from his labor, and partly from his stock. To him, land is only the instrument which enables him to earn the wages of this labor, and to make the profits of this stock. All taxes, and all the revenue which is founded upon them, all salaries, pensions, and annuities of every kind, are ultimately derived from some one or other of those three original sources of revenue, and are paid either immediately or mediately from the wages of labor, the profits of stock, or the rent of land.

When those three different sorts of revenue belong to different persons, they are readily distinguished; but when they belong to the same they are sometimes confounded with one another, at least in common language.

A gentleman who farms a part of his own estate, after paying the expense of cultivation, should gain both the rent of the landlord and the profit of the farmer. He is apt to de-

nominate, however, his whole gain "profit," and thus con-
founds rent with profit, at least in common language. The
greater part of our North American and West Indian planters
are in this situation. They farm, the greater part of them,
their own estates, and accordingly we seldom hear of the rent
of a plantation, but frequently of its profit.

Common farmers seldom employ any overseer to direct the
general operations of the farm. They generally too work a
good deal with their own hands, as plowmen, harrowers, etc.
What remains of the crop after paying the rent, therefore,
should not only replace to them their stock employed in
cultivation, together with its ordinary profits, but pay them
the wages which are due to them, both as laborers and over-
seers. Whatever remains, however, after paying the rent and
keeping up the stock, is called profit. But wages evidently
make a part of it. The farmer, by saving these wages, must
necessarily gain them. Wages, therefore, are in this case confounded with profit.

An independent manufacturer, who has stock enough both
to purchase materials and to maintain himself till he can
carry his work to market, should gain both the wages of a
journeyman who works under a master, and the profit which
that master makes by the sale of the journeyman's work. His
whole gains, however, are commonly called profit, and wages
are, in this case too, confounded with profit.

A gardener who cultivates his own garden with his own
hands unites in his own person the three different characters
of landlord, farmer, and laborer. His produce, therefore,
should pay him the rent of the first, the profit of the second,
and the wages of the third. The whole, however, is commonly considered as the earnings of his labor. Both rent and
profit are, in this case, confounded with wages.

As in a civilized country there are but few commodities of
which the exchangeable value arises from labor only, rent
and profit contributing largely to that of the far greater part
of them, so the annual produce of its labor will always be
sufficient to purchase or command a much greater quantity of

labor than what was employed in raising, preparing, and bringing that produce to market. If the society were annually to employ all the labor which it can annually purchase, as the quantity of labor would increase greatly every year, so the produce of every succeeding year would be of vastly greater value than that of the foregoing. But there is no country in which the whole annual produce is employed in maintaining the industrious. The idle everywhere consume a great part of it; and according to the different proportions in which it is annually divided between those two different orders of people, its ordinary or average value must either annually increase, or diminish, or continue the same from one year to another.

CHAPTER VII

OF THE NATURAL AND MARKET PRICE OF COMMODITIES

There is in every society or neighborhood an ordinary or average rate both of wages and profit in every different employment of labor and stock. This rate is naturally regulated, as I shall show hereafter,[1] partly by the general circumstances of the society, their riches or poverty, their advancing, stationary, or declining condition; and partly by the particular nature of each employment.

There is likewise in every society or neighborhood an ordinary or average rate of rent, which is regulated too, as I shall show hereafter,[2] partly by the general circumstances of the society or neighborhood in which the land is situated, and partly by the natural or improved fertility of the land.

1 [See Book I, Chapter III, 63-89; IX, 90-102.]
2 [See Book I, Chapter XI (not included in this edition).]

These ordinary or average rates may be called the natural rates of wages, profit, and rent, at the time and place in which they commonly prevail.

When the price of any commodity is neither more nor less than what is sufficient to pay the rent of the land, the wages of the labor, and the profits of the stock employed in raising, preparing, and bringing it to market according to their natural rates, the commodity is then sold for what may be called its natural price.

The commodity is then sold precisely for what it is worth, or for what it really costs the person who brings it to market; for though in common language what is called the prime cost of any commodity does not comprehend the profit of the person who is to sell it again, yet if he sells it at a price which does not allow him the ordinary rate of profit in his neighborhood, he is evidently a loser by the trade, since by employing his stock in some other way he might have made that profit. His profit, besides, is his revenue, the proper fund of his subsistence. As, while he is preparing and bringing the goods to market, he advances to his workmen their wages, or their subsistence, so he advances to himself, in the same manner, his own subsistence, which is generally suitable to the profit which he may reasonably expect from the sale of his goods. Unless they yield him this profit, therefore, they do not repay him what they may very properly be said to have really cost him.

Though the price, therefore, which leaves him this profit is not always the lowest at which a dealer may sometimes sell his goods, it is the lowest at which he is likely to sell them for any considerable time, at least where there is perfect liberty, or where he may change his trade as often as he pleases.

The actual price at which any commodity is commonly sold is called its market price. It may either be above, or below, or exactly the same with its natural price.

The market price of every particular commodity is regulated by the proportion between the quantity which is actually brought to market and the demand of those who are willing to pay the natural price of the commodity, or the whole value of the rent, labor, and profit which must be paid in order to bring it thither. Such people may be called the effectual demanders, and their demand, the effectual demand, since it may be sufficient to effectuate the bringing of the commodity to market. It is different from the absolute demand. A very poor man may be said in some sense to have a demand for a coach and six; he might like to have it; but his demand is not an effectual demand, as the commodity can never be brought to market in order to satisfy it.

When the quantity of any commodity which is brought to market falls short of the effectual demand, all those who are willing to pay the whole value of the rent, wages, and profit, which must be paid in order to bring it thither, cannot be supplied with the quantity which they want. Rather than want it altogether, some of them will be willing to give more. A competition will immediately begin among them, and the market price will rise more or less above the natural price, according as either the greatness of the deficiency or the wealth and wanton luxury of the competitors happen to animate more or less the eagerness of the competition. Among competitors of equal wealth and luxury the same deficiency will generally occasion a more or less eager competition, according as the acquisition of the commodity happens to be of more or less importance to them. Hence the exorbitant price of the necessities of life during the blockade of a town or in a famine.

When the quantity brought to market exceeds the effectual demand, it cannot be all sold to those who are willing to pay the whole value of the rent, wages, and profit, which must be paid in order to bring it thither. Some part must be sold to those who are willing to pay less, and the low price which they give for it must reduce the price of the whole. The market price will sink more or less below the natural price, according as the greatness of the excess increases more or less the competition of the sellers, or according as it happens to be more or less important to them to get immediately rid of the commodity. The same excess in the importation of perishables will occasion a much greater competition than in that of durable commodities, in the importation of oranges, for example, than in that of old iron.

When the quantity brought to market is just sufficient to supply the effectual demand and no more, the market price naturally comes to be either exactly, or as nearly as can be judged of, the same with the natural price. The whole quantity upon hand can be disposed of for this price and cannot be disposed of for more. The competition of the different dealers obliges them all to accept of this price, but does not oblige them to accept of less.

The quantity of every commodity brought to market naturally suits itself to the effectual demand. It is the interest of all those who employ their land, labor, or stock, in bringing any commodity to market, that the quantity never should exceed the effectual demand; and it is the interest of all other people that it never should fall short of that demand.

If at any time it exceeds the effectual demand, some of the component parts of its price must be paid below their natural rate. If it is rent, the interest of the landlords will immediately prompt them to withdraw a part of their land; and if it is wages or profit, the interest of the laborers in the one case, and of their employers in the other, will prompt them to withdraw a part of their labor or stock from this employment. The quantity brought to market will soon be no more than sufficient to supply the effectual demand. All the different parts of its price will rise to their natural rate, and the whole price to its natural price.

If, on the contrary, the quantity brought to market should at any time fall short of the effectual demand, some of the component parts of its price must rise above their natural rate. If it is rent, the interest of all other landlords will naturally prompt them to prepare more land for the raising of this commodity; if it is wages or profit, the interest of all other laborers and dealers will soon prompt them to employ more labor and stock in preparing and bringing it to market.

The quantity brought thither will soon be sufficient to supply the effectual demand. All the different parts of its price will soon sink to their natural rate, and the whole price to its natural price.

The natural price, therefore, is, as it were, the central price, to which the prices of all commodities are continually gravitating. Different accidents may sometimes keep them suspended a good deal above it, and sometimes force them down even somewhat below it. But whatever may be the obstacles which hinder them from settling in this center of repose and continuance, they are constantly tending towards it.

The whole quantity of industry annually employed in order to bring any commodity to market naturally suits itself in this manner to the effectual demand. It naturally aims at bringing always that precise quantity thither which may be sufficient to supply, and no more than supply, that demand.

But in some employments the same quantity of industry will in different years produce very different quantities of commodities; while in others it will produce always the same, or very nearly the same. The same number of laborers in husbandry will, in different years, produce very different quantities of corn, wine, oil, hops, etc. But the same number of spinners and weavers will every year produce the same or very nearly the same quantity of linen and woolen cloth. It is only the average produce of the one species of industry which can be suited in any respect to the effectual demand; and as its actual produce is frequently much greater and frequently much less than its average produce, the quantity of the commodities brought to market will sometimes exceed a good deal, and sometimes fall short a good deal, of the effectual demand. Even though that demand therefore should continue always the same, their market price will be liable to great fluctuations, will sometimes fall a good deal below, and sometimes rise a good deal above, their natural price. In the other species of industry, the produce of equal quantities of labor being always the same, or very nearly the same, it can be more exactly suited to the effectual demand. While that demand

continues the same, therefore, the market price of the commodities is likely to do so too, and to be either altogether, or
as nearly as can be judged, the same with the natural price.
That the price of linen and woolen cloth is liable neither to
such frequent nor to such great variations as the price of corn,
every man's experience will inform him. The price of the one
species of commodities varies only with the variations in the
demand, that of the other varies not only with the variations
in the demand, but with the much greater and more frequent
variations in the quantity of what is brought to market in
order to supply that demand.

The occasional and temporary fluctuations in the market
price of any commodity fall chiefly upon those parts of its
price which resolve themselves into wages and profit. That
part which resolves itself into rent is less affected by them. A
rent certain in money is not in the least affected by them either
in its rate or in its value. A rent which consists either in a
certain proportion or in a certain quantity of the rude
produce is no doubt affected in its yearly value by all the
occasional and temporary fluctuations in the market price of
that rude produce; but it is seldom affected by them in its
yearly rate. In settling the terms of the lease, the landlord and
farmer endeavor, according to their best judgment, to adjust
that rate, not to the temporary and occasional, but to the
average and ordinary price of the produce.

Such fluctuations affect both the value and the rate either of
wages or of profit, accordingly as the market happens to be
either overstocked or understocked with commodities or with
labor—with work done or with work to be done. A public
mourning raises the price of black cloth (with which the market is almost always understocked upon such occasions) and
augments the profits of the merchants who possess any considerable quantity of it. It has no effect upon the wages of the
weavers. The market is understocked with commodities, not
with labor—with work done, not with work to be done. It
raises the wages of journeymen tailors. The market is here
understocked with labor. There is an effectual demand for

more labor, for more work to be done than can be had. It
sinks the price of colored silks and cloths, and thereby reduces
the profits of the merchants who have any considerable quantity of them upon hand. It sinks, too, the wages of the workmen employed in preparing such commodities, for which all
demand is stopped for six months, perhaps for a twelvemonth.
The market is here overstocked both with commodities and
with labor.

But though the market price of every particular commodity
is in this manner continually gravitating, if one may say so,
towards the natural price, yet sometimes particular accidents,
sometimes natural causes, and sometimes particular regulations of police [3] may, in many commodities, keep up the market price, for a long time together, a good deal above the
natural price.

When by an increase in the effectual demand the market
price of some particular commodity happens to rise a good
deal above the natural price, those who employ their stocks
in supplying that market are generally careful to conceal this
change. If it was commonly known, their great profit would
tempt so many new rivals to employ their stocks in the same
way that, the effectual demand being fully supplied, the market price would soon be reduced to the natural price, and
perhaps for some time even below it. If the market is at a
great distance from the residence of those who supply it, they
may sometimes be able to keep the secret for several years together, and may so long enjoy their extraordinary profits without any new rivals. Secrets of this kind, however, it must be
acknowledged, can seldom be long kept; and the extraordinary
profit can last very little longer than they are kept.

Secrets in manufactures are capable of being kept longer

---

[3] [In his *Lectures on Justice, Police, Revenue and Arms,* Smith treated
the objects of police as "cheapness of commodities, public security and
cleanliness." It was under this heading that he placed the opulence of a
state. Smith took the word from the French which, in turn, had derived
it from the Greek word "politeia," signifying the policy of civil government.—M.]

than secrets in trade. A dyer who has found the means of producing a particular color with materials which cost only half
the price of those commonly made use of may, with good
management, enjoy the advantage of his discovery as long as
he lives, and even leave it as a legacy to his posterity. His
extraordinary gains arise from the high price which is paid
for his private labor. They properly consist in the high wages
of that labor. But as they are repeated upon every part of
his stock, and as their whole amount bears, upon that account,
a regular proportion to it, they are commonly considered as
extraordinary profits of stock.

Such enhancements of the market price are evidently the
effects of particular accidents, of which, however, the operation may sometimes last for many years together.

Some natural productions require such a singularity of soil
and situation that all the land in a great country, which is
fit for producing them, may not be sufficient to supply the
effectual demand. The whole quantity brought to market,
therefore, may be disposed of to those who are willing to give
more than what is sufficient to pay the rent of the land which
produced them, together with the wages of the labor and the
profits of the stock which were employed in preparing and
bringing them to market according to their natural rates. Such
commodities may continue for whole centuries together to be
sold at this high price; and that part of it which resolves itself
into the rent of land is in this case the part which is generally
paid above its natural rate. The rent of the land which affords
such singular and esteemed productions, like the rent of some
vineyards in France of a peculiarly happy soil and situation,
bears no regular proportion to the rent of other equally fertile
and equally well-cultivated land in its neighborhood. The
wages of the labor and the profits of the stock employed in
bringing such commodities to market, on the contrary, are
seldom out of their natural proportion to those of the other
employments of labor and stock in their neighborhood.

Such enhancements of the market price are evidently the effect of natural causes which may hinder the effectual demand

from ever being fully supplied, and which may continue, therefore, to operate forever.

A monopoly granted either to an individual or to a trading company has the same effect as a secret in trade or manufactures. The monopolists, by keeping the market constantly understocked, by never fully supplying the effectual demand, sell their commodities much above the natural price, and raise their emoluments, whether they consist in wages or profit, greatly above their natural rate.

The price of monopoly is upon every occasion the highest which can be got. The natural price, or the price of free competition, on the contrary, is the lowest which can be taken, not upon every occasion indeed, but for any considerable time together. The one is upon every occasion the highest which can be squeezed out of the buyers, or which, it is supposed, they will consent to give: The other is the lowest which the sellers can commonly afford to take and at the same time continue their business.

The exclusive privileges of corporations, statutes of apprenticeship, and all those laws which restrain, in particular employments, the competition to a smaller number than might otherwise go into them, have the same tendency, though in a lesser degree. They are a sort of enlarged monopolies, and may frequently, for ages together, and in whole classes of employments, keep up the market price of particular commodities above the natural price, and maintain both the wages of the labor and the profits of the stock employed about them somewhat above their natural rate.

Such enhancements of the market price may last as long as the regulations of police which give occasion to them.

The market price of any particular commodity, though it may continue long above, can seldom continue long below, its natural price. Whatever part of it was paid below the natural rate, the persons whose interest it affected would immediately feel the loss, and would immediately withdraw either so much land, or so much labor, or so much stock, from being employed about it, that the quantity brought to market would soon be no more than sufficient to supply the effectual demand. Its market price, therefore, would soon rise to the natural price. This at least would be the case where there was perfect liberty.

The same statutes of apprenticeship and other corporation laws, indeed, which, when a manufacture is in prosperity, enable the workman to raise his wages a good deal above their natural rate, sometimes oblige him, when it decays, to let them down a good deal below it. As in the one case they exclude many people from his employment, so in the other they exclude him from many employments. The effect of such regulations, however, is not near so durable in sinking the workman's wages below, as in raising them above, their natural rate. Their operation in the one way may endure for many centuries, but in the other it can last no longer than the lives of some of the workmen who were bred to the business in the time of its prosperity. When they are gone, the number of those who are afterwards educated to the trade will naturally suit itself to the effectual demand. The police must be as violent as that of Indostan [India] or ancient Egypt [4] (where every man was bound by a principle of religion to follow the occupation of his father, and was supposed to commit the most horrid sacrilege if he changed it for another), which can in any particular employment, and for several generations together, sink either the wages of labor or the profits of stock below their natural rate.

This is all that I think necessary to be observed at present concerning the deviations, whether occasional or permanent, of the market price of commodities from the natural price.

The natural price itself varies with the natural rate of each of its component parts, of wages, profit, and rent; and in every society this rate varies according to their circumstances, according to their riches or poverty, their advancing, stationary,

[4] [In *Lectures*, p. 168, the Egyptian practice is attributed to a "law of Sesostris."—C. (Sesostris, a legendary king of Egypt, who, according to Herodotus, conquered the entire world, divided Egypt into districts, was a great lawgiver, and introduced a system of caste.—M.)]

or declining condition. I shall, in the four following chapters, endeavor to explain, as fully and distinctly as I can, the causes of those different variations.[5]

First, I shall endeavor to explain what are the circumstances which naturally determine the rate of wages, and in what manner those circumstances are affected by the riches or poverty, by the advancing, stationary, or declining state of the society.

Secondly, I shall endeavor to show what are the circumstances which naturally determine the rate of profit, and in what manner too those circumstances are affected by the like variations in the state of the society.

Though pecuniary wages and profit are very different in the different employments of labor and stock, yet a certain proportion seems commonly to take place between both the pecuniary wages in all the different employments of labor, and the pecuniary profits in all the different employments of stock. This proportion, it will appear hereafter, depends partly upon the nature of the different employments, and partly upon the different laws and policy of the society in which they are carried on. But though in many respects dependent upon the laws and policy, this proportion seems to be little affected by the riches or poverty of that society, by its advancing, stationary, or declining condition, but to remain the same or very nearly the same in all those different states. I shall, in the third place, endeavor to explain all the different circumstances which regulate this proportion.

In the fourth and last place, I shall endeavor to show what are the circumstances which regulate the rent of land, and which either raise or lower the real price of all the different substances which it produces.

[5] [Of the four chapters mentioned by Smith, we reprint only the first two in their entirety and the concluding part of the fourth.—M.]

CHAPTER VIII

OF THE WAGES OF LABOR

The produce of labor constitutes the natural recompense or wages of labor.

In that original state of things, which precedes both the appropriation of land and the accumulation of stock, the whole produce of labor belongs to the laborer. He has neither landlord nor master to share with him.[1]

Had this state continued, the wages of labor would have augmented with all those improvements in its productive powers to which the division of labor gives occasion. All things would gradually have become cheaper. They would have been produced by a smaller quantity of labor, and as the commodities produced by equal quantities of labor would naturally in this state of things be exchanged for one another, they would have been purchased likewise with the produce of a smaller quantity.

But though all things would have become cheaper in reality, in appearance many things might have become dearer than before, or have been exchanged for a greater quantity of other goods. Let us suppose, for example, that in the greater part of employments the productive powers of labor had been im-

[1] [It is interesting to compare Smith's "original state of things," a time without landlord or master, with John Locke's "state of nature" as depicted in *The Second Treatise of Civil Government* (Chapter Two and *passim*). Did Smith believe such a state of nature had actually existed as an historical fact? His close friend, David Hume, it may be noted, wrote an essay opposing the existence of an "original state of things." Whatever Smith's real beliefs, his statements supply the ground for an equalitarian philosophy and could easily serve the turn of a Karl Marx, who saw in capitalism the exploitation of the worker and who accused the capitalist of deducting from the worker what rightfully belonged to him. Both Smith and Marx tend to neglect the fact that, without entrepreneurs, the division of labor might never have expanded.—M.]

proved to tenfold, or that a day's labor could produce ten times the quantity of work which it had done originally; but that in a particular employment they had been improved only to double, or that a day's labor could produce only twice the quantity of work which it had done before. In exchanging the produce of a day's labor in the greater part of employments for that of a day's labor in this particular one, ten times the original quantity of work in them would purchase only twice the original quantity in it. Any particular quantity in it, therefore, a pound weight, for example, would appear to be five times dearer than before. In reality, however, it would be twice as cheap. Though it required five times the quantity of other goods to purchase it, it would require only half the quantity of labor either to purchase or to produce it. The acquisition, therefore, would be twice as easy as before.

But this original state of things, in which the laborer enjoyed the whole produce of his own labor, could not last beyond the first introduction of the appropriation of land and the accumulation of stock. It was at an end, therefore, long before the most considerable improvements were made in the productive powers of labor, and it would be to no purpose to trace further what might have been its effects upon the recompense or wages of labor.

As soon as land becomes private property, the landlord demands a share of almost all the produce which the laborer can either raise or collect from it. His rent makes the first deduction from the produce of the labor which is employed upon land.

It seldom happens that the person who tills the ground has wherewithal to maintain himself till he reaps the harvest. His maintenance is generally advanced to him from the stock of a master, the farmer who employs him, and who would have no interest to employ him, unless he was to share in the produce of his labor, or unless his stock was to be replaced to him with a profit. This profit makes a second deduction from the produce of the labor which is employed upon land.

The produce of almost all other labor is liable to the like

deduction of profit. In all arts and manufactures the greater part of the workmen stand in need of a master to advance them the materials of their work, and their wages and maintenance till it be completed. He shares in the produce of their labor, or in the value which it adds to the materials upon which it is bestowed; and in this share consists his profit.

It sometimes happens, indeed, that a single independent workman has stock sufficient both to purchase the materials of nis work, and to maintain himself till it is completed. He is both master and workman, and enjoys the whole produce of his own labor, or the whole value which it adds to the materials upon which it is bestowed. It includes what are usually two distinct revenues, belonging to two distinct persons, the profits of stock, and the wages of labor.

Such cases, however, are not very frequent, and in every part of Europe twenty workmen serve under a master for one that is independent; and the wages of labor are everywhere understood to be, what they usually are, when the laborer is one person, and the owner of the stock which employs him another.

What are the common wages of labor depends everywhere upon the contract usually made between those two parties, whose interests are by no means the same. The workmen desire to get as much, the masters to give as little as possible. The former are disposed to combine in order to raise, the latter in order to lower, the wages of labor.

It is not, however, difficult to foresee which of the two parties must, upon all ordinary occasions, have the advantage in the dispute, and force the other into a compliance with their terms. The masters, being fewer in number, can combine much more easily; and the law, besides, authorizes, or at least does not prohibit their combinations, while it prohibits those of the workmen. We have no acts of Parliament against combining to lower the price of work; but many against combining to raise it. In all such disputes the masters can hold out much longer. A landlord, a farmer, a master manufacturer, or merchant, though they did not employ a single workman, could generally live a year or two upon the stocks which they have already acquired. Many workmen could not subsist a week, few could subsist a month, and scarcely any a year without employment. In the long run the workman may be as necessary to his master as his master is to him, but the necessity is not so immediate.

We rarely hear, it has been said, of the combinations of masters, though frequently of those of workmen. But whoever imagines, upon this account, that masters rarely combine, is as ignorant of the world as of the subject. Masters are always and everywhere in a sort of tacit, but constant and uniform, combination, not to raise the wages of labor above their actual rate. To violate this combination is everywhere a most unpopular action, and a sort of reproach to a master among his neighbors and equals. We seldom, indeed, hear of this combination, because it is the usual and, one may say, the natural state of things which nobody ever hears of. Masters, too, sometimes enter into particular combinations to sink the wages of labor even below this rate. These are always conducted with the utmost silence and secrecy, till the moment of execution, and when the workmen yield, as they sometimes do, without resistance, though severely felt by them, they are never heard of by other people. Such combinations, however, are frequently resisted by a contrary defensive combination of the workmen, who sometimes, too, without any provocation of this kind, combine of their own accord to raise the price of their labor. Their usual pretenses [2] are sometimes the high price of provisions, sometimes the great profit which their masters make by their work. But whether their combinations be offensive or defensive, they are always abundantly heard of. In order to bring the point to a speedy decision, they have always recourse to the loudest clamor, and sometimes to the most shocking violence and outrage. They are desperate, and act with the folly and extravagance of desperate men, who

[2] [The word is used as elsewhere in Adam Smith without the implication of falsity now attached to it: a pretense is simply something put forward.—C.]

must either starve or frighten their masters into an immediate compliance with their demands. The masters upon these occasions are just as clamorous upon the other side, and never cease to call aloud for the assistance of the civil magistrate and the rigorous execution of those laws which have been enacted with so much severity against the combinations of servants, laborers, and journeymen. The workmen, accordingly, very seldom derive any advantage from the violence of those tumultuous combinations, which, partly from the interposition of the civil magistrate, partly from the superior steadiness of the masters, partly from the necessity which the greater part of the workmen are under of submitting for the sake of present subsistence, generally end in nothing but the punishment or ruin of the ringleaders.

But though in disputes with their workmen masters must generally have the advantage, there is however a certain rate below which it seems impossible to reduce, for any considerable time, the ordinary wages even of the lowest species of labor.

A man must always live by his work, and his wages must at least be sufficient to maintain him. They must even upon most occasions be somewhat more, otherwise it would be impossible for him to bring up a family, and the race of such workmen could not last beyond the first generation. Mr. Cantillon seems, upon this account, to suppose that the lowest species of common laborers must everywhere earn at least double their own maintenance, in order that one with another they may be enabled to bring up two children; the labor of the wife, on account of her necessary attendance on the children, being supposed no more than sufficient to provide for herself.[3] But one half the children born, it is computed, die before the age of manhood. The poorest laborers, therefore, according to this account, must, one with another, attempt to rear at least four

[3] [*Essai sur la nature du commerce en général*, 1755, pp. 42-47. The "seems" is not meaningless, as Cantillon is unusually obscure in the passage referred to. It is not clear whether he intends to include the woman's earnings or not.—C.]

children, in order that two may have an equal chance of living
to that age. But the necessary maintenance of four children,
it is supposed, may be nearly equal to that of one man. The
labor of an able-bodied slave, the same author adds, is computed to be worth double his maintenance; and that of the
meanest laborer, he thinks, cannot be worth less than that of
an able-bodied slave. Thus far at least [it] seems certain that, in
order to bring up a family, the labor of the husband and wife
together must, even in the lowest species of common labor, be
able to earn something more than what is precisely necessary
for their own maintenance; but in what proportion, whether
in that above mentioned, or in any other, I shall not take
upon me to determine.[4]

There are certain circumstances, however, which sometimes
give the laborers an advantage, and enable them to raise their
wages considerably above this rate, evidently the lowest which
is consistent with common humanity.

When in any country the demand for those who live by
wages, laborers, journeymen, servants of every kind, is continually increasing, when every year furnishes employment
for a greater number than had been employed the year before, the workmen have no occasion to combine in order to
raise their wages. The scarcity of hands occasions a competition among masters, who bid against one another, in order to
get workmen, and thus voluntarily break through the natural
combination of masters not to raise wages.

The demand for those who live by wages, it is evident, cannot increase but in proportion to the increase of the funds
which are destined for the payment of wages. These funds are
of two kinds: first, the revenue which is over and above what
is necessary for the maintenance; and, secondly, the stock
which is over and above what is necessary for the employment
of their masters.

When the landlord, annuitant, or moneyed man has a

4 [Cantillon himself, p. 44, says: *"C'est une matière qui n'admet pas un
calcul exact, et dans laquelle la précision n'est pas même fort nécessaire, il
suffit qu'on ne s'y éloigne pas beaucoup de la réalité."*—C.]

greater revenue than what he judges sufficient to maintain his own family, he employs either the whole or a part of the surplus in maintaining one or more menial servants. Increase this surplus, and he will naturally increase the number of those servants.

When an independent workman, such as a weaver or shoemaker, has got more stock than what is sufficient to purchase the materials of his own work, and to maintain himself till he can dispose of it, he naturally employs one or more journeyman with the surplus, in order to make a profit by their work. Increase this surplus, and he will naturally increase the number of his journeymen.

The demand for those who live by wages, therefore, necessarily increases with the increase of the revenue and stock of every country, and cannot possibly increase without it. The increase of revenue and stock is the increase of national wealth.[5] The demand for those who live by wages, therefore, naturally increases with the increase of national wealth, and cannot possibly increase without it.

It is not the actual greatness of national wealth, but its continual increase, which occasions a rise in the wages of labor. It is not, accordingly, in the richest countries, but in the most thriving, or in those which are growing rich the fastest, that the wages of labor are highest. England is certainly, in the present times, a much richer country than any part of North America. The wages of labor, however, are much higher in North America than in any part of England. In the province of New York, common laborers earn [6] three shillings and sixpence currency, equal to two shillings sterling, a day; ship carpenters, ten shillings and sixpence currency, with a pint of rum worth sixpence sterling, equal in all to six shillings and sixpence sterling; house carpenters and bricklayers, eight shil-

[5] [Above, in the Introduction and Plan of the Work, the wealth of a nation was treated as synonymous with its annual produce, and there has been hitherto no suggestion that its stock must be considered.—C.]

[6] This was written in 1773, before the commencement of the late disturbances.

lings currency, equal to four shillings and sixpence sterling; journeymen tailors, five shillings currency, equal to about two shillings and ten pence sterling. These prices are all above the London price, and wages are said to be as high in the other colonies as in New York. The price of provisions is everywhere in North America much lower than in England. A dearth has never been known there. In the worst seasons, they have always had a sufficiency for themselves, though less for exportation. If the money price of labor, therefore, be higher than it is anywhere in the mother country, its real price, the real command of the necessities and conveniences of life which it conveys to the laborer, must be higher in a still greater proportion.

But though North America is not yet so rich as England, it is much more thriving, and advancing with much greater rapidity to the further acquisition of riches. The most decisive mark of the prosperity of any country is the increase of the number of its inhabitants.[7] In Great Britain, and most other European countries, they are not supposed to double in less than five hundred years. In the British colonies in North America, it has been found, that they double in twenty or twenty-five years. Nor in the present times is this increase principally owing to the continual importation of new inhabitants, but to the great multiplication of the species. Those who live to old age, it is said, frequently see there from fifty to a hundred, and sometimes many more, descendants from their own body. Labor is there so well rewarded that a numerous family of children, instead of being a burden, is a source of opulence and prosperity to the parents. The labor of each child, before it can leave their house, is computed to be worth a hundred pounds clear gain to them. A young

---

[7] [This was a typical eighteenth-century view. Rousseau, for example, in Ch. IX of the *Social Contract,* answers the question as to "what are the marks of a good government?" by the statement: "numbers and population." In our time, however, with the threat of over-population rather than de-population, we are not so sure that increased population is a "decisive mark" of either prosperity or good government.—M.]

widow with four or five young children, who, among the
middling or inferior ranks of people in Europe, would have
so little chance for a second husband, is there frequently
courted as a sort of fortune. The value of children is the greatest of all encouragements to marriage. We cannot, therefore,
wonder that the people in North America should generally
marry very young. Notwithstanding the great increase occasioned by such early marriages, there is a continual complaint of the scarcity of hands in North America. The demand
for laborers, the funds destined for maintaining them, increase, it seems, still faster than they can find laborers to employ.

Though the wealth of a country should be very great, yet
if it has been long stationary, we must not expect to find the
wages of labor very high in it. The funds destined for the
payment of wages, the revenue and stock of its inhabitants,
may be of the greatest extent; but if they have continued for
several centuries of the same, or very nearly of the same extent, the number of laborers employed every year could easily
supply, and even more than supply, the number wanted the
following year. There could seldom be any scarcity of hands,
nor could the masters be obliged to bid against one another
in order to get them. The hands, on the contrary, would, in
this case, naturally multiply beyond their employment. There
would be a constant scarcity of employment, and the laborers
would be obliged to bid against one another in order to get it.
If in such a country the wages of labor had ever been more
than sufficient to maintain the laborer, and to enable him to
bring up a family, the competition of the laborers and the
interest of the masters would soon reduce them to this lowest
rate which is consistent with common humanity. China has
been long one of the richest, that is, one of the most fertile,
best cultivated, most industrious, and most populous countries in the world.[8] It seems, however, to have been long stationary. Marco Polo, who visited it more than five hundred

[8] [Here we have a third method of calculating the riches or wealth of a
country, namely by the amount of produce per acre.—C.]

years ago, describes its cultivation, industry, and populousness, almost in the same terms in which are described by travellers in the present times. It had perhaps, even long before his time, acquired that full complement of riches which the nature of its laws and institutions permits it to acquire. The accounts of all travellers, inconsistent in many other respects, agree in the low wages of labor, and in the difficulty which a laborer finds in bringing up a family in China. If by digging the ground a whole day he can get what will purchase a small quantity of rice in the evening, he is contented. The condition of artificers is, if possible, still worse. Instead of waiting indolently in their workhouses for the calls of their customers, as in Europe, they are continually running about the streets with the tools of their respective trades, offering their service and, as it were, begging employment. The poverty of the lower ranks of people in China far surpasses that of the most beggarly nations in Europe. In the neighborhood of Canton many hundred, it is commonly said, many thousand families have no habitation on the land, but live constantly in little fishing boats upon the rivers and canals. The subsistence which they find there is so scanty that they are eager to fish up the nastiest garbage thrown overboard from any European ship. Any carrion, the carcass of a dead dog or cat, for example, though half putrid and stinking, is as welcome to them as the most wholesome food to the people of other countries. Marriage is encouraged in China, not by the profitableness of children, but by the liberty of destroying them. In all great towns several are every night exposed in the street, or drowned like puppies in the water. The performance of this horrid office is even said to be the avowed business by which some people earn their subsistence.

China, however, though it may perhaps stand still, does not seem to go backwards. Its towns are nowhere deserted by their inhabitants. The lands which had once been cultivated are nowhere neglected. The same or very nearly the same annual labor must therefore continue to be performed, and the funds destined for maintaining it must not, consequently, be sensibly diminished. The lowest class of laborers, therefore, notwithstanding their scanty subsistence, must some way or another make shift to continue their race so far as to keep up their usual numbers.

But it would be otherwise in a country where the funds destined for the maintenance of labor were sensibly decaying. Every year the demand for servants and laborers would, in all the different classes of employments, be less than it had been the year before. Many who had been bred in the superior classes, not being able to find employment in their own business, would be glad to seek it in the lowest. The lowest class being not only overstocked with its own workmen, but with the overflowings of all the other classes, the competition for employment would be so great in it as to reduce the wages of labor to the most miserable and scanty subsistence of the laborer. Many would not be able to find employment even upon these hard terms, but would either starve, or be driven to seek a subsistence either by begging, or by the perpetration perhaps of the greatest enormities. Want, famine, and mortality would immediately prevail in that class, and from thence extend themselves to all the superior classes, till the number of inhabitants in the country was reduced to what could easily be maintained by the revenue and stock which remained in it, and which had escaped either the tyranny or calamity which had destroyed the rest. This perhaps is nearly the present state of Bengal, and of some other of the English settlements in the East Indies. In a fertile country which had before been much depopulated, where subsistence, consequently, should not be very difficult, and where, notwithstanding, three or four hundred thousand people die of hunger in one year, we may be assured that the funds destined for the maintenance of the laboring poor are fast decaying. The difference between the genius of the British constitution which protects and governs North America and that of the mercantile company which oppresses and domineers in the East Indies cannot perhaps be better illustrated than by the different state of those countries.

The liberal reward of labor, therefore, as it is the necessary effect, so it is the natural symptom, of increasing national wealth. The scanty maintenance of the laboring poor, on the other hand, is the natural symptom that things are at a stand, and their starving condition that they are going fast backward.

In Great Britain the wages of labor seem, in the present times, to be evidently more than what is precisely necessary to enable the laborer to bring up a family. In order to satisfy ourselves upon this point it will not be necessary to enter into any tedious or doubtful calculation of what may be the lowest sum upon which it is possible to do this. There are many plain symptoms that the wages of labor are nowhere in this country regulated by this lowest rate which is consistent with common humanity.

First, in almost every part of Great Britain there is a distinction, even in the lowest species of labor, between summer and winter wages. Summer wages are always highest. But on account of the extraordinary expense of fuel, the maintenance of a family is most expensive in winter. Wages, therefore, being highest when this expense is lowest, it seems evident that they are not regulated by what is necessary for this expense, but by the quantity and supposed value of the work. A laborer, it may be said indeed, ought to save part of his summer wages in order to defray his winter expense, and that through the whole year they do not exceed what is necessary to maintain his family through the whole year. A slave, however, or one absolutely dependent on us for immediate subsistence, would not be treated in this manner. His daily subsistence would be proportioned to his daily necessities.

Secondly, the wages of labor do not in Great Britain fluctuate with the price of provisions. These vary everywhere from year to year, frequently from month to month. But in many places the money price of labor remains uniformly the same sometimes for half a century together. If in these places, therefore, the laboring poor can maintain their families in dear years, they must be at their ease in times of moderate plenty, and in affluence in those of extraordinary cheapness. The high price of provisions during these ten years past has not, in many parts of the kingdom, been accompanied with any sensible rise in the money price of labor. It has, indeed, in some, owing probably more to the increase of the demand for labor than to that of the price of provisions.

Thirdly, as the price of provisions varies more from year to year than the wages of labor, so, on the other hand, the wages of labor vary more from place to place than the price of provisions. The prices of bread and butcher's meat are generally the same or very nearly the same through the greater part of the United Kingdom. These and most other things which are sold by retail, the way in which the laboring poor buy all things, are generally fully as cheap or cheaper in great towns than in the remoter parts of the country for reasons which I shall have occasion to explain hereafter.[9] But the wages of labor in a great town and its neighborhood are frequently a fourth or a fifth part, twenty or five-and-twenty per cent higher than at a few miles distance. Eighteen pence a day may be reckoned the common price of labor in London and its neighborhood. At a few miles distance it falls to fourteen and fifteen pence. Ten pence may be reckoned its price in Edinburgh and its neighborhood. At a few miles distance it falls to eight pence, the usual price of common labor through the greater part of the low country of Scotland, where it varies a good deal less than in England. Such a difference of prices, which it seems is not always sufficient to transport a man from one parish to another, would necessarily occasion so great a transportation of the most bulky commodities, not only from one parish to another, but from one end of the kingdom, almost from one end of the world to the other, as would soon reduce them more nearly to a level. After all that has been said of the levity and inconstancy of human nature, it appears evident from experience that a man is of all sorts of luggage the most difficult to be transported. If the laboring

[9] [See Book I, Chapter X—C. (not included in this edition).]

poor, therefore, can maintain their families in those parts of the kingdom where the price of labor is lowest, they must be in affluence where it is highest.

Fourthly, the variations in the price of labor not only do not correspond either in place or time with those in the price of provisions, but they are frequently quite opposite.

Grain, the food of the common people, is dearer in Scotland than in England, whence Scotland receives almost every year very large supplies. But English corn must be sold dearer in Scotland, the country to which it is brought, than in England, the country from which it comes; and in proportion to its quality it cannot be sold dearer in Scotland than the Scotch corn that comes to the same market in competition with it. The quality of grain depends chiefly upon the quantity of flour or meal which it yields at the mill, and in this respect English grain is so much superior to the Scotch that, though often dearer in appearance, or in proportion to the measure of its bulk, it is generally cheaper in reality, or in proportion to its quality, or even to the measure of its weight. The price of labor, on the contrary, is dearer in England than in Scotland. If the laboring poor, therefore, can maintain their families in the one part of the United Kingdom, they must be in affluence in the other. Oatmeal indeed supplies the common people in Scotland with the greatest and the best part of their food, which is in general much inferior to that of their neighbors of the same rank in England. This difference, however, in the mode of their subsistence is not the cause, but the effect, of the difference in their wages; though, by a strange misapprehension, I have frequently heard it represented as the cause. It is not because one man keeps a coach while his neighbor walks on foot, that the one is rich and the other poor; but because the one is rich he keeps a coach, and because the other is poor he walks on foot.

During the course of the last century, taking one year with another, grain was dearer in both parts of the United Kingdom than during that of the present. This is a matter of fact which cannot now admit of any reasonable doubt; and the proof of it is, if possible, still more decisive with regard to Scotland than with regard to England. It is in Scotland supported by the evidence of the public fiars, annual valuations made upon oath, according to the actual state of the markets, of all the different sorts of grain in every different county of Scotland. If such direct proof could require any collateral evidence to confirm it, I would observe that this has likewise been the case in France, and probably in most other parts of Europe. With regard to France there is the clearest proof. But though it is certain that in both parts of the United Kingdom grain was somewhat dearer in the last century than in the present, it is equally certain that labor was much cheaper. If the laboring poor, therefore, could bring up their families then, they must be much more at their ease now. In the last century, the most usual day wages of common labor through the greater part of Scotland were sixpence in summer and fivepence in winter. Three shillings a week, the same price very nearly, still continues to be paid in some parts of the Highlands and Western Islands. Through the greater part of the low country the most usual wages of common labor are now eightpence a day; tenpence, sometimes a shilling about Edinburgh, in the counties which border upon England, probably on account of that neighborhood, and in a few other places where there has lately been a considerable rise in the demand for labor, about Glasgow, Carron, Ayrshire, etc. In England the improvements of agriculture, manufactures and commerce began much earlier than in Scotland. The demand for labor, and consequently its price, must necessarily have increased with those improvements. In the last century, accordingly, as well as in the present, the wages of labor were higher in England than in Scotland. They have risen, too, considerably since that time, though, on account of the greater variety of wages paid there in different places, it is more difficult to ascertain how much. In 1614, the pay of a foot soldier was the same as in the present times, eight pence a day.[10] When it was first established it would naturally be regulated by the usual wages of common laborers, the rank of people from which foot soldiers are commonly drawn. Lord Chief Justice Hales,[11] who wrote in the time of Charles II, computes the necessary expense of a laborer's family, consisting of six persons, the father and mother and two children able to do something, two not able, at ten shillings a week, or twenty-six pounds a year. If they cannot earn this by their labor, they must make it up, he supposes, either by begging or stealing. He appears to have inquired very carefully into this subject.[12] In 1688, Mr. Gregory King, whose skill in political arithmetic is so much extolled by Doctor Davenant,[13] computed the ordinary income of laborers and out-servants to be fifteen pounds a year to a family, which he supposed to consist, one with another, of three and a half persons.[14] His calculation, therefore, though different in appearance, corresponds very nearly at bottom with that of Judge Hales. Both suppose the weekly expense of such families to be about twenty pence a head. Both the pecuniary income and expense of such families have increased considerably since that time through the greater part of the kingdom, in some places more, and in some less; though perhaps scarcely anywhere so much as some exaggerated accounts of the present wages of labor have lately represented them to the public. The price of labor, it must be observed, cannot be ascertained very accurately anywhere, different prices being often paid at the same place and for the same sort of labor, not only according to the different abilities of the workmen, but according to the easiness or hardness of

10 [Hume, *History*, ed. of 1773, vol. vi., p. 178, quoting Rymer's *Foedera*, tom. xvi., p. 717. This was for service in Germany.—C.]

11 [Sir Matthew Hale.—C.]

12 See his scheme for the maintenance of the Poor, in Burn's *History of the Poor Laws* [London, 1764].

13 [Davenant, *Essay upon the probable Methods of Making a People Gainers in the Balance of Trade*, 1699, pp. 15, 16; in *Works*, ed. Whitworth, vol. ii., p. 175.—C.]

14 [Scheme D in Davenant, *Balance of Trade*, in *Works* Scheme B, vol. ii., p. 184.—C.]

the masters. Where wages are not regulated by law, all that we can pretend to determine is what are the most usual; and experience seems to show that law can never regulate them properly, though it has often pretended to do so.

The real recompense of labor, the real quantity of the necessities and conveniences of life which it can procure to the laborer, has, during the course of the present century, increased perhaps in a still greater proportion than its money price. Not only grain has become somewhat cheaper, but many other things, from which the industrious poor derive an agreeable and wholesome variety of food, have become a great deal cheaper. Potatoes, for example, do not at present, through the greater part of the kingdom, cost half the price which they used to do thirty or forty years ago. The same thing may be said of turnips, carrots, cabbages, things which were formerly never raised but by the spade, but which are now commonly raised by the plow. All sort of garden stuff too has become cheaper. The greater part of the apples and even of the onions consumed in Great Britain were in the last century imported from Flanders. The great improvements in the coarser manufactures of both linen and woolen cloth furnish the laborers with cheaper and better clothing; and those in the manufactures of the coarser metals, with cheaper and better instruments of trade, as well as with many agreeable and convenient pieces of household furniture. Soap, salt, candles, leather, and fermented liquors, have, indeed, become a good deal dearer, chiefly from the taxes which have been laid upon them. The quantity of these, however, which the laboring poor are under any necessity of consuming, is so very small, that the increase in their price does not compensate the diminution in that of so many other things. The common complaint that luxury extends itself even to the lowest ranks of the people, and that the laboring poor will not now be contented with the same food, clothing and lodging which satisfied them in former times, may convince us that it is not the money price of labor only, but its real recompense, which has augmented.

Is this improvement in the circumstances of the lower ranks

of the people to be regarded as an advantage or as an inconvenience to the society? The answer seems at first sight
abundantly plain. Servants, laborers, and workmen of different
kinds make up the far greater part of every great political
society. But what improves the circumstances of the greater
part can never be regarded as an inconvenience to the whole.
No society can surely be flourishing and happy, of which the
far greater part of the members are poor and miserable. It is
but equity, besides, that they who feed, clothe, and lodge the
whole body of the people should have such a share of the
produce of their own labor as to be themselves tolerably well
fed, clothed and lodged.

Poverty, though it no doubt discourages, does not always
prevent marriage. It seems even to be favorable to generation.
A half-starved Highland woman frequently bears more than
twenty children, while a pampered fine lady is often incapable
of bearing any, and is generally exhausted by two or three.
Barrenness, so frequent among women of fashion, is very rare
among those of inferior station. Luxury in the fair sex, while
it inflames perhaps the passion for enjoyment, seems always
to weaken, and frequently to destroy altogether, the powers of
generation.

But poverty, though it does not prevent the generation, is
extremely unfavorable to the rearing of children. The tender
plant is produced, but in so cold a soil, and so severe a climate,
soon withers and dies. It is not uncommon, I have been frequently told, in the Highlands of Scotland for a mother who
has borne twenty children not to have two alive. Several
officers of great experience have assured me, that so far from
recruiting their regiment, they have never been able to supply
it with drums and fifes from all the soldiers' children that
were born in it. A greater number of fine children, however, is
seldom seen anywhere than about a barrack of soldiers. Very
few of them, it seems, arrive at the age of thirteen or fourteen.
In some places one half the children born die before they are
four years of age, in many places before they are seven, and in
almost all places before they are nine or ten. This great mor-

tality, however, will everywhere be found chiefly among the children of the common people, who cannot afford to tend them with the same care as those of better station. Though their marriages are generally more fruitful than those of people of fashion, a smaller proportion of their children arrive at maturity. In foundling hospitals, and among the children brought up by parish charities, the mortality is still greater than among those of the common people.

Every species of animals naturally multiplies in proportion to the means of their subsistence, and no species can ever multiply beyond it. But in civilized society it is only among the inferior ranks of people that the scantiness of subsistence can set limits to the further multiplication of the human species; and it can do so in no other way than by destroying a great part of the children which their fruitful marriages produce.

The liberal reward of labor, by enabling them to provide better for their children, and consequently to bring up a greater number, naturally tends to widen and extend those limits. It deserves to be remarked, too, that it necessarily does this as nearly as possible in the proportion which the demand for labor requires. If this demand is continually increasing, the reward of labor must necessarily encourage in such a manner the marriage and multiplication of laborers, as may enable them to supply that continually increasing demand by a continually increasing population. If the reward should at any time be less than what was requisite for this purpose, the deficiency of hands would soon raise it; and if it should at any time be more, their excessive multiplication would soon lower it to this necessary rate. The market would be so much understocked with labor in the one case, and so much overstocked in the other, as would soon force back its price to that proper rate which the circumstances of the society required. It is in this manner that the demand for men, like that for any other commodity, necessarily regulates the production of men; quickens it when it goes on too slowly, and stops it when it advances too fast. It is this demand which regulates and determines the state of propagation in all the different countries of the world, in North America, in Europe, and in China; which renders it rapidly progressive in the first, slow and gradual in the second, and altogether stationary in the last.

The wear and tear of a slave, it has been said, is at the expense of his master, but that of a free servant is at his own expense. The wear and tear of the latter, however, is, in reality, as much at the expense of his master as that of the former. The wages paid to journeymen and servants of every kind must be such as may enable them, one with another, to continue the race of journeymen and servants, according as the increasing, diminishing, or stationary demand of the society may happen to require. But though the wear and tear of a free servant be equally at the expense of his master, it generally costs him much less than that of a slave. The fund destined for replacing or repairing, if I may say so, the wear and tear of the slave, is commonly managed by a negligent master or careless overseer. That destined for performing the same office with regard to the freeman is managed by the freeman himself. The disorders which generally prevail in the economy of the rich naturally introduce themselves into the management of the former: The strict frugality and parsimonious attention of the poor as naturally establish themselves in that of the latter. Under such different management, the same purpose must require very different degrees of expense to execute it. It appears, accordingly, from the experience of all ages and nations, I believe, that the work done by freemen comes cheaper in the end than that performed by slaves. It is found to do so even at Boston, New York, and Philadelphia, where the wages of common labor are so very high.

The liberal reward of labor, therefore, as it is the effect of increasing wealth, so it is the cause of increasing population. To complain of it is to lament over the necessary effect and cause of the greatest public prosperity.

It deserves to be remarked, perhaps, that it is in the progressive state, while the society is advancing to the further acquisition, rather than when it has acquired its full complement of riches, that the condition of the laboring poor, of the great body of the people, seems to be the happiest and the most comfortable. It is hard in the stationary, and miserable in the declining state. The progressive state is in reality the cheerful and the hearty state to all the different orders of the society. The stationary is dull; the declining melancholy.

The liberal reward of labor, as it encourages the propagation, so it increases the industry of the common people. The wages of labor are the encouragement of industry, which, like every other human quality, improves in proportion to the encouragement it receives. A plentiful subsistence increases the bodily strength of the laborer; and the comfortable hope of bettering his condition, and of ending his days perhaps in ease and plenty, animates him to exert that strength to the utmost. Where wages are high, accordingly, we shall always find the workmen more active, diligent, and expeditious, than where they are low; in England, for example, than in Scotland; in the neighborhood of great towns, than in remote country places. Some workmen, indeed, when they can earn in four days what will maintain them through the week, will be idle the other three. This, however, is by no means the case with the greater part. Workmen, on the contrary, when they are liberally paid by the piece, are very apt to overwork themselves, and to ruin their health and constitution in a few years. A carpenter in London, and in some other places, is not supposed to last in his utmost vigor above eight years. Something of the same kind happens in many other trades in which the workmen are paid by the piece, as they generally are in manufactures, and even in country labor, wherever wages are higher than ordinary. Almost every class of artificers is subject to some peculiar infirmity occasioned by excessive application to their peculiar species of work. Ramuzzini, an eminent Italian physician, has written a particular book concerning such diseases. We do not reckon our soldiers the most industrious set of people among us. Yet when soldiers have been employed in some particular sorts of work, and liberally paid by the piece, their officers have frequently been obliged to stipulate with the undertaker, that they should not be allowed to earn above a certain sum every day, according to the rate at which they were paid. Till this stipulation was made, mutual emulation and the desire of greater gain frequently prompted them to overwork themselves, and to hurt their health by excessive labor. Excessive application during four days of the week is frequently the real cause of the idleness of the other three, so much and so loudly complained of. Great labor, either of mind or body, continued for several days together, is in most men naturally followed by a great desire of relaxation, which, if not restrained by force or by some strong necessity, is almost irresistible. It is the call of nature, which requires to be relieved by some indulgence, sometimes of ease only, but sometimes too of dissipation and diversion. If it is not complied with, the consequences are often dangerous, and sometimes fatal, and such as almost always, sooner or later, bring on the peculiar infirmity of the trade. If masters would always listen to the dictates of reason and humanity, they have frequently occasion rather to moderate than to animate the application of many of their workmen. It will be found, I believe, in every sort of trade, that the man who works so moderately as to be able to work constantly, not only preserves his health the longest, but, in the course of the year, executes the greatest quantity of work.

In cheap years, it is pretended, workmen are generally more idle, and in dear ones, more industrious than ordinary. A plentiful subsistence therefore, it has been concluded, relaxes, and a scanty one quickens their industry. That a little more plenty than ordinary may render some workmen idle cannot well be doubted; but that it should have this effect upon the greater part, or that men in general should work better when they are ill fed than when they are well fed, when they are disheartened than when they are in good spirits, when they are frequently sick than when they are generally in good health, seems not very probable. Years of dearth, it is to be observed, are generally among the common people years of sickness and mortality, which cannot fail to diminish the produce of their industry.

In years of plenty, servants frequently leave their masters and trust their subsistence to what they can make by their own industry. But the same cheapness of provisions, by increasing the fund which is destined for the maintenance of servants, encourages masters, farmers especially, to employ a greater number. Farmers upon such occasions expect more profit from their corn by maintaining a few more laboring servants, than by selling it at a low price in the market. The demand for servants increases, while the number of those who offer to supply that demand diminishes. The price of labor, therefore, frequently rises in cheap years.

In years of scarcity, the difficulty and uncertainty of subsistence make all such people eager to return to service. But the high price of provisions, by diminishing the funds destined for the maintenance of servants, disposes masters rather to diminish than to increase the number of those they have. In dear years, too, poor independent workmen frequently consume the little stocks with which they had used to supply themselves with the materials of their work, and are obliged to become journeymen for subsistence. More people want employment than can easily get it; many are willing to take it upon lower terms than ordinary, and the wages of both servants and journeymen frequently sink in dear years.

Masters of all sorts, therefore, frequently make better bargains with their servants in dear than in cheap years, and find them more humble and dependent in the former than in the latter. They naturally, therefore, commend the former as more favorable to industry. Landlords and farmers, besides, two of the largest classes of masters, have another reason for being pleased with dear years. The rents of the one and the profits of the other depend very much upon the price of provisions. Nothing can be more absurd, however, than to imagine that men in general should work less when they work for themselves, than when they work for other people. A poor independent workman will generally be more industrious than even a journeyman who works by the piece. The one enjoys the whole produce of his own industry; the other shares it with his master. The one, in his separate independent state, is less liable to the temptations of bad company, which in large manufactories so frequently ruin the morals of the other. The superiority of the independent workman over those servants who are hired by the month or by the year, and whose wages and maintenance are the same whether they do much or do little, is likely to be still greater. Cheap years tend to increase the proportion of independent workmen to journeymen and servants of all kinds, and dear years to diminish it.

A French author of great knowledge and ingenuity, Mr. Messance, receiver of the tailles [15] in the election of St. Etienne, endeavors to show that the poor do more work in cheap than in dear years, by comparing the quantity and value of the goods made upon those different occasions in three different manufactures; one of coarse woolens carried on at Elbeuf; one of linen, and another of silk, both of which extend through the whole generality of Rouen. It appears from his account, which is copied from the registers of the public offices, that the quantity and value of the goods made in all those three manufactures has generally been greater in cheap than in dear years; and that it has always been greatest in the cheapest, and least in the dearest years. All the three seem to be stationary manufactures, or which, though their produce may vary somewhat from year to year, are upon the whole neither going backwards nor forwards.

The manufacture of linen in Scotland, and that of coarse woolens in the west riding of Yorkshire, are growing manufactures, of which the produce is generally, though with some variations, increasing both in quantity and value. Upon examining, however, the accounts which have been published of their annual produce, I have not been able to observe that

[15] [The *taille* was a French land tax.—M.]

its variations have had any sensible connection with the dearness or cheapness of the seasons. In 1740, a year of great scarcity, both manufactures, indeed, appear to have declined very considerably. But in 1756, another year of great scarcity, the Scotch manufacture made more than ordinary advances. The Yorkshire manufacture, indeed, declined, and its produce did not rise to what it had been in 1755 till 1766, after the repeal of the American Stamp Act. In that and the following year it greatly exceeded what it had ever been before, and it has continued to advance ever since.

The produce of all great manufactures for distant sale must necessarily depend, not so much upon the dearness or cheapness of the seasons in the countries where they are carried on, as upon the circumstances which affect the demand in the countries where they are consumed, upon peace or war, upon the prosperity or declension of other rival manufactures, and upon the good or bad humor of their principal customers. A great part of the extraordinary work, besides, which is probably done in cheap years, never enters the public registers of manufactures. The menservants who leave their masters become independent laborers. The women return to their parents, and commonly spin in order to make clothes for themselves and their families. Even the independent workmen do not always work for public sale, but are employed by some of their neighbors in manufactures for family use. The produce of their labor, therefore, frequently makes no figure in those public registers of which the records are sometimes published with so much parade, and from which our merchants and manufacturers would often vainly pretend to announce the prosperity or declension of the greatest empires.

Though the variations in the price of labor, not only do not always correspond with those in the price of provisions, but are frequently quite opposite, we must not, upon this account, imagine that the price of provisions has no influence upon that of labor. The money price of labor is necessarily regulated by two circumstances: the demand for labor, and the price of the necessities and conveniences of life. The demand for labor,

according as it happens to be increasing, stationary, or declining, or to require an increasing, stationary, or declining population, determines the quantity of the necessities and conveniences of life which must be given to the laborer; and the
money price of labor is determined by what is requisite for
purchasing this quantity. Though the money price of labor,
therefore, is sometimes high where the price of provisions is
low, it would be still higher, the demand continuing the same,
if the price of provisions was high.

It is because the demand for labor increases in years of
sudden and extraordinary plenty, and diminishes in those of
sudden and extraordinary scarcity, that the money price of
labor sometimes rises in the one, and sinks in the other.

In a year of sudden and extraordinary plenty, there are
funds in the hands of many of the employers of industry,
sufficient to maintain and employ a greater number of industrious people than had been employed the year before, and
this extraordinary number cannot always be had. Those
masters, therefore, who want more workmen, bid against one
another in order to get them, which sometimes raises both the
real and the money price of their labor.

The contrary of this happens in a year of sudden and extraordinary scarcity. The funds destined for employing industry are less than they had been the year before. A considerable number of people are thrown out of employment,
who bid against one another in order to get it, which sometimes lowers both the real and the money price of labor. In
1740, a year of extraordinary scarcity, many people were willing to work for bare subsistence. In the succeeding years of
plenty, it was more difficult to get laborers and servants.

The scarcity of a dear year, by diminishing the demand for
labor, tends to lower its price, as the high price of provisions
tends to raise it. The plenty of a cheap year, on the contrary,
by increasing the demand, tends to raise the price of labor, as
the cheapness of provisions tends to lower it. In the ordinary
variations of the price of provisions, those two opposite causes
seem to counterbalance one another, which is probably in

part the reason why the wages of labor are everywhere so much more steady and permanent than the price of provisions.

The increase in the wages of labor necessarily increases the price of many commodities, by increasing that part of it which resolves itself into wages, and so far tends to diminish their consumption both at home and abroad. The same cause, however, which raises the wages of labor, the increase of stock, tends to increase its productive powers, and to make a smaller quantity of labor produce a greater quantity of work. The owner of the stock which employs a great number of laborers necessarily endeavors, for his own advantage, to make such a proper division and distribution of employment that they may be enabled to produce the greatest quantity of work possible. For the same reason, he endeavors to supply them with the best machinery which either he or they can think of. What takes place among the laborers in a particular workhouse takes place, for the same reason, among those of a great society. The greater their number, the more they naturally divide themselves into different classes and subdivisions of employment. More heads are occupied in inventing the most proper machinery for executing the work of each, and it is, therefore, more likely to be invented. There are many commodities, therefore, which, in consequence of these improvements, come to be produced by so much less labor than before, that the increase of its price is more than compensated by the diminution of its quantity.

CHAPTER IX

OF THE PROFITS OF STOCK [1]

The rise and fall in the profits of stock depend upon the same causes with the rise and fall in the wages of labor, the increasing or declining state of the wealth of the society; but those causes affect the one and the other very differently.

The increase of stock, which raises wages, tends to lower profit. When the stocks of many rich merchants are turned into the same trade, their mutual competition naturally tends to lower its profit; and when there is a like increase of stock in all the different trades carried on in the same society, the same competition must produce the same effect in them all.

It is not easy, it has already been observed, to ascertain what are the average wages of labor even in a particular place, and at a particular time. We can, even in this case, seldom determine more than what are the most usual wages. But even this can seldom be done with regard to the profits of stock. Profit is so very fluctuating, that the person who carries on a particular trade cannot always tell you himself what is the average of his annual profit. It is affected, not only by every variation of price in the commodities which he deals in, but by the good or bad fortune both of his rivals and of his customers, and by a thousand other accidents to which goods when carried either by sea or by land, or even when stored in a warehouse, are liable. It varies, therefore, not only from year to year, but from day to day, and almost from hour to hour. To ascertain what is the average profit of all the different trades carried on in a great kingdom must be much more difficult; and to judge of what it may have been formerly, or

1 [This chapter deals more with rates of interest, as indicative of rates of profit, than it does with the direct question of profits of stock.—M.]

in remote periods of time, with any degree of precision, must be altogether impossible.

But though it may be impossible to determine, with any degree of precision, what are or were the average profits of stock, either in the present or in ancient times, some notion may be formed of them from the interest of money. It may be laid down as a maxim, that wherever a great deal can be made by the use of money, a great deal will commonly be given for the use of it; and that wherever little can be made by it, less will commonly be given for it.[2] Accordingly, therefore, as the usual market rate of interest varies in any country, we may be assured that the ordinary profits of stock must vary with it, must sink as it sinks, and rise as it rises. The progress of interest, therefore, may lead us to form some notion of the progress of profit.

By the 37th of Henry VIII all interest above ten per cent was declared unlawful. More, it seems, had sometimes been taken before that. In the reign of Edward VI religious zeal prohibited all interest. This prohibition, however, like all others of the same kind, is said to have produced no effect, and probably rather increased than diminished the evil of usury. The statute of Henry VIII was revived by the 13th of Elizabeth, cap. 8, and ten per cent continued to be the legal rate of interest till the 21st of James I, when it was restricted to eight per cent. It was reduced to six per cent soon after the Restoration, and by the 12th of Queen Anne, to five per cent. All these different statutory regulations seem to have been made with great propriety. They seem to have followed and not to have gone before the market rate of interest, or the rate at which people of good credit usually borrowed. Since the time of Queen Anne, five per cent seems to have been rather above than below the market rate. Before the late war,[3] the government borrowed at three per cent, and people of

---

[2] [But that interest will not always bear the same proportion to profit is recognized below, (pp. 99ff.)—C.]

[3] [That of 1756-1763.—C.]

good credit in the capital, and in many other parts of the kingdom, at three and a half, four, and four and a half per cent.

Since the time of Henry VIII, the wealth and revenue of the country have been continually advancing, and, in the course of their progress, their pace seems rather to have been gradually accelerated than retarded. They seem, not only to have been going on, but to have been going on faster and faster. The wages of labor have been continually increasing during the same period, and in the greater part of the different branches of trade and manufactures the profits of stock have been diminishing.

It generally requires a greater stock to carry on any sort of trade in a great town than in a country village. The great stocks employed in every branch of trade, and the number of rich competitors, generally reduce the rate of profit in the former below what it is in the latter. But the wages of labor are generally higher in a great town than in a country village. In a thriving town the people who have great stocks to employ frequently cannot get the number of workmen they want, and therefore bid against one another in order to get as many as they can, which raises the wages of labor and lowers the profits of stock. In the remote parts of the country there is frequently not stock sufficient to employ all the people, who therefore bid against one another in order to get employment, which lowers the wages of labor, and raises the profits of stock.

In Scotland, though the legal rate of interest is the same as in England, the market rate is rather higher. People of the best credit there seldom borrow under five per cent. Even private bankers in Edinburgh give four per cent upon their promissory notes, of which payment either in whole or in part may be demanded at pleasure. Private bankers in London give no interest for the money which is deposited with them. There are few trades which cannot be carried on with a smaller stock in Scotland than in England. The common rate of profit, therefore, must be somewhat greater. The wages of labor, it has already been observed, are lower in Scotland than in England. The country too is not only much poorer, but the steps by which it advances to a better condition, for it is evidently advancing, seem to be much slower and more tardy.

The legal rate of interest in France has not, during the course of the present century, been always regulated by the market rate. In 1720 interest was reduced from the twentieth to the fiftieth penny, or from five to two per cent. In 1724 it was raised to the thirtieth penny, or to 3 1/3 per cent. In 1725 it was again raised to the twentieth penny, or to five per cent. In 1766, during the administration of Mr. Laverdy, it was reduced to the twenty-fifth penny, or to four per cent. The Abbé Terray raised it afterwards to the old rate of five per cent. The supposed purposes of many of those violent reductions of interest was to prepare the way for reducing that of the public debts, a purpose which has sometimes been executed. France is perhaps in the present times not so rich a country as England; and though the legal rate of interest has in France frequently been lower than in England, the market rate has generally been higher; for there, as in other countries, they have several very safe and easy methods of evading the law. The profits of trade, I have been assured by British merchants who had traded in both countries, are higher in France than in England; and it is no doubt upon this account that many British subjects choose rather to employ their capitals in a country where trade is in disgrace, than in one where it is highly respected. The wages of labor are lower in France than in England. When you go from Scotland to England, the difference which you may remark between the dress and countenance of the common people in the one country and in the other sufficiently indicates the difference in their condition. The contrast is still greater when you return from France. France, though no doubt a richer country than Scotland, seems not to be going forward so fast. It is a common and even a popular opinion in the country that it is going backward; an opinion which, I apprehend, is ill-founded even with regard to France, but which nobody can possibly entertain with regard to Scotland who sees the country now, and who saw it twenty or thirty years ago.

The province of Holland, on the other hand, in proportion to the extent of its territory and the number of its people, is a richer country than England. The government there borrows at two per cent, and private people of good credit at three. The wages of labor are said to be higher in Holland than in England, and the Dutch, it is well known, trade upon lower profits than any people in Europe. The trade of Holland, it has been pretended by some people, is decaying, and it may perhaps be true that some particular branches of it are so. But these symptoms seem to indicate sufficiently that there is no general decay. When profit diminishes, merchants are very apt to complain that trade decays, though the diminution of profits is the natural effect of its prosperity, or of a greater stock being employed in it than before. During the late war the Dutch gained the whole carrying trade of France, of which they still retain a very large share. The great property which they possess both in the French and English funds, about forty millions, it is said, in the latter (in which I suspect, however, there is a considerable exaggeration), the great sums which they lend to private people in countries where the rate of interest is higher than in their own, are circumstances which no doubt demonstrate the redundancy of their stock, or that it has increased beyond what they can employ with tolerable profit in the proper business of their own country; but they do not demonstrate that that business has decreased. As the capital of a private man, though acquired by a particular trade, may increase beyond what he can employ in it, and yet that trade continue to increase too, so may likewise the capital of a great nation.

In our North American and West Indian colonies, not only the wages of labor, but the interest of money, and consequently the profits of stock, are higher than in England. In the different colonies both the legal and the market rate of interest run from six to eight per cent. High wages of labor and high profits of stock, however, are things, perhaps, which scarcely ever go together, except in the peculiar circumstances of new colonies. A new colony must always for some time be more understocked in proportion to the extent of its territory, and more underpeopled in proportion to the extent of its stock, than the greater part of other countries. They have more land than they have stock to cultivate. What they have, therefore, is applied to the cultivation only of what is most fertile and most favorably situated, the land near the seashore and along the banks of navigable rivers. Such land too is frequently purchased at a price below the value even of its natural produce. Stock employed in the purchase and improvement of such lands must yield a very large profit, and consequently afford to pay a very large interest. Its rapid accumulation in so profitable an employment enables the planter to increase the number of his hands faster than he can find them in a new settlement. Those whom he can find, therefore, are very liberally rewarded. As the colony increases, the profits of stock gradually diminish. When the most fertile and best situated lands have been all occupied, less profit can be made by the cultivation of what is inferior both in soil and situation, and less interest can be afforded for the stock which is so employed. In the greater part of our colonies, accordingly, both the legal and the market rate of interest have been considerably reduced during the course of the present century. As riches, improvement, and population have increased, interest has declined. The wages of labor do not sink with the profits of stock. The demand for labor increases with the increase of stock, whatever be its profits; and after these are diminished, stock may not only continue to increase, but to increase much faster than before. It is with industrious nations who are advancing in the acquisition of riches as with industrious individuals. A great stock, though with small profits, generally increases faster than a small stock with great profits. Money, says the proverb, makes money. When you have got a little, it is often easy to get more. The great difficulty is to get that little. The connection between the increase of stock and that of industry, or of the demand for useful labor, has

partly been explained already,[4] but will be explained more
fully hereafter [5] in treating of the accumulation of stock.

The acquisition of new territory, or of new branches of
trade, may sometimes raise the profits of stock, and with them
the interest of money, even in a country which is fast advancing in the acquisition of riches. The stock of the country not
being sufficient for the whole accession of business, which
such acquisitions present to the different people among whom
it is divided, is applied to those particular branches only
which afford the greatest profit. Part of what had before been
employed in other trades is necessarily withdrawn from them,
and turned into some of the new and more profitable ones.
In all those old trades, therefore, the competition comes to be
less than before. The market comes to be less fully supplied
with many different sorts of goods. Their price necessarily
rises more or less, and yields a greater profit to those who deal
in them, who can, therefore, afford to borrow at a higher interest. For some time after the conclusion of the late war, not
only private people of the best credit, but some of the greatest
companies in London commonly borrowed at five per cent
who before that had not been used to pay more than four,
and four and a half per cent. The great accession both of
territory and trade by our acquisitions in North America and
the West Indies will sufficiently account for this, without supposing any diminution in the capital stock of the society. So
great an accession of new business to be carried on by the old
stock must necessarily have diminished the quantity employed
in a great number of particular branches, in which the competition being less, the profits must have been greater. I shall
hereafter [6] have occasion to mention the reasons which dispose
me to believe that the capital stock of Great Britain was not
diminished even by the enormous expense of the late war.

The diminution of the capital stock of the society, or of the
funds destined for the maintenance of industry, however, as it

---

[4] [See pp. 63-68.]   [5] [See pp. 111-34.]
[6] [See pp. 284ff. See also Book II, Chapter III (not included in this
edition).]

lowers the wages of labor, so it raises the profits of stock, and consequently the interest of money. By the wages of labor being lowered, the owners of what stock remains in the society can bring their goods at less expense to market than before, and less stock being employed in supplying the market than before, they can sell them dearer. Their goods cost them less, and they get more for them. Their profits, therefore, being augmented at both ends, can well afford a large interest. The great fortunes so suddenly and so easily acquired in Bengal and the other British settlements in the East Indies may satisfy us that, as the wages of labor are very low, so the profits of stock are very high in those ruined countries. The interest of money is proportionably so. In Bengal, money is frequently lent to the farmers at forty, fifty, and sixty per cent, and the succeeding crop is mortgaged for the payment. As the profits which can afford such an interest must eat up almost the whole rent of the landlord, so such enormous usury must in its turn eat up the greater part of those profits. Before the fall of the Roman republic, a usury of the same kind seems to have been common in the provinces, under the ruinous administration of their proconsuls. The virtuous Brutus lent money in Cyprus at eight-and-forty per cent, as we learn from the letters of Cicero.[7]

In a country which had acquired that full complement of riches which the nature of its soil and climate, and its situation with respect to other countries, allowed it to acquire; which could, therefore, advance no further, and which was not going backward; both the wages of labor and the profits of stock would probably be very low. In a country fully peopled in proportion to what either its territory could maintain or

---

[7] *Ad Atticum*, VI., i., 5, 6. Cicero had arranged that a six-year-old debt should be repaid with interest at the rate of twelve per cent per annum, the principal being increased by that amount for each of the six years. This would have very nearly doubled the principal, but Brutus, through his agent, kept asking for forty-eight per cent, which would have multiplied it by more than fifteen. However, Cicero asserted that the twelve per cent would have satisfied the cruelest usurers.—C.]

its stock employ, the competition for employment would necessarily be so great as to reduce the wages of labor to what was barely sufficient to keep up the number of laborers, and, the country being already fully peopled, that number could never be augmented. In a country fully stocked in proportion to all the business it had to transact, as great a quantity of stock would be employed in every particular branch as the nature and extent of the trade would admit. The competition, therefore, would everywhere be as great, and consequently the ordinary profit as low as possible.

But perhaps no country has ever yet arrived at this degree of opulence. China seems to have been long stationary, and had probably long ago acquired that full complement of riches which is consistent with the nature of its laws and institutions. But this complement may be much inferior to what, with other laws and institutions, the nature of its soil, climate, and situation might admit of. A country which neglects or despises foreign commerce, and which admits the vessels of foreign nations into one or two of its ports only, cannot transact the same quantity of business which it might do with different laws and institutions. In a country, too, where, though the rich or the owners of large capitals enjoy a good deal of security, the poor or the owners of small capitals enjoy scarcely any, but are liable, under the pretense of justice, to be pillaged and plundered at any time by the inferior mandarins; the quantity of stock employed in all the different branches of business transacted within it can never be equal to what the nature and extent of that business might admit. In every different branch, the oppression of the poor must establish the monopoly of the rich, who, by engrossing the whole trade to themselves, will be able to make very large profits. Twelve per cent accordingly is said to be the common interests of money in China, and the ordinary profits of stock must be sufficient to afford this large interest.

A defect in the law may sometimes raise the rate of interest considerably above what the condition of the country, as to wealth or poverty, would require. When the law does not enforce the performance of contracts, it puts all borrowers nearly upon the same footing with bankrupts or people of doubtful credit in better regulated countries. The uncertainty of recovering his money makes the lender exact the same usurious interest which is usually required from bankrupts. Among the barbarous nations who overran the western provinces of the Roman Empire, the performance of contracts was left for many ages to the faith of the contracting parties. The courts of justice of their kings seldom intermeddled in it. The high rate of interest which took place in those ancient times may perhaps be partly accounted for from this cause.

When the law prohibits interest altogether, it does not prevent it. Many people must borrow, and nobody will lend without such a consideration for the use of their money as is suitable, not only to what can be made by the use of it, but to the difficulty and danger of evading the law. The high rate of interest among all Mohammedan nations is accounted for by Mr. Montesquieu, not from their poverty, but partly from this,[8] and partly from the difficulty of recovering the money.[9]

The lowest ordinary rate of profit must always be something more than what is sufficient to compensate the occasional losses to which every employment of stock is exposed. It is this surplus only which is net or clear profit. What is called gross profit comprehends frequently, not only this surplus, but what is retained for compensating such extraordinary losses. The interest which the borrower can afford to pay is in proportion to the clear profit only.

The lowest ordinary rate of interest must, in the same manner, be something more than sufficient to compensate the occasional losses to which lending, even with tolerable prudence, is exposed. Were it not more, charity or friendship could be the only motives for lending.

In a country which had acquired its full complement of riches, where in every particular branch of business there was the greatest quantity of stock that could be employed in it, as

8 [*I.e.*, the danger of evading the law.—C.]
9 [*Esprit des lois*, liv. xxii., ch. 19.—C.]

the ordinary rate of clear profit would be very small, so the usual market rate of interest which could be afforded out of it would be so low as to render it impossible for any but the very wealthiest people to live upon the interest of their money. All people of small or middling fortunes would be obliged to superintend themselves the employment of their own stocks. It would be necessary that almost every man should be a man of business, or engage in some sort of trade. The province of Holland seems to be approaching near to this state. It is there unfashionable not to be a man of business. Necessity makes it usual for almost every man to be so, and custom everywhere regulates fashion. As it is ridiculous not to dress, so is it, in some measure, not to be employed, like other people. As a man of a civil profession seems awkward in a camp or a garrison, and is even in some danger of being despised there, so does an idle man among men of business.

The highest ordinary rate of profit may be such as, in the price of the greater part of commodities, eats up the whole of what should go to the rent of the land, and leaves only what is sufficient to pay the labor of preparing and bringing them to market, according to the lowest rate at which labor can anywhere be paid, the bare subsistence of the laborer. The workman must always have been fed in some way or other while he was about the work; but the landlord may not always have been paid. The profits of the trade which the servants of the East India Company carry on in Bengal may not perhaps be very far from this rate.

The proportion which the usual market rate of interest ought to bear to the ordinary rate of clear profit necessarily varies as profit rises or falls. Double interest is in Great Britain reckoned what the merchants call a good, moderate, reasonable profit—terms which I apprehend mean no more than a common and usual profit. In a country where the ordinary rate of clear profit is eight or ten per cent, it may be reasonable that one half of it should go to interest, wherever business is carried on with borrowed money. The stock is at the risk of the borrower, who, as it were, insures it to the lender; and four or five per cent may, in the greater part of trades, be both a sufficient profit upon the risk of this insurance, and a sufficient recompense for the trouble of employing the stock. But the proportion between interest and clear profit might not be the same in countries where the ordinary rate of profit was either a good deal lower, or a good deal higher. If it were a good deal lower, one half of it perhaps could not be afforded for interest; and more might be afforded if it were a good deal higher.

In countries which are fast advancing to riches, the low rate of profit may, in the price of many commodities, compensate the high wages of labor, and enable those countries to sell as cheaply as their less thriving neighbors, among whom the wages of labor may be lower.

In reality high profits tend much more to raise the price of work than high wages. If in the linen manufacture, for example, the wages of the different working people, the flax-dressers, the spinners, the weavers, etc., should, all of them, be advanced twopence a day, it would be necessary to heighten the price of a piece of linen only by a number of twopences equal to the number of people that had been employed about it, multiplied by the number of days during which they had been so employed. That part of the price of the commodity which resolved itself into wages would, through all the different stages of the manufacture, rise only in arithmetical proportion to this rise of wages. But if the profits of all the different employers of those working people should be raised five per cent, that part of the price of the commodity which resolved itself into profit would, through all the different stages of the manufacture, rise in geometrical proportion to this rise of profit. The employer of the flax-dressers would, in selling his flax, require an additional five per cent upon the whole value of the materials and wages which he advanced to his workmen. The employer of the spinners would require an additional five per cent both upon the advanced price of the flax and upon the wages of the spinners. And the employer of the weavers would require a like five per cent both upon the advanced price of the linen yarn and upon the wages of the weavers. In raising the price of commodities the rise of wages operates in the same manner as simple interest does in the accumulation of debt. The rise of profit operates like compound interest.[10] Our merchants and master manufacturers complain much of the bad effects of high wages in raising the price, and thereby lessening the sale of their goods both at home and abroad. They say nothing concerning the bad effects of high profits. They are silent with regard to the pernicious effects of their own gains. They complain only of those of other people.

[10] [According to the view of the subject here set forth, if the three employers each spend £100 in wages and materials, and profits are at first 5 per cent and then rise to 10 per cent, the finished commodity must rise from £331 0s. 3d. to £364 2s., while if, on the other hand, the wages rise from £100 to £105, the commodity will only rise to £347 11s. 3d. It is assumed either that profits mean profits on turnover and not on capital per annum, or else that the employers each have their capital turned over once a year. But even when one or other of these assumptions is granted, it is clear that the "simple interest" may easily be greater than the "compound." In the examples just given we doubled profits, but only added one-twentieth to wages. If we double wages and leave profits at 5 per cent, the commodity should rise from £331 0s. 3d. to £662 0s. 6d.—C. (Here again, Smith's prejudice in favor of the laboring class seems to intrude on his analysis.—M.)]

[CHAPTERS X AND XI (PARTS I - III)]

[Editor's Summary]

Chapter X deals with "Wages and Profit in the different Employments of Labor and Stock," and Smith analyzes inequalities arising both from the "Nature of the Employments themselves" and from the "Policy of Europe." Under the first heading, Smith sees as factors:

> first, the agreeableness or disagreeableness of the employments themselves; secondly, the easiness and cheapness, or the difficulty and expense of learning them; thirdly, the constancy or inconstancy of employment in them; fourthly, the small or great trust which must be reposed in those who exercise them; and fifthly, the probability or improbability of success in them.

Under the second heading, he lists inequalities occasioned:

> first, by restraining the competition in some employments to a smaller number than would otherwise be disposed to enter into them; secondly, by increasing it in others beyond what it naturally would be; and, thirdly, by obstructing the free circulation of labor and stock, both from employment to employment and from place to place.

Smith also discusses such matters as monopolies, apprenticeship laws, and poor laws. His appeal throughout is to "natural liberty."

Chapter XI is concerned with the third factor, after wages and profits, in the price of a commodity: the rent of land. Smith's view was that "Rent . . . enters into the composition of the price of commodities in a different way from wages and profit. High or low wages and profit are the causes of high or low price; high or low rent is the effect of it." Smith also undertakes a long historical "Digression concerning the Variations in the Value of Silver during the Course of the Four last Centuries," in the course of which he once again attacks the mercantilist theory that national wealth consists of abundant gold and silver, and, instead, emphasizes that land is the most durable part of a country's wealth. We reprint the Conclusion to this chapter, with the exception of the tables of the comparative prices of wheat, the average of different prices, and the average price of each year in money of the present times.

[CHAPTER XI]

[OF THE RENT OF LAND]

Conclusion of the Chapter

I shall conclude this very long chapter with observing that every improvement in the circumstances of the society tends either directly or indirectly to raise the real rent of land, to increase the real wealth of the landlord, his power of purchasing the labor, or the produce of the labor of other people.

The extension of improvement and cultivation tends to raise it directly. The landlord's share of the produce necessarily increases with the increase of the produce.

That rise in the real price of those parts of the rude produce of land, which is first the effect of extended improvement and cultivation, and afterwards the cause of their being still further extended, the rise in the price of cattle, for example, tends too to raise the rent of land directly, and in a still greater proportion. The real value of the landlord's share, his real command of the labor of other people, not only rises with the real value of the produce, but the proportion of his share to the whole produce rises with it. That produce, after the rise in its real price, requires no more labor to collect it than before. A smaller proportion of it will, therefore, be sufficient to replace, with the ordinary profit, the stock which employs that labor. A greater proportion of it must, consequently, belong to the landlord.[1]

1 [Smith states the opposite of this on p. 116f.—M.]

All those improvements in the productive powers of labor, which tend directly to reduce the real price of manufactures, tend indirectly to raise the real rent of land. The landlord exchanges that part of his rude produce which is over and above his own consumption, or what comes to the same thing, the price of that part of it, for manufactured produce. Whatever reduces the real price of the latter raises that of the former. An equal quantity of the former becomes thereby equivalent to a greater quantity of the latter; and the landlord is enabled to purchase a greater quantity of the conveniences, ornaments, or luxuries which he has occasion for.

Every increase in the real wealth of the society, every increase in the quantity of useful labor employed within it, tends indirectly to raise the real rent of land. A certain proportion of this labor naturally goes to the land. A greater number of men and cattle are employed in its cultivation, the produce increases with the increase of the stock which is thus employed in raising it, and the rent increases with the produce.

The contrary circumstances, the neglect of cultivation and improvement, the fall in the real price of any part of the rude produce of land, the rise in the real price of manufactures from the decay of manufacturing art and industry, the declension of the real wealth of the society, all tend, on the other hand, to lower the real rent of land, to reduce the real wealth of the landlord, to diminish his power of purchasing either the labor, or the produce of the labor, of other people.

The whole annual produce of the land and labor of every country, or what comes to the same thing, the whole price of that annual produce, naturally divides itself, it has already been observed,[2] into three parts: the rent of land, the wages of labor, and the profits of stock; and constitutes a revenue to three different orders of people: to those who live by rent, to those who live by wages, and to those who live by profit. These are the three great, original, and constituent orders of

[2] [See pp. 49f.]

every civilized society, from whose revenue that of every other order is ultimately derived.

The interest of the first of those three great orders, it appears from what has been just now said, is strictly and inseparably connected with the general interest of the society. Whatever either promotes or obstructs the one necessarily promotes or obstructs the other. When the public deliberates concerning any regulation of commerce or police, the proprietors of land never can mislead it, with a view to promote the interest of their own particular order, at least, if they have any tolerable knowledge of that interest. They are, indeed, too often defective in this tolerable knowledge. They are the only one of the three orders whose revenue costs them neither labor nor care, but comes to them, as it were, of its own accord, and independent of any plan or project of their own. That indolence, which is the natural effect of the ease and security of their situation, renders them too often not only ignorant, but incapable of that application of mind which is necessary in order to foresee and understand the consequences of any public regulation.

The interest of the second order, that of those who live by wages, is as strictly connected with the interest of the society as that of the first. The wages of the laborer, it has already been shown,[3] are never so high as when the demand for labor is continually rising, or when the quantity employed is every year increasing considerably. When this real wealth of the society becomes stationary, his wages are soon reduced to what is barely enough to enable him to bring up a family, or to continue the race of laborers. When the society declines, they fall even below this. The order of proprietors may, perhaps, gain more by the prosperity of the society than that of laborers, but there is no order that suffers so cruelly from its decline. But though the interest of the laborer is strictly connected with that of the society, he is incapable either of comprehending that interest, or of understanding its connec-

[3] [See pp. 68-72.]

tion with his own. His condition leaves him no time to receive the necessary information, and his education and habits are commonly such as to render him unfit to judge even though he was fully informed. In the public deliberations, therefore, his voice is little heard and less regarded, except upon some particular occasions, when his clamor is animated, set on, and supported by his employers, not for his, but their own particular purposes.

His employers constitute the third order, that of those who live by profit. It is the stock that is employed for the sake of profit, which puts into motion the greater part of the useful labor of every society. The plans and projects of the employers of stock regulate and direct all the most important operations of labor, and profit is the end proposed by all those plans and projects. But the rate of profit does not, like rent and wages, rise with the prosperity, and fall with the declension, of the society. On the contrary, it is naturally low in rich, and high in poor countries, and it is always highest in the countries which are going fastest to ruin. The interest of this third order, therefore, has not the same connection with the general interest of the society as that of the other two. Merchants and master manufacturers are, in this order, the two classes of people who commonly employ the largest capitals, and who by their wealth draw to themselves the greatest share of the public consideration. As during their whole lives they are engaged in plans and projects, they have frequently more acuteness of understanding than the greater part of country gentlemen. As their thoughts, however, are commonly exercised rather about the interest of their own particular branch of business than about that of the society, their judgment, even when given with the greatest candor (which it has not been upon every occasion), is much more to be depended upon with regard to the former of those two objects, than with regard to the latter. Their superiority over the country gentleman is not so much in their knowledge of the public interest as in their having a better knowledge of their own interest than he has of his. It is by this superior knowledge of their own interest that they have frequently imposed upon his generosity, and persuaded him to give up both his own interest and that of the public, from a very simple but honest conviction that their interest, and not his, was the interest of the public. The interest of the dealers, however, in any particular branch of trade or manufactures, is always in some respects different from, and even opposite to, that of the public. To widen the market and to narrow the competition is always the interest of the dealers. To widen the market may frequently be agreeable enough to the interest of the public; but to narrow the competition must always be against it, and can serve only to enable the dealers, by raising their profits above what they naturally would be, to levy, for their own benefit, an absurd tax upon the rest of their fellow citizens. The proposal of any new law or regulation of commerce which comes from this order ought always to be listened to with great precaution, and ought never to be adopted till after having been long and carefully examined, not only with the most scrupulous, but with the most suspicious attention. It comes from an order of men whose interest is never exactly the same with that of the public, who have generally an interest to deceive and even to oppress the public, and who accordingly have, upon many occasions, both deceived and oppressed it.

BOOK TWO

OF THE NATURE, ACCUMULATION, AND EMPLOYMENT OF STOCK

[CHAPTERS I AND II]

[Editor's Summary]

Book II deals with "The Nature, Accumulation and Employment of Stock," by which Smith means capital accumulation. It is the latter which sets on and permits the division of labor and the expansion of production. In Chapter I, Smith takes up the division of stock into circulating and fixed capital (there is also that portion "which is reserved for immediate consumption"), and then further divides these into their component parts. Chapter II treats of money as a branch of the general stock, and concludes that, while money is a part of a society's capital (gold and silver are, after all, materials), it cannot be considered, like land and labor, a part of its revenue, i.e., money is simply the "great wheel of circulation." Smith then proceeds, in the bulk of the chapter, to discuss subjects such as banking, paper money, and gold and silver. Once again, his purpose is to dispel the illusion, fostered by mercantilist thinkers, that money is more important than land or labor.

CHAPTER III

OF THE ACCUMULATION OF CAPITAL, OR OF PRODUCTIVE AND UNPRODUCTIVE LABOR

There is one sort of labor which adds to the value of the subject upon which it is bestowed; there is another which has no such effect. The former, as it produces a value, may be called productive; the latter, unproductive [1] labor. Thus the

[1] Some French authors of great learning and ingenuity have used those words in a different sense. In the last chapter of the fourth book I shall endeavor to show that their sense is an improper one.

Productive labor : tangible obje[ct]
Unproductive labor : servant, ∅ tangible.

labor of a manufacturer [2] adds, generally, to the value of the materials which he works upon, that of his own maintenance, and of his master's profit. The labor of a menial servant, on the contrary, adds to the value of nothing. Though the manufacturer has his wages advanced to him by his master, he, in reality, costs him no expense, the value of those wages being generally restored, together with a profit, in the improved value of the subject upon which his labor is bestowed. But the maintenance of a menial servant never is restored. A man grows rich by employing a multitude of manufacturers; he grows poor by maintaining a multitude of menial servants.[3] The labor of the latter, however, has its value, and deserves its reward as well as that of the former. But the labor of the manufacturer fixes and realizes itself in some particular subject or vendible commodity, which lasts for some time at least after that labor is past. It is, as it were, a certain quantity of labor stocked and stored up to be employed, if necessary, upon some other occasion. That subject, or what is the same thing, the price of that subject, can afterwards, if necessary, put into motion a quantity of labor equal to that which had originally produced it. The labor of the menial servant, on the contrary, does not fix or realize itself in any particular subject or vendible commodity. His services generally perish in the very instant of their performance, and seldom leave any trace or value behind them, for which an equal quantity of service could afterwards be procured.

The labor of some of the most respectable orders in the society is, like that of menial servants, unproductive of any value and does not fix or realize itself in any permanent sub-

[2] [As is clear from what follows, by "manufacturer" Smith means "worker" in current usage.—M.]

[3] [In the argument which follows in the text the fact is overlooked that this is only true when the manufacturers are employed to produce commodities for sale and when the menial servants are employed merely for the comfort of the employer. A man may and often does grow poor by employing people to make "particular subjects or vendible commodities" for his own consumption, and an innkeeper may and often does grow rich by employing menial servants.—C.]

ject, or vendible commodity, which endures after that labor is past, and for which an equal quantity of labor could afterwards be procured. The sovereign, for example, with all the officers both of justice and war who serve under him, the whole army and navy, are unproductive laborers. They are the servants of the public, and are maintained by a part of the annual produce of the industry of other people. Their service, how honorable, how useful,[4] or how necessary soever, produces nothing for which an equal quantity of service can afterwards be procured. The protection, security, and defense of the commonwealth, the effect of their labor this year, will not purchase its protection, security, and defense for the year to come. In the same class must be ranked some both of the gravest and most important, and some of the most frivolous professions: churchmen, lawyers, physicians, men of letters of all kinds; players, buffoons, musicians, opera singers, opera dancers, etc. The labor of the meanest of these has a certain value, regulated by the very same principles which regulate that of every other sort of labor; and that of the noblest and most useful produces nothing which could afterwards purchase or procure an equal quantity of labor. Like the declamation of the actor, the harangue of the orator, or the tune of the musician, the work of all of them perishes in the very instant of its production.

Both productive and unproductive laborers, and those who do not labor at all, are all equally maintained by the annual produce of the land and labor of the country. This produce, how great soever, can never be infinite, but must have certain limits. Accordingly, therefore, as a smaller or greater proportion of it is in any one year employed in maintaining unproductive hands, the more in the one case and the less in the other will remain for the productive, and the next year's produce will be greater or smaller accordingly, the whole annual produce, if we except the spontaneous productions of the earth, being the effect of productive labor.

4 [But in the "Introduction and Plan of the Work," "useful" is coupled with "productive," and used as equivalent to it.—C.]

Though the whole annual produce of the land and labor of every country is, no doubt, ultimately destined for supplying the consumption of its inhabitants, and for procuring a revenue to them; yet when it first comes either from the ground, or from the hands of the productive laborers, it naturally divides itself into two parts. One of them, and frequently the largest, is, in the first place, destined for replacing a capital, or for renewing the provisions, materials, and finished work which had been withdrawn from a capital; the other for constituting a revenue either to the owner of this capital, as the profit of his stock; or to some other person, as the rent of his land. Thus, of the produce of land, one part replaces the capital of the farmer; the other pays his profit and the rent of the landlord, and thus constitutes a revenue both to the owner of this capital, as the profits of his stock, and to some other person, as the rent of his land. Of the produce of a great manufactory, in the same manner, one part, and that always the largest, replaces the capital of the undertaker of the work; the other pays his profit, and thus constitutes a revenue to the owner of this capital.

That part of the annual produce of the land and labor of any country which replaces a capital never is immediately employed to maintain any but productive hands. It pays the wages of productive labor only. That which is immediately destined for constituting a revenue, either as profit or as rent, may maintain indifferently either productive or unproductive hands.

Whatever part of his stock a man employs as a capital, he always expects it to be replaced to him with a profit. He employs it, therefore, in maintaining productive hands only, and after having served in the function of a capital to him, it constitutes a revenue to them. Whenever he employs any part of it in maintaining unproductive hands of any kind, that part is, from that moment, withdrawn from his capital and placed in his stock reserved for immediate consumption.

Unproductive laborers, and those who do not labor at all,

are all maintained by revenue; either, first, by that part of the annual produce which is originally destined for constituting a revenue to some particular persons, either as the rent of land or as the profits of stock; or, secondly, by that part which, though originally destined for replacing a capital and for maintaining productive laborers only, yet when it comes into their hands, whatever part of it is over and above their necessary subsistence, may be employed in maintaining indifferently either productive or unproductive hands. Thus, not only the great landlord or the rich merchant, but even the common workman, if his wages are considerable, may maintain a menial servant; or he may sometimes go to a play or a puppet show, and so contribute his share toward maintaining one set of unproductive laborers; or he may pay some taxes, and thus help to maintain another set, more honorable and useful, indeed, but equally unproductive. No part of the annual produce, however, which had been originally destined to replace a capital, is ever directed toward maintaining unproductive hands, till after it has put into motion its full complement of productive labor, or all that it could put into motion in the way in which it was employed. The workman must have earned his wages by work done, before he can employ any part of them in this manner. That part too is generally but a small one. It is his spare revenue only, of which productive laborers have seldom a great deal. They generally have some, however, and in the payment of taxes the greatness of their number may compensate, in some measure, the smallness of their contribution. The rent of land and the profits of stock are everywhere, therefore, the principal sources from which unproductive hands derive their subsistence. These are the two sorts of revenue of which the owners have generally most to spare. They might both maintain indifferently either productive or unproductive hands. They seem, however, to have some predilection for the latter. The expense of a great lord feeds generally more idle than industrious people. The rich merchant, though with his capital he maintains industrious people only, yet by his expense, that is, by the employment of his revenue, he feeds commonly the very same sort as the great lord.

The proportion, therefore, between the productive and unproductive hands depends very much in every country upon the proportion between that part of the annual produce which, as soon as it comes either from the ground or from the hands of the productive laborers, is destined for replacing a capital, and that which is destined for constituting a revenue, either as rent, or as profit. This proportion is very different in rich from what it is in poor countries.

Thus, at present, in the opulent countries of Europe, a very large, frequently the largest portion of the produce of the land, is destined for replacing the capital of the rich and independent farmer; the other, for paying his profits and the rent of the landlord. But anciently, during the prevalency of the feudal government, a very small portion of the produce was sufficient to replace the capital employed in cultivation. It consisted commonly in a few wretched cattle, maintained altogether by the spontaneous produce of uncultivated land, and which might, therefore, be considered as a part of that spontaneous produce. It generally, too, belonged to the landlord, and was by him advanced to the occupiers of the land. All the rest of the produce properly belonged to him too, either as rent for his land, or as profit upon this paltry capital. The occupiers of land were generally bondmen, whose persons and effects were equally his property. Those who were not bondmen were tenants at will, and though the rent which they paid was often nominally little more than a quitrent, it really amounted to the whole produce of the land. Their lord could at all times command their labor in peace and their service in war. Though they lived at a distance from his house, they were equally dependent upon him as his retainers who lived in it. But the whole produce of the land undoubtedly belongs to him who can dispose of the labor and service of all those whom it maintains. In the present state of Europe, the share of the landlord seldom exceeds a third, sometimes not a fourth part of the whole produce of the land. The rent of land, however, in all the improved parts of the country, has been tripled and quadrupled since those ancient times; and this third or fourth part of the annual produce is, it seems, three or four times greater than the whole had been before. In the progress of improvement, rent, though it increases in proportion to the extent, diminishes in proportion to the produce of the land.

In the opulent countries of Europe, great capitals are at present employed in trade and manufactures. In the ancient state, the little trade that was stirring, and the few homely and coarse manufactures that were carried on, required but very small capitals. These, however, must have yielded very large profits. The rate of interest was nowhere less than ten per cent, and their profits must have been sufficient to afford this great interest. At present the rate of interest, in the improved parts of Europe, is nowhere higher than six per cent and in some of the most improved it is so low as four, three, and two per cent. Though that part of the revenue of the inhabitants which is derived from the profits of stock is always much greater in rich than in poor countries, it is because the stock is much greater: in proportion to the stock the profits are generally much less.

That part of the annual produce, therefore, which, as soon as it comes either from the ground, or from the hands of the productive laborers, is destined for replacing a capital, is not only much greater in rich than in poor countries, but bears a much greater proportion to that which is immediately destined for constituting a revenue either as rent or as profit. The funds destined for the maintenance of productive labor are not only much greater in the former than in the latter, but bear a much greater proportion to those which, though they may be employed to maintain either productive or unproductive hands, have generally a predilection for the latter.

The proportion between those different funds necessarily determines in every country the general character of the inhabitants as to industry or idleness. We are more industrious than our forefathers, because in the present times the funds destined for the maintenance of industry are much greater in proportion to those which are likely to be employed in the maintenance of idleness than they were two or three centuries ago. Our ancestors were idle for want of a sufficient encouragement to industry. It is better, says the proverb, to play for nothing, than to work for nothing. In mercantile and manufacturing towns, where the inferior ranks of people are chiefly maintained by the employment of capital, they are in general industrious, sober, and thriving, as in many English and in most Dutch towns. In those towns which are principally supported by the constant or occasional residence of a court, and in which the inferior ranks of people are chiefly maintained by the spending of revenue, they are in general idle, dissolute, and poor, as at Rome, Versailles, Compiègne, and Fontainebleau. If you except Rouen and Bordeaux, there is little trade or industry in any of the parliament towns of France; and the inferior ranks of people, being chiefly maintained by the expense of the members of the courts of justice, and of those who come to plead before them, are in general idle and poor. The great trade of Rouen and Bordeaux seems to be altogether the effect of their situation. Rouen is necessarily the entrepôt of almost all the goods which are brought either from foreign countries, or from the maritime provinces of France, for the consumption of the great city of Paris. Bordeaux is in the same manner the entrepôt of the wines which grow upon the banks of the Garonne, and of the rivers which run into it, one of the richest wine countries in the world, and which seems to produce the wine fittest for exportation, or best suited to the taste of foreign nations. Such advantageous situations necessarily attract a great capital by the great employment which they afford it; and the employment of this capital is the cause of the industry of those two cities. In the other parliament towns of France, very little more capital seems to be employed than what is necessary for supplying their own consumption, that is, little more than the smallest capital which can be employed in them. The same thing may be said of Paris, Madrid, and Vienna. Of those three cities, Paris is by far the most industrious; but Paris itself is the principal market of all the manufactures established at Paris, and its own consumption is the principal object of all the trade which it carries on. London, Lisbon, and Copenhagen are perhaps the only three cities in Europe which are both the constant residence of a court, and can at the same time be considered as trading cities, or as cities which trade not only for their own consumption, but for that of other cities and countries. The situation of all the three is extremely advantageous, and naturally fits them to be the entrepôts of a great part of the goods destined for the consumption of distant places. In a city where a great revenue is spent, to employ with advantage a capital for any other purpose than for supplying the consumption of that city, is probably more difficult than in one in which the inferior ranks of people have no other maintenance but what they derive from the employment of such a capital. The idleness of the greater part of the people who are maintained by the expense of revenue corrupts, it is probable, the industry of those who ought to be maintained by the employment of capital, and renders it less advantageous to employ a capital there than in other places. There was little trade or industry in Edinburgh before the union. When the Scotch parliament was no longer to be assembled in it, when it ceased to be the necessary residence of the principal nobility and gentry of Scotland, it became a city of some trade and industry. It still continues, however, to be the residence of the principal courts of justice in Scotland, of the boards of customs and excise, etc. A considerable revenue, therefore, still continues to be spent in it. In trade and industry it is much inferior to Glasgow, of which the inhabitants are chiefly maintained by the employment of capital. The inhabitants of a large village, it has sometimes been observed, after having made considerable progress in manufactures, have become idle and poor in consequence of a great lord's having taken up his residence in their neighborhood.

The proportion between capital and revenue, therefore, seems everywhere to regulate the proportion between industry and idleness. Wherever capital predominates, industry prevails; wherever revenue, idleness. Every increase or diminution of capital, therefore, naturally tends to increase or diminish the real quantity of industry, the number of productive hands, and consequently the exchangeable value of the annual produce of the land and labor of the country, the real wealth and revenue of all its inhabitants.

Capitals are increased by parsimony, and diminished by prodigality and misconduct.

Whatever a person saves from his revenue adds to his capital, and [he] either employs it himself in maintaining an additional number of productive hands, or enables some other person to do so, by lending it to him for an interest, that is, for a share of the profits. As the capital of an individual can be increased only by what he saves from his annual revenue or his annual gains, so the capital of a society, which is the same as that of all the individuals who compose it, can be increased only in the same manner.

Parsimony, and not industry, is the immediate cause of the increase of capital. Industry, indeed, provides the subject which parsimony accumulates. But whatever industry might acquire, if parsimony did not save and store up, the capital would never be the greater.

Parsimony, by increasing the fund which is destined for the maintenance of productive hands, tends to increase the number of those hands whose labor adds to the value of the subject upon which it is bestowed. It tends therefore to increase the exchangeable value of the annual produce of the land and labor of the country. It puts into motion an additional quantity of industry, which gives an additional value to the annual produce.

What is annually saved is as regularly consumed as what is annually spent, and nearly in the same time too; but it is consumed by a different set of people. That portion of his revenue which a rich man annually spends is in most cases consumed by idle guests and menial servants, who leave nothing behind them in return for their consumption. That portion which he annually saves, as for the sake of the profit it is immediately employed as a capital, is consumed in the same manner, and nearly in the same time too, but by a different set of people, by laborers, manufacturers, and artificers, who reproduce with a profit the value of their annual consumption. His revenue, we shall suppose, is paid him in money. Had he spent the whole, the food, clothing, and lodging, which the whole could have purchased, would have been distributed among the former set of people. By saving a part of it, as that part is for the sake of the profit immediately employed as a capital either by himself or by some other person, the food, clothing, and lodging, which may be purchased with it, are necessarily reserved for the latter. The consumption is the same, but the consumers are different.

By what a frugal man annually saves, he not only affords maintenance to an additional number of productive hands, for that or the ensuing year, but, like the founder of a public workhouse, he establishes as it were a perpetual fund for the maintenance of an equal number in all times to come. The perpetual allotment and destination of this fund, indeed, is not always guarded by any positive law, by any trust-right or deed of mortmain. It is always guarded, however, by a very powerful principle, the plain and evident interest of every individual to whom any share of it shall ever belong. No part of it can ever afterwards be employed to maintain any but productive hands without an evident loss to the person who thus perverts it from its proper destination.

The prodigal perverts it in this manner. By not confining his expense within his income, he encroaches upon his capital. Like him who perverts the revenues of some pious foundation to profane purposes, he pays the wages of idleness with those funds which the frugality of his forefathers had, as it were, consecrated to the maintenance of industry. By diminishing the funds destined for the employment of productive labor, he necessarily diminishes, so far as it depends upon him, the quantity of that labor which adds a value to the subject upon which it is bestowed, and, consequently, the value of the annual produce of the land and labor of the whole country, the real wealth and revenue of its inhabitants. If the prodigality of some was not compensated by the frugality of others, the conduct of every prodigal, by feeding the idle with the bread of the industrious, tends not only to beggar himself, but to impoverish his country.

Though the expense of the prodigal should be altogether in homemade, and no part of it in foreign, commodities, its effect upon the productive funds of the society would still be the same. Every year there would still be a certain quantity of food and clothing, which ought to have maintained productive, employed in maintaining unproductive hands. Every year, therefore, there would still be some diminution in what would otherwise have been the value of the annual produce of the land and labor of the country.

This expense, it may be said indeed, not being in foreign goods, and not occasioning any exportation of gold and silver, the same quantity of money would remain in the country as before. But if the quantity of food and clothing, which were thus consumed by unproductive, had been distributed among productive hands, they would have reproduced, together with a profit, the full value of their consumption. The same quantity of money would in this case equally have remained in the country, and there would besides have been a reproduction of an equal value of consumable goods. There would have been two values instead of one.

The same quantity of money, besides, cannot long remain in any country in which value of the annual produce diminishes. The sole use of money is to circulate consumable goods. By means of it provisions, materials, and finished work are bought and sold, and distributed to their proper consumers. The quantity of money, therefore, which can be annually employed in any country, must be determined by the value of the consumable goods annually circulated within it. These must consist either in the immediate produce of the land and labor of the country itself, or in something which had been purchased with some part of that produce. Their value, therefore, must diminish as the value of that produce diminishes, and along with it the quantity of money which can be employed in circulating them. But the money which by this annual diminution of produce is annually thrown out of domestic circulation will not be allowed to lie idle. The interest of whoever possesses it requires that it should be employed. But having no employment at home, it will, in spite of all laws and prohibitions, be sent abroad, and employed in purchasing consumable goods which may be of some use at home. Its annual exportation will in this manner continue for some time to add something to the annual consumption of the country beyond the value of its own annual produce. What in the days of its prosperity had been saved from that annual produce, and employed in purchasing gold and silver, will contribute for some little time to support its consumption in adversity. The exportation of gold and silver is, in this case, not the cause, but the effect of its declension, and may even, for some little time, alleviate the misery of that declension.

The quantity of money, on the contrary, must in every country naturally increase as the value of the annual produce increases. The value of the consumable goods annually circulated within the society being greater, will require a greater quantity of money to circulate them. A part of the increased produce, therefore, will naturally be employed in purchasing, wherever it is to be had, the additional quantity of gold and silver necessary for circulating the rest. The increase of those metals will in this case be the effect, not the cause, of the public prosperity. Gold and silver are purchased everywhere in the same manner. The food, clothing, and lodging, the revenue and maintenance of all those whose labor or stock is employed in bringing them from the mine to the market, is the price paid for them in Peru as well as in England. The country which has this price to pay will never be long without the quantity of those metals which it has occasion for; and no country will ever long retain a quantity which it has no occasion for.

Whatever, therefore, we may imagine the real wealth and revenue of a country to consist in, whether in the value of the annual produce of its land and labor, as plain reason seems to dictate, or in the quantity of the precious metals which circulate within it, as vulgar prejudices suppose—in either view of the matter, every prodigal appears to be a public enemy, and every frugal man a public benefactor.

The effects of misconduct are often the same as those of prodigality. Every injudicious and unsuccessful project in agriculture, mines, fisheries, trade, or manufactures tends in the same manner to diminish the funds destined for the maintenance of productive labor. In every such project, though the capital is consumed by productive hands only, yet, as by the injudicious manner in which they are employed, they do not reproduce the full value of their consumption, there must always be some diminution in what would otherwise have been the productive funds of the society.

It can seldom happen, indeed, that the circumstances of a great nation can be much affected either by the prodigality or misconduct of individuals, the profusion or imprudence of some being always more than compensated by the frugality and good conduct of others.

With regard to profusion, the principle which prompts to expense is the passion for present enjoyment, which, though sometimes violent and very difficult to be restrained, is in general only momentary and occasional. But the principle which prompts to save is the desire of bettering our condition, a desire which, though generally calm and dispassionate, comes with us from the womb, and never leaves us till we go into the grave. In the whole interval which separates those two moments, there is scarcely perhaps a single instant in which any man is so perfectly and completely satisfied with his situation as to be without any wish of alteration or improvement of any kind. An augmentation of fortune is the means by which the greater part of men propose and wish to better their condition. It is the means the most vulgar and the most obvious; and the most likely way of augmenting their fortune is to save and accumulate some part of what they acquire, either regularly and annually, or upon some extraordinary occasions. Though the principle of expense, therefore, prevails in almost all men upon some occasions, and in some men upon almost all occasions, yet in the greater part of men, taking the whole course of their life at an average, the principle of frugality seems not only to predominate, but to predominate very greatly.

With regard to misconduct, the number of prudent and successful undertakings is everywhere much greater than that of injudicious and unsuccessful ones. After all our complaints of the frequency of bankruptcies, the unhappy men who fall into this misfortune make but a very small part of the whole number engaged in trade and all other sorts of business, not much more perhaps than one in a thousand. Bankruptcy is perhaps the greatest and most humiliating calamity which can befall an innocent man. The greater part of men, therefore, are sufficiently careful to avoid it. Some, indeed, do not avoid it, as some do not avoid the gallows.

Great nations are never impoverished by private, though they sometimes are by public, prodigality and misconduct. The whole, or almost the whole, public revenue is in most countries employed in maintaining unproductive hands. Such are the people who compose a numerous and splendid court, a great ecclesiastical establishment, great fleets and armies, who in time of peace produce nothing, and in time of war acquire nothing which can compensate the expense of maintaining them, even while the war lasts. Such people, as they themselves produce nothing, are all maintained by the produce of other men's labor. When multiplied, therefore, to an unnecessary number, they may in a particular year consume so great a share of this produce as not to leave a sufficiency for maintaining the productive laborers who should reproduce it next year. The next year's produce, therefore, will be less than that of the foregoing, and if the same disorder should continue, that of the third year will be still less than that of the second. Those unproductive hands, who should be maintained by a part only of the spare revenue of the people, may consume so great a share of their whole revenue, and therefore oblige so great a number to encroach upon their capitals, upon the funds destined for the maintenance of productive labor, that all the frugality and good conduct of individuals may not be able to compensate the waste and degradation of produce occasioned by this violent and forced encroachment.

This frugality and good conduct, however, is upon most occasions, it appears from experience, sufficient to compensate not only the private prodigality and misconduct of individuals, but the public extravagance of government. The uniform, constant, and uninterrupted effort of every man to better his condition, the principle from which public and national, as well as private opulence is originally derived, is frequently powerful enough to maintain the natural progress of things toward improvement, in spite both of the extravagance of government, and of the greatest errors of administration. Like the unknown principle of animal life, it frequently restores health and vigor to the constitution, in spite, not only of the disease, but of the absurd prescriptions of the doctor.

The annual produce of the land and labor of any nation can be increased in its value by no other means, but by increasing either the number of its productive laborers, or the productive powers of those laborers who had before been employed. The number of its productive laborers, it is evident, can never be much increased but in consequence of an increase of capital, or of the funds destined for maintaining them. The productive powers of the same number of laborers cannot be increased, but in consequence either of some addition and improvement to those machines and instruments which facilitate and abridge labor; or of a more proper division and distribution of employment. In either case an additional capital is almost always required. It is by means of an additional capital only, that the undertaker of any work can either provide his workmen with better machinery, or make a more proper distribution of employment among them. When the work to be done consists of a number of parts, to keep every man constantly employed in one way requires a much greater capital than where every man is occasionally employed in every different part of the work. When we compare, therefore, the state of a nation at two different periods, and find that the annual produce of its land and labor is evidently greater at the latter than at the former, that its lands are better cultivated, its manufactures more numerous and more flourishing, and its trade more extensive, we may be assured that its capital must have increased during the interval between those two periods, and that more must have been added to it by the good conduct of some, than had been taken from it either by the private misconduct of others, or by the public extravagance of government. But we shall find this to have been the case of almost all nations, in all tolerably quiet and peaceful times, even of those who have not enjoyed the most prudent and parsimonious governments. To form a right judgment of it, indeed, we must compare the state of the country at periods somewhat distant from one another. The progress is frequently so gradual that, at near periods, the improvement is not only not sensible, but from the declension either of certain branches of industry, or of certain districts of the country, things which sometimes happen though the country in general be in great prosperity, there frequently arises a suspicion that the riches and industry of the whole are decaying.

The annual produce of the land and labor of England, for example, is certainly much greater than it was a little more than a century ago, at the restoration of Charles II. Though, at present, few people, I believe, doubt of this, yet during this period, five years have seldom passed away in which some book or pamphlet has not been published, written, too, with such abilities as to gain some authority with the public, and pretending to demonstrate that the wealth of the nation was fast declining, that the country was depopulated, agriculture neglected, manufactures decaying, and trade undone. Nor have these publications been all party pamphlets, the wretched offspring of falsehood and venality. Many of them have been written by very candid and very intelligent people, who wrote nothing but what they believed, and for no other reason but because they believed it.

The annual produce of the land and labor of England, again, was certainly much greater at the Restoration, than we can suppose it to have been about a hundred years before, at the accession of Elizabeth. At this period, too, we have all reason to believe, the country was much more advanced in improvement than it had been about a century before, toward the close of the dissensions between the houses of York and Lancaster. Even then it was, probably, in a better condition than it had been at the Norman Conquest, and at the Norman Conquest, than during the confusion of the Saxon Heptarchy. Even at this early period, it was certainly a more improved country than at the invasion of Julius Caesar, when its inhabitants were nearly in the same state as the savages in North America.

In each of those periods, however, there was not only much private and public profusion, many expensive and unnecessary wars, great perversion of the annual produce from maintaining productive, to maintaining unproductive hands; but sometimes, in the confusion of civil discord, such absolute waste and destruction of stock as might be supposed not only to retard, as it certainly did, the natural accumulation of riches, but to have left the country, at the end of the period, poorer than at the beginning. Thus, in the happiest and most fortunate period of them all, that which has passed since the Restoration, how many disorders and misfortunes have occurred, which, could they have been foreseen, not only the impoverishment, but the total ruin of the country would have been expected from them? The fire and the plague of London, the two Dutch wars, the disorders of the revolution, the war in Ireland, the four expensive French wars of 1688,

1702, 1742, and 1756, together with the two rebellions of 1715 and 1745. In the course of the four French wars, the nation has contracted more than a hundred and forty-five millions of debt, over and above all the other extraordinary annual expenses which they occasioned, so that the whole cannot be computed at less than two hundred millions. So great a share of the annual produce of the land and labor of the country, has, since the revolution, been employed upon different occasions, in maintaining an extraordinary number of unproductive hands. But had not those wars given this particular direction to so large a capital, the greater part of it would naturally have been employed in maintaining productive hands, whose labor would have replaced, with a profit, the whole value of their consumption. The value of the annual produce of the land and labor of the country would have been considerably increased by it every year, and every year's increase would have augmented still more that of the following year. More houses would have been built, more lands would have been improved, and those which had been improved before would have been better cultivated; more manufactures would have been established, and those which had been established before would have been more extended; and to what height the real wealth and revenue of the country might, by this time, have been raised, it is not perhaps very easy even to imagine.

But though the profusion of government must, undoubtedly, have retarded the natural progress of England toward wealth and improvement, it has not been able to stop it. The annual produce of its land and labor is, undoubtedly, much greater at present than it was either at the Restoration or at the Revolution. The capital, therefore, annually employed in cultivating this land, and in maintaining this labor, must likewise be much greater. In the midst of all the exactions of government, this capital has been silently and gradually accumulated by the private frugality and good conduct of individuals, by their universal, continual, and uninterrupted effort to better their own condition. It is this effort, protected by law and allowed by liberty to exert itself in the manner that is most advantageous, which has maintained the progress of England toward opulence and improvement in almost all former times, and which, it is to be hoped, will do so in all future times. England, however, as it has never been blessed with a very parsimonious government, so parsimony has at no time been the characteristical virtue of its inhabitants. It is the highest impertinence and presumption, therefore, in kings and ministers, to pretend to watch over the economy of private people and to restrain their expense, either by sumptuary laws, or by prohibiting the importation of foreign luxuries. They are themselves always, and without any exception, the greatest spendthrifts in the society. Let them look well after their own expense, and they may safely trust private people with theirs. If their own extravagance does not ruin the state, that of their subjects never will.

As frugality increases and prodigality diminishes the public capital, so the conduct of those whose expense just equals their revenue, without either accumulating or encroaching, neither increases nor diminishes it. Some modes of expense, however, seem to contribute more to the growth of public opulence than others.

The revenue of an individual may be spent, either in things which are consumed immediately, and in which one day's expense can neither alleviate nor support that of another; or it may be spent in things more durable, which can therefore be accumulated, and in which every day's expense may, as he chooses, either alleviate or support and heighten the effect of that of the following day. A man of fortune, for example, may either spend his revenue in a profuse and sumptuous table, and in maintaining a great number of menial servants and a multitude of dogs and horses; or contenting himself with a frugal table and few attendants, he may lay out the greater part of it in adorning his house or his country villa, in useful or ornamental buildings, in useful or ornamental furniture, in collecting books, statues, pictures; or in things more frivolous, jewels, baubles, ingenious trinkets of different kinds; or, what is most trifling of all, in amassing a great wardrobe of fine clothes, like the favorite and minister of a great prince who died a few years ago.[5] Were two men of equal fortune to spend their revenue, the one chiefly in the one way, the other in the other, the magnificence of the person whose expense had been chiefly in durable commodities would be continually increasing, every day's expense contributing something to support and heighten the effect of that of the following day; that of the other, on the contrary, would be no greater at the end of the period than at the beginning. The former, too, would, at the end of the period, be the richer man of the two. He would have a stock of goods of some kind or other which, though it might not be worth all that it cost, would always be worth something. No trace or vestige of the expense of the latter would remain, and the effects of ten or twenty years profusion would be as completely annihilated as if they had never existed.

As the one mode of expense is more favorable than the other to the opulence of an individual, so is it likewise to that of a nation. The houses, the furniture, the clothing of the rich, in a little time, become useful to the inferior and middling ranks of people. They are able to purchase them when their superiors grow weary of them, and the general accommodation of the whole people is thus gradually improved when this mode of expense becomes universal among men of fortune. In countries which have long been rich, you

[5] [As suggested by Germain Garnier's note on this passage (*Recherches sur la Nature et les Causes de la Richesse des Nations*, 1802, tom. ii., p. 346), this was doubtless the Count of Brühl, Minister and Great Chamberlain to the King of Poland, who left at his death 365 suits of clothes, all very rich. Jonas Hanway (*Historical Account of the British Trade over the Caspian Sea, with a Journal of Travels from London through Russia into Persia, and back through Russia, Germany and Holland*, 1753, vol. ii, p. 230) says this Count had 300 or 400 suits of rich clothes, and had "collected all the finest colors of all the finest cloths, velvets, and silks of all the manufactures, not to mention the different kinds of lace and embroideries of Europe," and also pictures and books, at Dresden. He died in 1764.—C.]

will frequently find the inferior ranks of people in possession both of houses and furniture perfectly good and entire, but of which neither the one could have been built, nor the other have been made for their use. What was formerly a seat of the family of Seymour, is now an inn upon the Bath road. The marriage bed of James the First of Great Britain, which his Queen brought with her from Denmark as a present fit for a sovereign to make to a sovereign, was, a few years ago, the ornament of an alehouse at Dunfermline. In some ancient cities, which either have been long stationary, or have gone somewhat to decay, you will sometimes scarcely find a single house which could have been built for its present inhabitants. If you go into those houses, too, you will frequently find many excellent, though antiquated, pieces of furniture which are still very fit for use, and which could as little have been made for them. Noble palaces, magnificent villas, great collections of books, statues, pictures, and other curiosities, are frequently both an ornament and an honor, not only to the neighborhood, but to the whole country to which they belong. Versailles is an ornament and an honor to France, Stowe and Wilton to England. Italy still continues to command some sort of veneration by the number of monuments of this kind which it possesses, though the wealth which produced them has decayed, and though the genius which planned them seems to be extinguished, perhaps from not having the same employment.

The expense, too, which is laid out in durable commodities, is favorable, not only to accumulation, but to frugality. If a person should at any time exceed in it, he can easily reform without exposing himself to the censure of the public. To reduce very much the number of his servants, to reform his table from great profusion to great frugality, to lay down his equipage after he has once set it up, are changes which cannot escape the observation of his neighbors, and which are supposed to imply some acknowledgment of preceding bad conduct. Few, therefore, of those who have once been so unfortunate as to launch out too far into this sort of expense, have afterwards the courage to reform, till ruin and bankruptcy oblige them. But if a person has, at any time, been at too great an expense in building, in furniture, in books or pictures, no imprudence can be inferred from his changing his conduct. These are things in which further expense is frequently rendered unnecessary by former expense; and when a person stops short, he appears to do so, not because he has exceeded his fortune, but because he has satisfied his fancy.

The expense, besides, that is laid out in durable commodities gives maintenance, commonly, to a greater number of people than that which is employed in the most profuse hospitality. Of two or three hundredweight of provisions, which may sometimes be served up at a great festival, one half, perhaps, is thrown to the dunghill, and there is always a great deal wasted and abused. But if the expense of this entertainment had been employed in setting to work masons, carpenters, upholsterers, mechanics, etc., a quantity of provisions, of equal value, would have been distributed among a still greater number of people who would have bought them in pennyworths and pound weights, and not have lost or thrown away a single ounce of them. In the one way, besides, this expense maintains productive, in the other, unproductive hands. In the one way, therefore, it increases, in the other, it does not increase, the exchangeable value of the annual produce of the land and labor of the country.

I would not, however, by all this be understood to mean that the one species of expense always betokens a more liberal or generous spirit than the other. When a man of fortune spends his revenue chiefly in hospitality, he shares the greater part of it with his friends and companions; but when he employs it in purchasing such durable commodities, he often spends the whole upon his own person, and gives nothing to anybody without an equivalent. The latter species of expense, therefore, especially when directed toward frivolous objects, the little ornaments of dress and furniture, jewels, trinkets, gewgaws, frequently indicates not only a trifling, but a base and selfish disposition. All that I mean is that the one sort of expense, as it always occasions some accumulation of valuable commodities, as it is more favorable to private frugality, and, consequently, to the increase of the public capital, and as it maintains productive rather than unproductive hands, conduces more than the other to the growth of public opulence.

[CHAPTERS IV AND V]

[Editor's Summary]

The rest of Book II is concerned with a brief treatment of the question of interest on capital (Chapter IV), and with the various ways—agriculture, manufacturing, and wholesale or retail trade—in which capital may be employed (Chapter V). One of the points which Smith makes is that the agriculture of his time was capable of absorbing a much greater capital than was then employed in it. In this context, he remarks that "it has been the principal cause of the rapid progress of our American colonies toward wealth and greatness that almost their whole capitals have hitherto been employed in agriculture." From this sort of observation, Smith is naturally led to the consideration of different policies (i.e., those favoring trade or agriculture) and different forms of progress which make up the substance of his Books III and IV.

BOOK THREE

OF THE DIFFERENT PROGRESS OF OPULENCE IN DIFFERENT NATIONS

CHAPTER I

OF THE NATURAL PROGRESS OF OPULENCE

The great commerce of every civilized society is that carried on between the inhabitants of the town and those of the country. It consists in the exchange of rude for manufactured produce, either immediately, or by the intervention of money, or of some sort of paper which represents money. The country supplies the town with the means of subsistence and the materials of manufacture. The town repays this supply by sending back a part of the manufactured produce to the inhabitants of the country. The town, in which there neither is nor can be any reproduction of substances, may very properly be said to gain its whole wealth and subsistence from the country. We must not, however, upon this account, imagine that the gain of the town is the loss of the country. The gains of both are mutual and reciprocal, and the division of labor is in this, as in all other cases, advantageous to all the different persons employed in the various occupations into which it is subdivided. The inhabitants of the country purchase of the town a greater quantity of manufactured goods, with the produce of a much smaller quantity of their own labor, than they must have employed had they attempted to prepare them themselves. The town affords a market for the surplus produce of the country, or what is over and above the maintenance of the cultivators, and it is there that the inhabitants of the country exchange it for something else which is in demand among them. The greater the number and revenue of the inhabitants of the town, the more extensive is the market which it affords to those of the country; and the more extensive that market, it is always the more advantageous to a great number. The corn which grows within a mile of the town sells there for the same price with that which comes from twenty miles distance. But the price of the latter must generally not only pay the expense of raising and bringing it to market, but afford, too, the ordinary profits of agriculture to the farmer. The proprietors and cultivators of the country, therefore, which lies in the neighborhood of the town, over and above the ordinary profits of agriculture gain, in the price of what they sell, the whole value of the carriage of the like produce that is brought from more distant parts, and they save, besides, the whole value of this carriage in the price of what they buy. Compare the cultivation of the lands in the neighborhood of any considerable town with that of those which lie at some distance from it, and you will easily satisfy yourself how much the country is benefited by the commerce of the town. Among all the absurd speculations that have been propagated concerning the balance of trade, it has never been pretended that either the country loses by its commerce with the town, or the town by that with the country which maintains it.

As subsistence is, in the nature of things, prior to convenience and luxury, so the industry which procures the former must necessarily be prior to that which ministers to the latter. The cultivation and improvement of the country, therefore, which affords subsistence, must, necessarily, be prior to the increase of the town, which furnishes only the means of convenience and luxury. It is the surplus produce of the country only, or what is over and above the maintenance of the cultivators, that constitutes the subsistence of the town, which can therefore increase only with the increase of this surplus produce. The town, indeed, may not always derive its whole subsistence from the country in its neighborhood, or even from the territory to which it belongs, but from very distant countries; and this, though it forms no exception from the general rule, has occasioned considerable variations in the progress of opulence in different ages and nations.

That order of things which necessity imposes in general, though not in every particular country, is, in every particular country, promoted by the natural inclinations of man. If hu-

man institutions had never thwarted those natural inclinations, the towns could nowhere have increased beyond what
the improvement and cultivation of the territory in which
they were situated could support, till such time, at least, as
the whole of that territory was completely cultivated and improved. Upon equal, or nearly equal, profits, most men will
choose to employ their capitals rather in the improvement and
cultivation of land, than either in manufactures or in foreign
trade. The man who employs his capital in land has it more
under his view and command, and his fortune is much less
liable to accidents than that of the trader, who is obliged
frequently to commit it, not only to the winds and the waves,
but to the more uncertain elements of human folly and injustice, by giving great credits in distant countries to men
with whose character and situation he can seldom be
thoroughly acquainted. The capital of the landlord, on the
contrary, which is fixed in the improvement of his land, seems
to be as well secured as the nature of human affairs can admit
of. The beauty of the country, besides the pleasures of a country life, the tranquillity of mind which it promises, and wherever the injustice of human laws does not disturb it, the independence which it really affords, have charms that more or
less attract everybody; and as to cultivate the ground was the
original destination of man, so in every stage of his existence
he seems to retain a predilection for this primitive employment.

Without the assistance of some artificers, indeed, the cultivation of land cannot be carried on, but with great inconvenience and continual interruption. Smiths, carpenters, wheel-
wrights, and plowwrights, masons, and bricklayers, tanners,
shoemakers, and tailors are people whose service the farmer
has frequent occasion for. Such artificers, too, stand, occasionally, in need of the assistance of one another; and as their
residence is not, like that of the farmer, necessarily tied down
to a precise spot, they naturally settle in the neighborhood of
one another, and thus form a small town or village. The
butcher, the brewer, and the baker soon join them, together

with many other artificers and retailers, necessary or useful for supplying their occasional wants, and who contribute still further to augment the town. The inhabitants of the town and those of the country are mutually the servants of one another. The town is a continual fair or market, to which the inhabitants of the country resort, in order to exchange their rude for manufactured produce. It is this commerce which supplies the inhabitants of the town both with the materials of their work, and the means of their subsistence. The quantity of the finished work which they sell to the inhabitants of the country necessarily regulates the quantity of the materials and provisions which they buy. Neither their employment nor subsistence, therefore, can augment but in proportion to the augmentation of the demand from the country for finished work; and this demand can augment only in proportion to the extension of improvement and cultivation. Had human institutions, therefore, never disturbed the natural course of things, the progressive wealth and increase of the towns would, in every political society, be consequential, and in proportion to the improvement and cultivation of the territory or country.

In our North American colonies, where uncultivated land is still to be had upon easy terms, no manufactures for distant sale have ever yet been established in any of their towns. When an artificer has acquired a little more stock than is necessary for carrying on his own business in supplying the neighboring country, he does not, in North America, attempt to establish with it a manufacture for more distant sale, but employs it in the purchase and improvement of uncultivated land. From artificer he becomes planter, and neither the large wages nor the easy subsistence which that country affords to artificers can bribe him rather to work for other people than for himself. He feels that an artificer is the servant of his customers, from whom he derives his subsistence; but that a planter who cultivates his own land, and derives his necessary subsistence from the labor of his own family, is really a master, and independent of all the world.

In countries, on the contrary, where there is either no uncultivated land, or none that can be had upon easy terms, every artificer who has acquired more stock than he can employ in the occasional jobs of the neighborhood, endeavors to prepare work for more distant sale. The smith erects some sort of iron, the weaver some sort of linen or woolen manufactory. Those different manufactures come, in process of time, to be gradually subdivided, and thereby improved and refined in a great variety of ways, which may easily be conceived, and which it is therefore unnecessary to explain any further.

In seeking for employment of a capital, manufactures are, upon equal or nearly equal profits, naturally preferred to foreign commerce, for the same reason that agriculture is naturally preferred to manufactures. As the capital of the landlord or farmer is more secure than that of the manufacturer, so the capital of the manufacturer, being at all times more within his view and command, is more secure than that of the foreign merchant. In every period, indeed, of every society, the surplus part both of the rude and manufactured produce, or that for which there is no demand at home, must be sent abroad in order to be exchanged for something for which there is some demand at home. But whether the capital which carries this surplus produce abroad be a foreign or a domestic one is of very little importance. If the society has not acquired sufficient capital both to cultivate all its lands, and to manufacture in the most complete manner the whole of its rude produce, there is even a considerable advantage that the rude produce should be exported by a foreign capital, in order that the whole stock of the society may be employed in more useful purposes. The wealth of ancient Egypt, that of China and Indostan sufficiently demonstrate that a nation may attain a very high degree of opulence, though the greater part of its exportation trade be carried on by foreigners. The progress of our North American and West Indian colonies would have been much less rapid, had not capital but what belonged to themselves been employed in exporting their surplus produce.

According to the natural course of things, therefore, the

greater part of the capital of every growing society is, first, directed to agriculture, afterwards to manufactures, and last of all to foreign commerce. This order of things is so very natural that, in every society that had any territory, it has always, I believe, been in some degree observed. Some of their lands must have been cultivated before any considerable towns could be established, and some sort of coarse industry of the manufacturing kind must have been carried on in those towns, before they could well think of employing themselves in foreign commerce.

But though this natural order of things must have taken place in some degree in every such society, it has, in all the modern states of Europe, been, in many respects, entirely inverted. The foreign commerce of some of their cities has introduced all their finer manufactures, or such as were fit for distant sale; and manufactures and foreign commerce together have given birth to the principal improvements of agriculture. The manners and customs which the nature of their original government introduced, and which remained after that government was greatly altered, necessarily forced them into this unnatural and retrograde order.

[CHAPTERS II AND III]

[Editor's Summary]

In the next two chapters of Book III, Smith investigates the manner in which Europe perverted the "natural order of things." In Chapter II, he describes the "Discouragement of Agriculture," and in Chapter III, the "Rise and Progress of Cities and Towns" after the fall of the Roman Empire. It is an interesting historical sketch of Europe in its feudal period. In the course of the chapters, Smith shows, by concrete examples, how government policies and institutions hampered the "natural" trend toward progress but could not completely block it. This theme is continued in Chapter IV.

CHAPTER IV

HOW THE COMMERCE OF THE TOWNS CONTRIBUTED TO THE IMPROVEMENT OF THE COUNTRY

The increase and riches of commercial and manufacturing towns contributed to the improvement and cultivation of the countries to which they belonged in three different ways.

First, by affording a great and ready market for the rude produce of the country, they gave encouragement to its cultivation and further improvement. This benefit was not even confined to the countries in which they were situated, but extended more or less to all those with which they had any dealings. To all of them they afforded a market for some part either of their rude or manufactured produce, and consequently gave some encouragement to the industry and improvement of all. Their own country, however, on account of its neighborhood, necessarily derived the greatest benefit from this market. Its rude produce being charged with less carriage, the traders could pay the growers a better price for it, and yet afford it as cheap to the consumers as that of more distant countries.

Secondly, the wealth acquired by the inhabitants of cities was frequently employed in purchasing such lands as were to be sold, of which a great part would frequently be uncultivated. Merchants are commonly ambitious of becoming country gentlemen, and when they do, they are generally the best of all improvers. A merchant is accustomed to employ his money chiefly in profitable projects; whereas a mere country gentleman is accustomed to employ it chiefly in expense. The one often sees his money go from him and return to him again with a profit; the other, when once he parts with it, very seldom expects to see any more of it. Those different habits naturally affect their temper and disposition in every sort of business. A merchant is commonly a bold, a country gentleman a timid, undertaker. The one is not afraid to lay out at once a large capital upon the improvement of his land, when he has a probable prospect of raising the value of it in proportion to the expense. The other, if he has any capital, which is not always the case, seldom ventures to employ it in this manner. If he improves at all, it is commonly not with a capital, but with what he can save out of his annual revenue. Whoever has had the fortune to live in a mercantile town situated in an unimproved country must have frequently observed how much more spirited the operations of merchants were in this way than those of mere country gentlemen. The habits, besides, of order, economy and attention, to which mercantile business naturally forms a merchant, render him much fitter to execute, with profit and success, any project of improvement.

Thirdly, and lastly, commerce and manufactures gradually introduced order and good government, and with them, the liberty and security of individuals among the inhabitants of the country, who had before lived almost in a continual state of war with their neighbors, and of servile dependence upon their superiors. This, though it has been the least observed, is by far the most important of all their effects. Mr. Hume [1] is the only writer who, so far as I know, has hitherto taken notice of it.

In a country which has neither foreign commerce, nor any of the finer manufactures, a great proprietor, having nothing for which he can exchange the greater part of the produce of his lands which is over and above the maintenance of the cultivators, consumes the whole in rustic hospitality at home. If this surplus produce is sufficient to maintain a hundred or a thousand men, he can make use of it in no other way than by maintaining a hundred or a thousand men. He is at all times, therefore, surrounded with a multitude of retainers and dependents, who, having no equivalent to give in return for their maintenance, but being fed entirely by his bounty, must obey him, for the same reason that soldiers must obey the prince who pays them. Before the extension of commerce and manufactures in Europe, the hospitality of the rich and the great, from the sovereign down to the smallest baron, exceeded everything which in the present times we can easily form a notion of. Westminster Hall was the dining room of William Rufus, and might frequently, perhaps, not be too large for his company. It was reckoned a piece of magnificence in Thomas Becket that he strewed the floor of his hall with clean hay or rushes in the season, in order that the knights and squires who could not get seats might not spoil their fine clothes when they sat down on the floor to eat their dinner. The great Earl of Warwick is said to have entertained every day at his different manors thirty thousand people; and though the number here may have been exaggerated, it must, however, have been very great to admit of such exaggeration. A hospitality nearly of the same kind was exercised not many

[1] ["Of Commerce" and "Of Luxury" in *Political Discourses*, 1752, and *History*, ed. of 1773, vol. iii., p. 400.—C.]

years ago in many different parts of the Highlands of Scotland. It seems to be common in all nations to whom commerce and manufactures are little known. I have seen, says Doctor Pocock, an Arabian chief dine in the streets of a town where he had come to sell his cattle, and invite all passengers, even common beggars, to sit down with him and partake of his banquet.

The occupiers of land were in every respect as dependent upon the great proprietor as his retainers. Even such of them as were not in a state of villenage were tenants at will, who paid a rent in no respect equivalent to the subsistence which the land afforded them. A crown, half a crown, a sheep, a lamb, was some years ago in the Highlands of Scotland a common rent for lands which maintained a family. In some places it is so at this day; nor will money at present purchase a greater quantity of commodities there than in other places. In a country where the surplus produce of a large estate must be consumed upon the estate itself, it will frequently be more convenient for the proprietor that part of it be consumed at a distance from his own house, provided they who consume it are as dependent upon him as either his retainers or his menial servants. He is thereby saved from the embarrassment of either too large a company or too large a family. A tenant at will, who possesses land sufficient to maintain his family for little more than a quitrent, is as dependent upon the proprietor as any servant or retainer whatever, and must obey him with as little reserve. Such a proprietor, as he feeds his servants and retainers at his own house, so he feeds his tenants at their houses. The subsistence of both is derived from his bounty, and its continuance depends upon his good pleasure.

Upon the authority which the great proprietors necessarily had in such a state of things over their tenants and retainers was founded the power of the ancient barons. They necessarily became the judges in peace, and the leaders in war, of all who dwelt upon their estates. They could maintain order and execute the law within their respective demesnes, because each of them could there turn the whole force of all the inhabitants against the injustice of anyone. No other person had sufficient authority to do this. The king in particular had not. In those ancient times he was little more than the greatest proprietor in his dominions, to whom, for the sake of common defense against their common enemies, the other great proprietors paid certain respects. To have enforced payment of a small debt within the lands of a great proprietor, where all the inhabitants were armed and accustomed to stand by one another, would have cost the king, had he attempted it by his own authority, almost the same effort as to extinguish a civil war. He was, therefore, obliged to abandon the administration of justice through the greater part of the country to those who were capable of administering it; and for the same reason to leave the command of the country militia to those whom that militia would obey.

It is a mistake to imagine that those territorial jurisdictions took their origin from the feudal law. Not only the highest jurisdictions both civil and criminal, but the power of levying troops, of coining money, and even that of making bylaws for the government of their own people, were all rights possessed alodially [2] by the great proprietors of land several centuries before even the name of the feudal law was known in Europe. The authority and jurisdiction of the Saxon lords in England appear to have been as great before the Conquest as that of any of the Norman lords after it. But the feudal law is not supposed to have become the common law of England till after the Conquest.[3] That the most extensive authority and jurisdictions were possessed by the great lords in France alodially, long before the feudal law was introduced into that country, is a matter of fact that admits of no doubt. That authority and those jurisdictions all necessarily flowed from the state of property and manners just now described. Without remounting to the remote antiquities of either the French or English monarchies, we may find in much later times many proofs that such effects must always flow from such causes. It

[2] [i.e., held in absolute independence, without being subject to any service or acknowledgment to a superior.—M.]

[3] [Hume, *History*, ed. of 1773, i., 224.—C.]

is not thirty years ago since Mr. Cameron of Lochiel, a gentleman of Lochaber in Scotland, without any legal warrant whatever, not being what was then called a lord of regality, nor
even a tenant in chief, but a vassal of the duke of Argyle, and
without being so much as a justice of peace, used, notwithstanding, to exercise the highest criminal jurisdiction over his
own people. He is said to have done so with great equity,
though without any of the formalities of justice; and it is not
improbable that the state of that part of the country at that
time made it necessary for him to assume this authority in
order to maintain the public peace. That gentleman, whose
rent never exceeded five hundred pounds a year, carried, in
1745, eight hundred of his own people into the rebellion with
him.

The introduction of the feudal law, so far from extending,
may be regarded as an attempt to moderate the authority of
the great alodial lords. It established a regular subordination, accompanied with a long train of services and duties,
from the king down to the smallest proprietor. During the
minority of the proprietor, the rent, together with the management of his lands, fell into the hands of his immediate
superior, and, consequently, those of all great proprietors into
the hands of the king, who was charged with the maintenance
and education of the pupil, and who, from his authority as
guardian, was supposed to have a right of disposing of him in
marriage, provided it was in a manner not unsuitable to his
rank. But though this institution necessarily tended to
strengthen the authority of the king, and to weaken that of
the great proprietors, it could not do either sufficiently for
establishing order and good government among the inhabitants of the country, because it could not alter sufficiently that
state of property and manners from which the disorders arose.
The authority of government still continued to be, as before,
too weak in the head and too strong in the inferior members,
and the excessive strength of the inferior members was the
cause of the weakness of the head. After the institution of
feudal subordination, the king was as incapable of restraining

the violence of the great lords as before. They still continued to make war according to their own discretion, almost continually upon one another, and very frequently upon the king; and the open country still continued to be a scene of violence, rapine, and disorder.

But what all the violence of the feudal institutions could never have effected, the silent and insensible operation of foreign commerce and manufactures gradually brought about. These gradually furnished the great proprietors with something for which they could exchange the whole surplus produce of their lands, and which they could consume themselves without sharing it either with tenants or retainers. All for ourselves, and nothing for other people, seems, in every age of the world, to have been the vile maxim of the masters of mankind. As soon, therefore, as they could find a method of consuming the whole value of their rents themselves, they had no disposition to share them with any other persons. For a pair of diamond buckles perhaps, or for something as frivolous and useless, they exchanged the maintenance, or what is the same thing, the price of the maintenance of a thousand men for a year, and with it the whole weight and authority which it could give them. The buckles, however, were to be all their own, and no other human creature was to have any share of them; whereas in the more ancient method of expense they must have shared with at least a thousand people. With the judges that were to determine the preference, this difference was perfectly decisive; and thus, for the gratification of the most childish, the meanest and the most sordid of all vanities, they gradually bartered their whole power and authority.[4]

In a country where there is no foreign commerce, nor any of the finer manufactures, a man of ten thousand a year cannot well employ his revenue in any other way than in maintaining, perhaps, a thousand families, who are all of them necessarily at his command. In the present state of Europe, a man of ten thousand a year can spend his whole revenue,

---

[4] [Hume, *History*, ed. of 1773, vol. iii., p. 400; vol. v., p. 488.—C.]

and he generally does so, without directly maintaining twenty people, or being able to command more than ten footmen not worth the commanding. Indirectly, perhaps, he maintains as great or even a greater number of people than he could have done by the ancient method of expense. For though the quantity of precious productions for which he exchanges his whole revenue be very small, the number of workmen employed in collecting and preparing it must necessarily have been very great. Its great price generally arises from the wages of their labor and the profits of all their immediate employers. By paying that price he indirectly pays all those wages and profits, and thus indirectly contributes to the maintenance of all the workmen and their employers. He generally contributes, however, but a very small proportion to that of each, to very few perhaps a tenth, to many not a hundredth, and to some not a thousandth, nor even a ten thousandth part of their whole annual maintenance. Though he contributes, therefore, to the maintenance of them all, they are all more or less independent of him, because generally they can all be maintained without him.

When the great proprietors of land spend their rents in maintaining their tenants and retainers, each of them maintains entirely all his own tenants and all his own retainers. But when they spend them in maintaining tradesmen and artificers, they may, all of them taken together, perhaps, maintain as great, or, on account of the waste which attends rustic hospitality, a greater number of people than before. Each of them, however, taken singly, contributes often but a very small share to the maintenance of any individual of this greater number. Each tradesman or artificer derives his subsistence from the employment, not of one, but of a hundred or a thousand different customers. Though in some measure obliged to them all, therefore, he is not absolutely dependent upon any one of them.

The personal expense of the great proprietors having in this manner gradually increased, it was impossible that the number of their retainers should not as gradually diminish, till they were at last dismissed altogether. The same cause grad-ually led them to dismiss the unnecessary part of their tenants. Farms were enlarged, and the occupiers of land, notwithstand-ing the complaints of depopulation, reduced to the number necessary for cultivating it, according to the imperfect state of cultivation and improvement in those times. By the re-moval of the unnecessary mouths, and by exacting from the farmer the full value of the farm, a greater surplus, or what is the same thing, the price of a greater surplus, was obtained for the proprietor, which the merchants and manufacturers soon furnished him with a method of spending upon his own person in the same manner as he had done the rest. The same cause continuing to operate, he was desirous to raise his rents above what his lands, in the actual state of their improvement, could afford. His tenants could agree to this upon one condi-tion only, that they should be secured in their possession, for such a term of years as might give them time to recover with profit whatever they should lay out in the further improve-ment of the land. The expensive vanity of the landlord made him willing to accept of this condition; and hence the origin of long leases.

Even a tenant at will, who pays the full value of the land, is not altogether dependent upon the landlord. The pecuniary advantages which they receive from one another are mutual and equal, and such a tenant will expose neither his life nor his fortune in the service of the proprietor. But if he has a lease for a long term of years, he is altogether independent; and his landlord must not expect from him even the most trifling service beyond what is either expressly stipulated in the lease, or imposed upon him by the common and known law of the country.

The tenants having in this manner become independent, and the retainers being dismissed, the great proprietors were no longer capable of interrupting the regular execution of justice, or of disturbing the peace of the country. Having sold their birthright, not like Esau for a mess of pottage in time of hunger and necessity, but in the wantonness of plenty, for trinkets and baubles, fitter to be the playthings of children than the serious pursuits of men, they became as insignificant as any substantial burgher or tradesman in a city. A regular government was established in the country as well as in the city, nobody having sufficient power to disturb its operations in the one any more than in the other.

It does not, perhaps, relate to the present subject, but I cannot help remarking on it, that very old families, such as have possessed some considerable estate from father to son for many successive generations, are very rare in commercial countries. In countries which have little commerce, on the contrary, such as Wales or the Highlands of Scotland, they are very common. The Arabian histories seem to be all full of genealogies, and there is a history written by a Tartar Khan, which has been translated into several European languages, and which contains scarcely anything else—a proof that ancient families are very common among those nations. In countries where a rich man can spend his revenue in no other way than by maintaining as many people as it can maintain, he is not apt to run out, and his benevolence it seems is seldom so violent as to attempt to maintain more than he can afford. But where he can spend the greatest revenue upon his own person, he frequently has no bounds to his expense because he frequently has no bounds to his vanity, or to his affection for his own person. In commercial countries, therefore, riches, in spite of the most violent regulations of law to prevent their dissipation, very seldom remain long in the same family. Among simple nations, on the contrary, they frequently do without any regulations of law, for among nations of shepherds, such as the Tartars and Arabs, the consumable nature of their property necessarily renders all such regulations impossible.

A revolution of the greatest importance to the public happiness was in this manner brought about by two different orders of people, who had not the least intention to serve the public. To gratify the most childish vanity was the sole motive of the great proprietors. The merchants and artificers, much less ridiculous, acted merely from a view to their own interest, and in pursuit of their own peddler principle of turning a penny wherever a penny was to be got. Neither of them had either knowledge or foresight of that great revolution which the folly of the one, and the industry of the other, was gradually bringing about.

It is thus that through the greater part of Europe the commerce and manufactures of cities, instead of being the effect, have been the cause and occasion of the improvement and cultivation of the country.

This order, however, being contrary to the natural course of things, is necessarily both slow and uncertain. Compare the slow progress of those European countries, of which the wealth depends very much upon their commerce and manufactures, with the rapid advances of our North American colonies, of which the wealth is founded altogether in agriculture. Through the greater part of Europe, the number of inhabitants is not supposed to double in less than five hundred years. In several of our North American colonies, it is found to double in twenty or five-and-twenty years. In Europe the law of primogeniture, and perpetuities of different kinds, prevent the division of great estates, and thereby hinder the multiplication of small proprietors. A small proprietor, however, who knows every part of his little territory, who views it all with the affection which property, especially small property, naturally inspires, and who upon that account takes pleasure not only in cultivating but in adorning it, is generally of all improvers the most industrious, the most intelligent, and the most successful. The same regulations, besides, keep so much land out of the market that there are always more capitals to buy than there is land to sell, so that what is sold always sells at a monopoly price. The rent never pays the interest of the purchase money, and is besides burdened with repairs and other occasional charges to which the interest of money is not liable. To purchase land is everywhere in Europe a most unprofitable employment of a small capital. For the sake of the superior security, indeed, a man of moderate circumstances, when he retires from business, will sometimes choose to lay out his little capital in land. A man of profession, too, whose revenue is derived from another source, often loves to secure his savings in the same way. But a young man, who, instead of applying to trade or to some profession, should employ a capital of two or three thousand pounds in the purchase and cultivation of a small piece of land, might indeed expect to live very happily, and very independently, but must bid adieu, forever, to all hope of either great fortune or great illustration, which by a different employment of his stock he might have had the same chance of acquiring with other people. Such a person, too, though he cannot aspire at being proprietor, will often disdain to be a farmer. The small quantity of land, therefore, which is brought to market, and the high price of what is brought thither, prevents a great number of capitals from being employed in its cultivation and improvement which would otherwise have taken that direction. In North America, on the contrary, fifty or sixty pounds is often found a sufficient stock to begin a plantation with. The purchase and improvement of uncultivated land is there the most profitable employment of the smallest as well as of the greatest capitals, and the most direct road to all the fortune and illustration which can be acquired in that country. Such land, indeed, is in North America to be had almost for nothing, or at a price much below the value of the natural produce, a thing impossible in Europe or, indeed, in any country where all lands have long been private property. If landed estates, however, were divided equally among all the children upon the death of any proprietor who left a numerous family, the estate would generally be sold. So much land would come to market that it could no longer sell at a monopoly price. The free rent of the land would go nearer to pay the interest of the purchase money, and a small capital might be employed in purchasing land as profitably as in any other way.

England, on account of the natural fertility of the soil, of the great extent of the seacoast in proportion to that of the whole country, and of the many navigable rivers which run through it and afford the convenience of water carriage to some of the most inland parts of it, is perhaps as well fitted by nature as any large country in Europe to be the seat of foreign commerce, and manufactures for distant sale, and of all the improvements which these can occasion. From the beginning of the reign of Elizabeth, too, the English legislature has been peculiarly attentive to the interests of commerce and manufactures, and in reality there is no country in Europe, Holland itself not excepted, of which the law is, upon the whole, more favorable to this sort of industry. Commerce and manufactures have accordingly been continually advancing during all this period. The cultivation and improvement of the country has, no doubt, been gradually advancing too: But it seems to have followed slowly, and at a distance, the more rapid progress of commerce and manufactures. The greater part of the country must probably have been cultivated before the reign of Elizabeth; and a very great part of it still remains uncultivated, and the cultivation of the far greater part, much inferior to what it might be. The law of England, however, favors agriculture not only indirectly by the protection of commerce, but by several direct encouragements. Except in times of scarcity, the exportation of corn is not only free, but encouraged by a bounty. In times of moderate plenty, the importation of foreign corn is loaded with duties that amount to a prohibition. The importation of live cattle, except from Ireland, is prohibited at all times, and it is but of late that it was permitted from thence. Those who cultivate the land, therefore, have a monopoly against their countrymen for the two greatest and most important articles of land produce, bread and butcher's meat. These encouragements, though at bottom, perhaps, as I shall endeavor to show hereafter,[5] altogether illusory, sufficiently demonstrate at least the good intention of the legislature to favor agriculture. But what is of much more importance than all of them, the yeomanry of England are rendered as secure, as independent,

[5] [See pp. 169-174; see also Book IV, Chapter V, section "Digression Concerning the Corn Trade etc.," (not included in this edition).]

and as respectable as law can make them. No country, therefore, in which the right of primogeniture takes place, which
pays tithes, and where perpetuities, though contrary to the
spirit of the law, are admitted in some cases, can give more encouragement to agriculture than England. Such, however, notwithstanding, is the state of its cultivation. What would it
have been, had the law given no direct encouragement to agriculture besides what arises indirectly from the progress of
commerce, and had left the yeomanry in the same condition
as in most other countries of Europe? It is now more than two
hundred years since the beginning of the reign of Elizabeth,
a period as long as the course of human prosperity usually endures.

France seems to have had a considerable share of foreign
commerce nearly a century before England was distinguished
as a commercial country. The marine of France was considerable, according to the notions of the times, before the expedi-
tion of Charles VIII to Naples.[6] The cultivation and improvement of France, however, is, upon the whole, inferior to that
of England. The law of the country has never given the same
direct encouragement to agriculture.

The foreign commerce of Spain and Portugal to the other
parts of Europe, though chiefly carried on in foreign ships,
is very considerable. That to their colonies is carried on in
their own, and is much greater, on account of the great riches
and extent of those colonies. But it has never introduced any
considerable manufactures for distant sale into either of those
countries, and the greater part of both still remains uncultivated. The foreign commerce of Portugal is of older standing
than that of any great country in Europe except Italy.

Italy is the only great country of Europe which seems to
have been cultivated and improved in every part, by means of
foreign commerce and manufactures for distant sale. Before
the invasion of Charles VIII, Italy, according to Guicciardin,[7]

6 [It seems likely that Charles VIII is here (though not on the next
page) confused with Charles of Anjou, brother of St. Louis.—C.]

7 [Guicciardini, *Della Istoria d'Italia*, Venice, 1738, vol. i., p. 2.—C.]

was cultivated not less in the most mountainous and barren parts of the country, than in the plainest and most fertile. The advantageous situation of the country, and the great number of independent states which at that time subsisted in it, probably contributed not a little to this general cultivation. It is not impossible too, notwithstanding this general expression of one of the most judicious and reserved of modern historians, that Italy was not at that time better cultivated than England is at present.

The capital, however, that is acquired to any country by commerce and manufactures is all a very precarious and uncertain possession, till some part of it has been secured and realized in the cultivation and improvement of its lands. A merchant, it has been said very properly, is not necessarily the citizen of any particular country. It is in a great measure indifferent to him from what place he carries on his trade; and a very trifling disgust will make him remove his capital, and together with it all the industry which it supports, from one country to another. No part of it can be said to belong to any particular country till it has been spread as it were over the face of that country, either in buildings, or in the lasting improvement of lands. No vestige now remains of the great wealth said to have been possessed by the greater part of the Hanse towns, except in the obscure histories of the thirteenth and fourteenth centuries. It is even uncertain where some of them were situated, or to what towns in Europe the Latin names given to some of them belong. But though the misfortunes of Italy in the end of the fifteenth and beginning of the sixteenth centuries greatly diminished the commerce and manufactures of the cities of Lombardy and Tuscany, those countries still continue to be among the most populous and best cultivated in Europe. The civil wars of Flanders, and the Spanish government which succeeded them, chased away the great commerce of Antwerp, Ghent, and Bruges. But Flanders still continues to be one of the richest, best cultivated, and most populous provinces of Europe. The ordinary revolutions of war and government easily dry up the sources of that wealth which arises from commerce only. That which arises from the more solid improvements of agriculture is much more durable, and cannot be destroyed but by those more violent convulsions occasioned by the depredations of hostile and barbarous nations continued for a century or two together, such as those that happened for some time before and after the fall of the Roman Empire in the western provinces of Europe.

BOOK FOUR

OF SYSTEMS OF POLITICAL ECONOMY

INTRODUCTION

Political economy, considered as a branch of the science of a statesman or legislator, proposes two distinct objects: first, to provide a plentiful revenue or subsistence for the people, or more properly to enable them to provide such a revenue or subsistence for themselves; and secondly, to supply the state or commonwealth with a revenue sufficient for the public services. It proposes to enrich both the people and the sovereign.

The different progress of opulence in different ages and nations has given occasion to two different systems of political economy with regard to enriching the people. The one may be called the system of commerce, the other that of agriculture. I shall endeavor to explain both as fully and distinctly as I can, and shall begin with the system of commerce. It is the modern system, and is best understood in our own country and in our own times.

[CHAPTER I]

[Editor's Summary]

In Chapter I of Book IV, Smith analyzes the "Principle of the Commercial, or Mercantile System." He attacks the following: 1) the "popular notion" that real wealth consists in the possession of money; 2) the mercantilist view that foreign trade must be regulated in order that a favorable balance of payments (i.e., more money entering than leaving the country) always obtains; and 3) the belief that, in conditions of war, gold and silver rather than land and labor are the real resources of a country. On the latter point, Smith gives a number of judgments on the general subject of what, today, we would call the economics of war. Smith concludes that the mercantile system is a faulty one. In comparison, he praises free trade with other countries on the grounds that it widens the market, enlarges the division of labor, and contributes to the benefit of all the countries involved. He continues this general theme in Chapter II, which we reprint; it is in this chapter that the famous reference to "an invisible hand" occurs.

CHAPTER II

OF RESTRAINTS UPON THE IMPORTATION FROM FOREIGN COUNTRIES OF SUCH GOODS AS CAN BE PRODUCED AT HOME

By restraining, either by high duties, or by absolute prohibitions, the importation of such goods from foreign countries as can be produced at home, the monopoly of the home market is more or less secured to the domestic industry employed in producing them. Thus the prohibition of importing either live cattle or salt provisions from foreign countries secures to the graziers of Great Britain the monopoly of the home market for butcher's meat. The high duties upon the importation of corn, which in times of moderate plenty amount to a prohibition, give a like advantage to the growers of that commodity. The prohibition of the importation of foreign woolens is equally favorable to the woolen manufacturers. The silk manufacture, though altogether employed upon foreign materials, has lately obtained the same advantage. The linen manufacture has not yet obtained it, but is making great strides toward it. Many other sorts of manufacturers have, in the same manner, obtained in Great Britain, either altogether, or very nearly, a monopoly against their countrymen. The variety of goods of which the importation into Great Britain is prohibited, either absolutely, or under certain circumstances, greatly exceeds what can easily be suspected by those who are not well acquainted with the laws of the customs.

That this monopoly of the home market frequently gives great encouragement to that particular species of industry which enjoys it, and frequently turns toward that employment a greater share of both the labor and stock of the society than would otherwise have gone to it, cannot be doubted. But whether it tends either to increase the general industry of the society, or to give it the most advantageous direction, is not, perhaps, altogether so evident.

The general industry of the society never can exceed what the capital of the society can employ. As the number of workmen that can be kept in employment by any particular person must bear a certain proportion to his capital, so the number of those that can be continually employed by all the members of a great society must bear a certain proportion to the whole capital of that society and never can exceed that proportion. No regulation of commerce can increase the quantity of industry in any society beyond what its capital can maintain. It can only divert a part of it into a direction into which it might not otherwise have gone; and it is by no means certain that this artificial direction is likely to be more advantageous to the society than that into which it would have gone of its own accord.

Every individual is continually exerting himself to find out the most advantageous employment for whatever capital he can command. It is his own advantage, indeed, and not that of the society, which he has in view. But the study of his own advantage naturally, or rather necessarily, leads him to prefer that employment which is most advantageous to the society.

First, every individual endeavors to employ his capital as near home as he can, and consequently as much as he can in the support of domestic industry, provided always that he can thereby obtain the ordinary, or not a great deal less than the ordinary, profits of stock.

Thus, upon equal or nearly equal profits, every wholesale merchant naturally prefers the home trade to the foreign trade of consumption, and the foreign trade of consumption to the carrying trade. In the home trade his capital is never so long out of his sight as it frequently is in the foreign trade of consumption. He can know better the character and situation of the persons whom he trusts, and if he should happen to be deceived, he knows better the laws of the country from which he must seek redress. In the carrying trade, the capital of the merchant is, as it were, divided between two foreign countries, and no part of it is ever necessarily brought home or placed under his own immediate view and command. The capital which an Amsterdam merchant employs in carrying corn from Königsberg to Lisbon, and fruit and wine from Lisbon to Königsberg, must generally be the one half of it at Königsberg and the other half at Lisbon. No part of it need ever come to Amsterdam. The natural residence of such a merchant should either be at Königsberg or Lisbon, and it can only be some very particular circumstances which can make him prefer the residence of Amsterdam. The uneasiness, however, which he feels at being separated so far from his capital generally determines him to bring part both of the Königsberg goods which he destines for the market of Lisbon, and of the Lisbon goods which he destines for that of Königsberg, to Amsterdam; and though this necessarily subjects him to a double charge of loading and unloading, as well as to the payment of some duties and customs, yet for the sake of having some part of his capital always under his own view and command, he willingly submits to this extraordinary charge; and it is in this manner that every country which has any considerable share of the carrying trade becomes always the emporium, or general market, for the goods of all the different countries whose trade it carries on. The merchant, in order to save a second loading and unloading, endeavors always to sell in the home market as much of the goods of all those different countries as he can, and thus, so far as he can, to convert his carrying trade into a foreign trade of consumption. A merchant, in the same manner, who is engaged in the foreign trade of consumption, when he collects goods for foreign markets, will always be glad, upon equal or nearly equal profits, to sell as great a part of them at home as he can. He saves himself the risk and trouble of exportation, when, so far as he can, he thus converts his foreign trade of consumption into a home trade. Home is in this manner the center, if I may say so, around which the capitals of the inhabitants of every country are continually circulating, and toward which they are always tending, though by particular causes they may sometimes be driven off and repelled from it toward more distant employments. But a capital employed in the home trade, it has already been shown,[1] necessarily puts into motion a greater quantity of domestic industry and gives revenue and employment to a greater number of the inhabitants of the country than an equal capital employed in the foreign trade of consumption; and one employed in the foreign trade of consumption has the same advantage over an equal capital employed in the carrying trade. Upon equal, or only nearly equal, profits, therefore, every individual naturally inclines to employ his capital

[1] [Smith has already shown this in Book II, Chapter V, which we have not reprinted.—M.]

in the manner in which it is likely to afford the greatest support to domestic industry, and to give revenue and employment to the greatest number of people of his own country.

Secondly, every individual who employs his capital in the support of domestic industry necessarily endeavors so to direct that industry that its produce may be of the greatest possible value.

The produce of industry is what it adds to the subject or materials upon which it is employed. In proportion as the value of this produce is great or small, so will likewise be the profits of the employer. But it is only for the sake of profit that any man employs a capital in the support of industry; and he will always, therefore, endeavor to employ it in the support of that industry of which the produce is likely to be of the greatest value, or to exchange for the greatest quantity either of money or of other goods.

But the annual revenue of every society is always precisely equal to the exchangeable value of the whole annual produce of its industry, or rather is precisely the same thing with that exchangeable value. As every individual, therefore, endeavors as much as he can both to employ his capital in the support of domestic industry and so to direct that industry that its produce may be of the greatest value; every individual necessarily labors to render the annual revenue of the society as great as he can. He generally, indeed, neither intends to promote the public interest, nor knows how much he is promoting it. By preferring the support of domestic to that of foreign industry, he intends only his own security; and by directing that industry in such a manner as its produce may be of the greatest value, he intends only his own gain, and he is in this, as in many other cases, led by an invisible hand to promote an end which was no part of his intention. Nor is it always the worse for the society that it was no part of it. By pursuing his own interest he frequently promotes that of the society more effectually than when he really intends to promote it. I have never known much good done by those who affected to trade for the public good. It is an affectation, indeed, not

Invisible Hand

very common among merchants, and very few words need be employed in dissuading them from it.

What is the species of domestic industry which his capital can employ, and of which the produce is likely to be of the greatest value, every individual, it is evident, can, in his local situation, judge much better than any statesman or lawgiver can do for him. The statesman, who should attempt to direct private people in what manner they ought to employ their capitals, would not only load himself with a most unnecessary attention, but assume an authority which could safely be trusted, not only to no single person, but to no council or senate whatever, and which would nowhere be so dangerous as in the hands of a man who had folly and presumption enough to fancy himself fit to exercise it.

To give the monopoly of the home market to the produce of domestic industry, in any particular art or manufacture, is in some measure to direct private people in what manner they ought to employ their capitals, and must, in almost all cases, be either a useless or a hurtful regulation. If the produce of domestic can be brought there as cheaply as that of foreign industry, the regulation is evidently useless. If it cannot, it must generally be hurtful. It is the maxim of every prudent master of a family, never to attempt to make at home what it will cost him more to make than to buy. The tailor does not attempt to make his own shoes, but buys them from the shoemaker. The shoemaker does not attempt to make his own clothes, but employs a tailor. The farmer attempts to make neither the one nor the other, but employs those different artificers. All of them find it for their interest to employ their whole industry in a way in which they have some advantage over their neighbors and to purchase with a part of its produce, or what is the same thing, with the price of a part of it, whatever else they have occasion for.

What is prudence in the conduct of every private family can scarcely be folly in that of a great kingdom. If a foreign country can supply us with a commodity cheaper than we ourselves can make it, better buy it from them with some part of the produce of our own industry, employed in a way in which we have some advantage. The general industry of the country, being always in proportion to the capital which employs it, will not thereby be diminished, no more than that of the above-mentioned artificers, but only left to find out the way in which it can be employed with the greatest advantage. It is certainly not employed to the greatest advantage, when it is thus directed toward an object which it can buy cheaper than it can make. The value of its annual produce is certainly more or less diminished when it is thus turned away from producing commodities evidently of more value than the commodity which it is directed to produce, according to the supposition that commodity could be purchased from foreign countries cheaper than it can be made at home. It could, therefore, have been purchased with a part only of the commodities, or, what is the same thing, with a part only of the price of the commodities, which the industry employed by an equal capital would have produced at home, had it been left to follow its natural course. The industry of the country, therefore, is thus turned away from a more to a less advantageous employment, and the exchangeable value of its annual produce, instead of being increased, according to the intention of the lawgiver, must necessarily be diminished by every such regulation.

By means of such regulations, indeed, a particular manufacture may sometimes be acquired sooner than it could have been otherwise, and after a certain time may be made at home as cheap or cheaper than in the foreign country. But though the industry of the society may be thus carried with advantage into a particular channel sooner than it could have been otherwise, it will by no means follow that the sum total, either of its industry or of its revenue, can ever be augmented by any such regulation. The industry of the society can augment only in proportion as its capital augments, and its capital can augment only in proportion to what can be gradually saved out of its revenue. But the immediate effect of every such regulation is to diminish its revenue, and what diminishes its revenue is certainly not very likely to augment its capital faster than it would have augmented of its own accord, had both capital and industry been left to find out their natural employments.

Though for want of such regulations the society should never acquire the proposed manufacture, it would not, upon that account, necessarily be the poorer in any one period of its duration. In every period of its duration its whole capital and industry might still have been employed, though upon different objects, in the manner that was most advantageous at the time. In every period its revenue might have been the greatest which its capital could afford, and both capital and revenue might have been augmented with the greatest possible rapidity.

The natural advantages which one country has over another in producing particular commodities are sometimes so great, that it is acknowledged by all the world to be in vain to struggle with them. By means of glasses, hotbeds, and hot-walls, very good grapes can be raised in Scotland, and very good wine too can be made of them at about thirty times the expense for which at least equally good can be brought from foreign countries. Would it be a reasonable law to prohibit the importation of all foreign wines, merely to encourage the making of claret and burgundy in Scotland? But if there would be a manifest absurdity in turning toward any employment thirty times more of the capital and industry of the country, than would be necessary to purchase from foreign countries an equal quantity of the commodities wanted, there must be an absurdity, though not altogether so glaring, yet exactly of the same kind, in turning toward any such employment a thirtieth, or even a three-hundredth, part more of either. Whether the advantages which one country has over another be natural or acquired is in this respect of no consequence. As long as the one country has those advantages, and the other wants them, it will always be more advantageous for the latter rather to buy of the former than to make. It is an acquired advantage only which one artificer has over his neighbor who exercises another trade; and yet they both find it more advantageous to buy of one another, than to make what does not belong to their particular trades.

Merchants and manufacturers are the people who derive the greatest advantage from this monopoly of the home market. The prohibition of the importation of foreign cattle, and of salt provisions, together with the high duties upon foreign corn, which in times of moderate plenty amount to a prohibition, are not nearly so advantageous to the graziers and farmers of Great Britain as other regulations of the same kind are to its merchants and manufacturers. Manufactures, those of the finer kind especially, are more easily transported from one country to another than corn or cattle. It is in the fetching and carrying manufactures, accordingly, that foreign trade is chiefly employed. In manufactures, a very small advantage will enable foreigners to undersell our own workmen, even in the home market. It will require a very great one to enable them to do so in the rude produce of the soil. If the free importation of foreign manufactures were permitted, several of the home manufactures would probably suffer, and some of them, perhaps, go to ruin altogether, and a considerable part of the stock and industry at present employed in them would be forced to find out some other employment. But the freest importation of the rude produce of the soil could have no such effect upon the agriculture of the country.

If the importation of foreign cattle, for example, were made ever so free, so few could be imported that the grazing trade of Great Britain could be little affected by it. Live cattle are, perhaps, the only commodity of which the transportation is more expensive by sea than by land. By land they carry themselves to market. By sea, not only the cattle, but their food and their water, too, must be carried at no small expense and inconvenience. The short sea between Ireland and Great Britain, indeed, renders the importation of Irish cattle more easy. But though the free importation of them, which was lately permitted only for a limited time, were rendered perpetual, it could have no considerable effect upon the interest of the graziers of Great Britain. Those parts of Great Britain which border upon the Irish Sea are all grazing countries. Irish cattle could never be imported for their use, but must be driven through those very extensive countries, at no small expense and inconvenience, before they could arrive at their proper market. Fat cattle could not be driven so far. Lean cattle, therefore, only could be imported, and such importation could interfere, not with the interest of the feeding or fattening countries, to which, by reducing the price of lean cattle, it would rather be advantageous, but with that of the breeding countries only. The small number of Irish cattle imported since their importation was permitted, together with the good price at which lean cattle still continue to sell, seem to demonstrate that even the breeding countries of Great Britain are never likely to be much affected by the free importation of Irish cattle. The common people of Ireland, indeed, are said to have sometimes opposed with violence the exportation of their cattle. But if the exporters had found any great advantage in continuing the trade, they could easily, when the law was on their side, have conquered this mobbish opposition.

Feeding and fattening countries, besides, must always be highly improved, whereas breeding countries are generally uncultivated. The high price of lean cattle, by augmenting the value of uncultivated land, is like a bounty against improvement. To any country which was highly improved throughout, it would be more advantageous to import its lean cattle than to breed them. The province of Holland, accordingly, is said to follow this maxim at present. The mountains of Scotland, Wales and Northumberland, indeed, are countries not capable of much improvement, and seem destined by nature to be the breeding countries of Great Britain. The freest importation of foreign cattle could have no other effect than to hinder those breeding countries from taking advantage of the increasing population and improvement of the rest of the kingdom, from raising their price to an exorbitant height, and from laying a real tax upon all the more improved and cultivated parts of the country.

The freest importation of salt provisions, in the same manner, could have as little effect upon the interest of the graziers of Great Britain as that of live cattle. Salt provisions are not only a very bulky commodity, but when compared with fresh meat, they are a commodity both of worse quality, and as they cost more labor and expense, of higher price. They could never, therefore, come into competition with the fresh meat, though they might with the salt provisions of the country. They might be used for victualing ships for distant voyages, and such like uses, but could never make any considerable part of the food of the people. The small quantity of salt provisions imported from Ireland since their importation was rendered free is an experimental proof that our graziers have nothing to apprehend from it. It does not appear that the price of butcher's meat has ever been sensibly affected by it.

Even the free importation of foreign corn could very little affect the interest of the farmers of Great Britain. Corn is a much more bulky commodity than butcher's meat. A pound of wheat at a penny is as dear as a pound of butcher's meat at fourpence. The small quantity of foreign corn imported even in times of the greatest scarcity may satisfy our farmers that they can have nothing to fear from the freest importation. The average quantity imported one year with another amounts only, according to the very well-informed author of the tracts upon the corn trade, to twenty-three thousand seven hundred and twenty-eight quarters of all sorts of grain, and does not exceed the five-hundredth and seventy-one part of the annual consumption. But as the bounty upon corn occasions a greater exportation in years of plenty, so it must of consequence occasion a greater importation in years of scarcity, than in the actual state of tillage would otherwise take place. By means of it, the plenty of one year does not compensate the scarcity of another, and as the average quantity exported is necessarily augmented by it, so must likewise, in the actual state of tillage, the average quantity imported. If there were no bounty, as less corn would be exported, so it is probable that, one year with another, less would be imported than at present. The corn merchants, the fetchers and carriers of corn between Great Britain and foreign countries, would have much less employment and might suffer considerably; but the country gentlemen and farmers could suffer very little. It is in the corn merchants, accordingly, rather than in the country gentlemen and farmers, that I have observed the greatest anxiety for the renewal and continuation of the bounty.

Country gentlemen and farmers are, to their great honor, of all people the least subject to the wretched spirit of monopoly. The undertaker of a great manufactory is sometimes alarmed if another work of the same kind is established within twenty miles of him. The Dutch undertaker of the woolen manufacture at Abbeville stipulated that no work of the same kind should be established within thirty leagues of that city. Farmers and country gentlemen, on the contrary, are generally disposed rather to promote than to obstruct the cultivation and improvement of their neighbors' farms and estates. They have no secrets, such as those of the greater part of manufacturers, but are generally rather fond of communicating to their neighbors, and of extending as far as possible any new practice which they have found to be advantageous. *Pius questus* [*quaestus*], says old Cato, *stabilissimusque, minimeque invidiosus; minimeque male cogitantes sunt, qui in eo studio occupati sunt.*[2] Country gentlemen and farmers, dispersed in different parts of the country, cannot so easily combine as merchants and manufacturers, who being collected into towns, and accustomed to that exclusive corporation spirit which prevails in them, naturally endeavor to obtain against all their countrymen the same exclusive privilege which they generally possess against the inhabitants of their respective towns.

[2] ["A god-fearing occupation is stablest, and least invites envy; and those engaged in it are least unwholesome in their outlook." Cato, *De re rustica, ad init.*–M.]

They accordingly seem to have been the original inventors of those restraints upon the importation of foreign goods which secure to them the monopoly of the home market. It was probably in imitation of them, and to put themselves upon a level with those who, they found, were disposed to oppress them, that the country gentlemen and farmers of Great Britain so far forgot the generosity which is natural to their station as to demand the exclusive privilege of supplying their countrymen with corn and butcher's meat. They did not perhaps take time to consider how much less their interest could be affected by the freedom of trade than that of the people whose example they followed.

To prohibit by a perpetual law the importation of foreign corn and cattle is in reality to enact that the population and industry of the country shall at no time exceed what the rude produce of its own soil can maintain.

There seem, however, to be two cases in which it will generally be advantageous to lay some burden upon foreign, for the encouragement of domestic, industry.

The first is, when some particular sort of industry is necessary for the defense of the country. The defense of Great Britain, for example, depends very much upon the number of its sailors and shipping. The Act of Navigation, therefore, very properly endeavors to give the sailors and shipping of Great Britain the monopoly of the trade of their own country, in some cases by absolute prohibitions, and in others by heavy burdens upon the shipping of foreign countries. The following are the principal dispositions of this act.

First, all ships of which the owners, masters, and three-fourths of the mariners are not British subjects are prohibited, upon pain of forfeiting ship and cargo, from trading to the British settlements and plantations, or from being employed in the coasting trade of Great Britain.

Secondly, a great variety of the most bulky articles of importation can be brought into Great Britain only, either in such ships as are above described, or in ships of the country where those goods are produced, and of which the owners,

masters, and three-fourths of the mariners are of that particular country; and when imported even in ships of this
latter kind, they are subject to double aliens' duty. If imported in ships of any other country, the penalty is forfeiture
of ship and goods. When this act was made, the Dutch were,
what they still are, the great carriers of Europe, and by this
regulation they were entirely excluded from being the carriers
to Great Britain, or from importing to us the goods of any
other European country.

Thirdly, a great variety of the most bulky articles of importation are prohibited from being imported, even in British
ships, from any country but that in which they are produced,
under pain of forfeiting ship and cargo. This regulation too
was probably intended against the Dutch. Holland was then,
as now, the great emporium for all European goods, and by
this regulation, British ships were hindered from loading in
Holland the goods of any other European country.

Fourthly, salt fish of all kinds, whale fins, whalebone, oil,
and blubber, not caught by and cured on board British
vessels, when imported into Great Britain, are subjected to
double aliens' duty. The Dutch, as they are still the principal,
were then the only fishers in Europe that attempted to supply
foreign nations with fish. By this regulation, a very heavy burden was laid upon their supplying Great Britain.

When the Act of Navigation was made, though England and
Holland were not actually at war, the most violent animosity
subsisted between the two nations. It had begun during the
government of the Long Parliament, which first framed this
act,[3] and it broke out soon after in the Dutch wars during that
of the Protector and of Charles the Second. It is not impossible, therefore, that some of the regulations of this famous
act may have proceeded from national animosity. They are as
wise, however, as if they had all been dictated by the most
deliberate wisdom. National animosity at that particular time

[3] [In 1651, by "An act for the increase of shipping and encouragement
of the navigation of this nation," p. 1,449 in the collection of Commonwealth Acts.—C.]

aimed at the very same object which the most deliberate wisdom would have recommended, the diminution of the naval power of Holland, the only naval power which could endanger the security of England.

The Act of Navigation is not favorable to foreign commerce, or to the growth of that opulence which can arise from it. The interest of a nation in its commercial relations to foreign nations is, like that of a merchant with regard to the different people with whom he deals, to buy as cheaply and to sell as dearly as possible. But it will be most likely to buy cheap when by the most perfect freedom of trade it encourages all nations to bring to it the goods which it has occasion to purchase; and, for the same reason, it will be most likely to sell dear when its markets are thus filled with the greatest number of buyers. The Act of Navigation, it is true, lays no burden upon foreign ships that come to export the produce of British industry. Even the ancient aliens duty, which used to be paid upon all goods exported as well as imported, has, by several subsequent acts, been taken off from the greater part of the articles of exportation. But if foreigners, either by prohibitions or high duties, are hindered from coming to sell, they cannot always afford to come to buy, because, coming without a cargo, they must lose the freight from their own country to Great Britain. By diminishing the number of sellers, therefore, we necessarily diminish that of buyers, and are thus likely not only to buy foreign goods dearer, but to sell our own cheaper, than if there was a more perfect freedom of trade. As defense, however, is of much more importance than opulence, the act of navigation is, perhaps, the wisest of all the commercial regulations of England.

The second case, in which it will generally be advantageous to lay some burden upon foreign for the encouragement of domestic industry, is, when some tax is imposed at home upon the produce of the latter. In this case, it seems reasonable that an equal tax should be imposed upon the like produce of the former. This would not give the monopoly of the home market to domestic industry, nor turn towards a particular employment a greater share of the stock and labor of the country than what would naturally go to it. It would only hinder any part of what would naturally go to it from being turned away by the tax into a less natural direction, and would leave the competition between foreign and domestic industry, after the tax, as nearly as possible upon the same footing as before it. In Great Britain, when any such tax is laid upon the produce of domestic industry, it is usual at the same time, in order to stop the clamorous complaints of our merchants and manufacturers that they will be undersold at home, to lay a much heavier duty upon the importation of all foreign goods of the same kind.

This second limitation of the freedom of trade according to some people should, upon some occasions, be extended much farther than to the precise foreign commodities which could come into competition with those which had been taxed at home. When the necessities of life have been taxed in any country, it becomes proper, they pretend, to tax not only the like necessities of life imported from other countries, but all sorts of foreign goods which can come into competition with anything that is the produce of domestic industry. Subsistence, they say, becomes necessarily dearer in consequence of such taxes; and the price of labor must always rise with the price of the laborers' subsistence. Every commodity, therefore, which is the produce of domestic industry, though not immediately taxed itself, becomes dearer in consequence of such taxes, because the labor which produces it becomes so. Such taxes, therefore, are really equivalent, they say, to a tax upon every particular commodity produced at home. In order to put domestic upon the same footing with foreign industry, therefore, it becomes necessary, they think, to lay some duty upon every foreign commodity, equal to this enhancement of the price of the home commodities with which it can come into competition.

Whether taxes upon the necessities of life, such as those in Great Britain upon soap, salt, leather, candles, etc., necessarily raise the price of labor, and consequently that of all other commodities, I shall consider hereafter when I come to treat of taxes. Supposing, however, in the meantime, that they have this effect, and they have it undoubtedly, this general enhancement of the price of all commodities, in consequence of that of labor, is a case which differs in the two following respects from that of a particular commodity, of which the price was enhanced by a particular tax immediately imposed upon it.

First, it might always be known with great exactness how far the price of such a commodity could be enhanced by such a tax, but how far the general enhancement of the price of labor might affect that of every different commodity about which labor was employed could never be known with any tolerable exactness. It would be impossible, therefore, to proportion with any tolerable exactness the tax upon every foreign, to this enhancement of the price of every home, commodity.

Secondly, taxes upon the necessities of life have nearly the same effect upon the circumstances of the people as a poor soil and a bad climate. Provisions are thereby rendered dearer in the same manner as if it required extraordinary labor and expense to raise them. As in the natural scarcity arising from soil and climate, it would be absurd to direct the people in what manner they ought to employ their capitals and industry, so is it likewise in the artificial scarcity arising from such taxes. To be left to accommodate, as well as they could, their industry to their situation and to find out those employments in which, notwithstanding their unfavorable circumstances, they might have some advantage either in the home or in the foreign market, is what in both cases would evidently be most for their advantage. To lay a new tax upon them, because they are already overburdened with taxes, and because they already pay too dearly for the necessities of life, to make them likewise pay too dearly for the greater part of other commodities, is certainly a most absurd way of making amends.

Such taxes, when they have grown up to a certain height, are a curse equal to the barrenness of the earth and the inclemency of the heavens, and yet it is in the richest and most industrious countries that they have been most generally imposed. No other countries could support so great a disorder. As the strongest bodies only can live and enjoy health under an unwholesome regimen, so the nations only, that in every sort of industry have the greatest natural and acquired advantages, can subsist and prosper under such taxes. Holland is the country in Europe in which they abound most, and which from peculiar circumstances continues to prosper, not by means of them, as has been most absurdly supposed, but in spite of them.

As there are two cases in which it will generally be advantageous to lay some burden upon foreign, for the encouragement of domestic, industry; so there are two others in which it may sometimes be a matter of deliberation: in the one, how far it is proper to continue the free importation of certain foreign goods, and in the other, how far, or in what manner, it may be proper to restore that free importation after it has been for some time interrupted.

The case in which it may sometimes be a matter of deliberation how far it is proper to continue the free importation of certain foreign goods is when some foreign nation restrains by high duties or prohibitions the importation of some of our manufactures into their country. Revenge in this case naturally dictates retaliation, and that we should impose the like duties and prohibitions upon the importation of some or all of their manufactures into ours. Nations accordingly seldom fail to retaliate in this manner. The French have been particularly forward to favor their own manufactures by restraining the importation of such foreign goods as could come into competition with them. In this consisted a great part of the policy of Mr. Colbert, who, notwithstanding his great abilities, seems in this case to have been imposed upon by the sophistry of merchants and manufacturers, who are always demanding a monopoly against their countrymen. It is at present the opinion of the most intelligent men in France that his operations of this kind have not been beneficial to his country. That minister, by the tariff of 1667, imposed very high duties

upon a great number of foreign manufactures. Upon his re-
fusing to moderate them in favor of the Dutch, they in 1671
prohibited the importation of the wines, brandies and manufactures of France. The war of 1672 seems to have been in part
occasioned by this commercial dispute. The peace of Nijmegen
put an end to it in 1678 by moderating some of those duties
in favor of the Dutch, who in consequence took off their prohibition. It was about the same time that the French and English began mutually to oppress each other's industry by the
like duties and prohibitions, of which the French, however,
seem to have set the first example. The spirit of hostility
which has subsisted between the two nations ever since has
hitherto hindered them from being moderated on either side.
In 1697, the English prohibited the importation of bone lace,
the manufacture of Flanders. The government of that country, at that time under the dominion of Spain, prohibited in
return the importation of English woolens. In 1700, the prohibition of importing bone lace into England was taken off
upon condition that the importation of English woolens into
Flanders should be put on the same footing as before.

There may be good policy in retaliations of this kind, when
there is a probability that they will procure the repeal of the
high duties or prohibitions complained of. The recovery of
a great foreign market will generally more than compensate
the transitory inconvenience of paying dearer during a short
time for some sorts of goods. To judge whether such retaliations are likely to produce such an effect does not, perhaps,
belong so much to the science of a legislator, whose deliberations ought to be governed by general principles which are
always the same, as to the skill of that insidious and crafty
animal, vulgarly called a statesman or politician, whose councils are directed by the momentary fluctuations of affairs.
When there is no probability that any such repeal can be procured, it seems a bad method of compensating the injury done
to certain classes of our people to do another injury ourselves, not only to those classes, but to almost all the other
classes of them. When our neighbors prohibit some manufac-

ture of ours, we generally prohibit not only the same, for that alone would seldom affect them considerably, but some other manufacture of theirs. This may no doubt give encouragement to some particular class of workmen among ourselves and, by excluding some of their rivals, may enable them to raise their price in the home market. Those workmen, however, who suffered by our neighbors' prohibition will not be benefited by ours. On the contrary, they and almost all the other classes of our citizens will thereby be obliged to pay dearer than before for certain goods. Every such law, therefore, imposes a real tax upon the whole country, not in favor of that particular class of workmen who were injured by our neighbors' prohibition, but of some other class.

The case in which it may sometimes be a matter of deliberation, how far, or in what manner, it is proper to restore the free importation of foreign goods after it has been for some time interrupted, is, when particular manufactures, by means of high duties or prohibitions upon all foreign goods which can come into competition with them, have been so far extended as to employ a great multitude of hands. Humanity may in this case require that the freedom of trade should be restored only by slow gradations, and with a good deal of reserve and circumspection. Were those high duties and prohibitions taken away all at once, cheaper foreign goods of the same kind might be poured so fast into the home market as to deprive all at once many thousands of our people of their ordinary employment and means of subsistence. The disorder which this would occasion might no doubt be very considerable. It would in all probability, however, be much less than is commonly imagined, for the two following reasons:

First, all those manufactures of which any part is commonly exported to other European countries without a bounty could be very little affected by the freest importation of foreign goods. Such manufactures must be sold as cheaply abroad as any other foreign goods of the same quality and kind, and consequently must be sold cheaper at home. They would still, therefore, keep possession of the home market, and though a

capricious man of fashion might sometimes prefer foreign
wares, merely because they were foreign, to cheaper and better goods of the same kind that were made at home, this folly
could, from the nature of things, extend .to so few, that it
could make no sensible impression upon the general employment of the people. But a great part of all the different
branches of our woolen manufacture, of our tanned leather,
and of our hardware, are annually exported to other European countries without any bounty, and these are the manufactures which employ the greatest number of hands. The silk,
perhaps, is the manufacture which would suffer the most by
this freedom of trade, and after it the linen, though the latter
much less than the former.

Secondly, though a great number of people should, by thus
restoring the freedom of trade, be thrown all at once out of
their ordinary employment and common method of subsistence, it would by no means follow that they would thereby
be deprived either of employment or subsistence. By the reduction of the army and navy at the end of the late war,[4]
more than a hundred thousand soldiers and seamen, a number equal to what is employed in the greatest manufactures,
were all at once thrown out of their ordinary employment;
but, though they no doubt suffered some inconvenience, they
were not thereby deprived of all employment and subsistence.
The greater part of the seamen, it is probable, gradually be-
took themselves to the merchant service as they could find
occasion, and in the meantime both they and the soldiers were
absorbed in the great mass of the people and employed in a
great variety of occupations. Not only no great convulsion, but
no sensible disorder arose from so great a change in the situation of more than a hundred thousand men, all accustomed
to the use of arms, and many of them to rapine and plunder.
The number of vagrants was scarcely anywhere sensibly in-

4 [When Smith talks of the American Revolution, he usually refers to it
as the "late" or "present" disturbances. Here, however, he is referring to
the war preceding the events of 1776, the Seven Years' War (1756-1763),
known in its American aspect as the French and Indian War.—M.]

creased by it; even the wages of labor were not reduced by it in any occupation, so far as I have been able to learn, except in that of seamen in the merchant service. But if we compare together the habits of a soldier and of any sort of manufacturer, we shall find that those of the latter do not tend so much to disqualify him from being employed in a new trade, as those of the former from being employed in any. The manufacturer has always been accustomed to look for his subsistence from his labor only; the soldier to expect it from his pay. Application and industry have been familiar to the one; idleness and dissipation to the other. But it is surely much easier to change the direction of industry from one sort of labor to another, than to turn idleness and dissipation to any. To the greater part of manufactures, besides, it has already been observed, there are other collateral manufactures of so similar a nature that a workman can easily transfer his industry from one of them to another. The greater part of such workmen too are occasionally employed in country labor. The stock which employed them in a particular manufacture before will still remain in the country to employ an equal number of people in some other way. The capital of the country remaining the same, the demand for labor will likewise be the same, or very nearly the same, though it may be exerted in different places and for different occupations. Soldiers and seamen, indeed, when discharged from the king's service, are at liberty to exercise any trade, within any town or place of Great Britain or Ireland. Let the same natural liberty of exercising what species of industry they please be restored to all his majesty's subjects, in the same manner as to soldiers and seamen; that is, break down the exclusive privileges of corporations and repeal the statute of apprenticeship, both which are real encroachments upon natural liberty, and add to these the repeal of the law of settlements, so that a poor workman, when thrown out of employment either in one trade or in one place, may seek for it in another trade or in another place, without the fear either of a prosecution or of a removal, and neither the public nor the individuals will suffer much more from the occasional disbanding of some particular classes of manufacturers, than from that of soldiers. Our manufacturers have no doubt great merit with their country, but they cannot have more than those who defend it with their blood, nor deserve to be treated with more delicacy.

To expect, indeed, that the freedom of trade should ever be entirely restored in Great Britain is as absurd as to expect that an Oceana or Utopia [5] should ever be established in it. Not only the prejudices of the public, but what is much more unconquerable, the private interests of many individuals, irresistibly oppose it. Were the officers of the army to oppose with the same zeal and unanimity any reduction in the number of forces with which master manufacturers set themselves against every law that is likely to increase the number of their rivals in the home market; were the former to animate their soldiers, in the same manner as the latter enflame their workmen, to attack with violence and outrage the proposers of any such regulation; to attempt to reduce the army would be as dangerous as it has now become to attempt to diminish in any respect the monopoly which our manufacturers have obtained against us. This monopoly has so much increased the number of some particular tribes of them, that, like an overgrown standing army, they have become formidable to the government, and upon many occasions intimidate the legislature. The member of parliament who supports every proposal for strengthening this monopoly is sure to acquire not only the reputation of understanding trade, but great popularity and influence with an order of men whose numbers and wealth render them of great importance. If he opposes them, on the contrary, and still more if he has authority enough to be able to thwart them, neither the most acknowledged probity, nor the highest rank, nor the greatest public services, can protect him from the most infamous abuse and

[5] [Oceana refers to *The Commonwealth of Oceana* (1756) by James Harrington, and Utopia to the book of the same name, written by Thomas More in 1515-1516. Both Oceana and Utopia are, of course, imaginary commonwealths.—M.]

detraction, from personal insults, nor sometimes from real danger, arising from the insolent outrage of furious and disappointed monopolists.

The undertaker of a great manufacture, who, by the home markets being suddenly laid open to the competition of foreigners, should be obliged to abandon his trade, would no doubt suffer very considerably. That part of his capital which had usually been employed in purchasing materials and in paying his workmen might, without much difficulty, perhaps, find another employment. But that part of it which was fixed in workhouses, and in the instruments of trade, could scarcely be disposed of without considerable loss. The equitable regard, therefore, to his interest requires that changes of this kind should never be introduced suddenly, but slowly, gradually, and after a very long warning. The legislature, were it possible that its deliberations could be always directed, not by the clamorous importunity of partial interests, but by an extensive view of the general good, ought upon this very account, perhaps, to be particularly careful neither to establish any new monopolies of this kind, nor to extend further those which are already established. Every such regulation introduces some degree of real disorder into the constitution of the state, which it will be difficult afterwards to cure without occasioning another disorder.

How far it may be proper to impose taxes upon the importation of foreign goods, in order not to prevent their importation, but to raise a revenue for government, I shall consider hereafter when I come to treat of taxes. Taxes imposed with a view to prevent, or even to diminish importation, are evidently as destructive of the revenue of the customs as of the freedom of trade.

[CHAPTERS III, IV, V, VI, AND VII]

[Editor's Summary]

Smith continues his discussion of the unreasonableness of restraints upon trade in Chapter III, and stresses that increased commerce between England and France would be of mutual advantage. Chapters IV and V are concerned with particular evils stemming from the mercantile principle: drawbacks ("a duty which is paid upon the importation of foreign goods, to be drawn back upon their exportation to any foreign country") and bounties. Under this general topic, Smith gives a substantial "Digression concerning the Corn Trade and Corn Laws," in which he once again pleads for free trade. In Chapter VI, Smith briefly examines treaties of commerce in general, and then discusses some specific examples.

In Chapter VII, Smith takes up the subject of colonies. The first part raises the question of "the Motives for establishing New Colonies," and the answer is given by way of a short historical analysis of colonization from the Greeks to the Spaniards. We reprint only the second part of the chapter, which deals with the "Causes of the Prosperity of New Colonies"; it is in this section of his work that Smith airs, directly and indirectly, many of his opinions about the American colonies and their grievances.

[CHAPTER VII]

PART II

Causes of the Prosperity of New Colonies

The colony of a civilized nation which takes possession either of a waste country, or of one so thinly inhabited that the natives easily give place to the new settlers, advances more rapidly to wealth and greatness than any other human society.

The colonists carry out with them a knowledge of agriculture and of other useful arts, superior to what can grow up of its own accord in the course of many centuries among savage and barbarous nations. They carry out with them too the habit of subordination, some notion of the regular government which takes place in their own country, of the system of laws which supports it, and of a regular administration of justice; and they naturally establish something of the same kind in the new settlement. But among savage and barbarous nations, the natural progress of law and government is still slower than the natural progress of arts, after law and government have been so far established as is necessary for their protection. Every colonist gets more land than he can possibly cultivate. He has no rent, and scarcely any taxes to pay. No landlord shares with him in its produce, and the share of the sovereign is commonly but a trifle. He has every motive to render as great as possible a produce which is thus to be almost entirely his own. But his land is commonly so extensive that with all his own industry, and with all the industry of other people whom he can get to employ, he can seldom make it produce the tenth part of what it is capable of producing. He is eager, therefore, to collect laborers from all quarters and to reward them with the most liberal wages. But those liberal wages, joined to the plenty and cheapness of land, soon make those laborers leave him, in order to become landlords themselves, and to reward, with equal liberality, other laborers, who soon leave them for the same reason that they left their first master. The liberal reward of labor encourages marriage. The children, during the tender years of infancy, are well fed and properly taken care of, and when they are grown up, the value of their labor greatly overpays their maintenance. When arrived at maturity, the high price of labor and the low price of land enable them to establish themselves in the same manner as their fathers did before them.

In other countries, rent and profit eat up wages, and the two superior orders of people oppress the inferior one. But in new colonies, the interest of the two superior orders obliges them to treat the inferior one with more generosity and humanity; at least where that inferior one is not in a state of slavery. Wastelands of the greatest natural fertility are to be had for a trifle. The increase of revenue which the proprietor, who is always the undertaker, expects from their improvement constitutes his profit, which in these circumstances is commonly very great. But this great profit cannot be made without employing the labor of other people in clearing and cultivating the land; and the disproportion between the great extent of the land and the small number of the people, which commonly takes place in new colonies, makes it difficult for him to get this labor. He does not, therefore, dispute about wages, but is willing to employ at any price. The high wages of labor encourage population. The cheapness and plenty of good land encourage improvement and enable the proprietor to pay those high wages. In those wages consists almost the whole price of the land; and though they are high, considered as the wages of labor, they are low, considered as the price of what is so very valuable. What encourages the progress of population and improvement, encourages that of real wealth and greatness.

The progress of many of the ancient Greek colonies toward wealth and greatness seems accordingly to have been very rapid. In the course of a century or two, several of them appear to have rivaled and even to have surpassed their mother cities. Syracuse and Agrigentum in Sicily, Tarentum and Locri in Italy, Ephesus and Miletus in Lesser Asia, appear by all accounts to have been at least equal to any of the cities of ancient Greece. Though posterior in their establishment, yet all the arts of refinement, philosophy, poetry, and eloquence seem to have been cultivated as early, and to have been improved as highly in them as in any part of the mother country. The schools of the two oldest Greek philosophers, those of Thales and Pythagoras, were established, it is remarkable, not in ancient Greece, but the one in an Asiatic, the other in an Italian, colony.[1] All those colonies had established them-

---

[1] [Miletus and Crotona.—C.]

selves in countries inhabited by savage and barbarous nations, who easily gave place to the new settlers. They had plenty of good land, and as they were altogether independent of the mother city, they were at liberty to manage their own affairs in the way that they judged was most suitable to their own interest.

The history of the Roman colonies is by no means so brilliant. Some of them, indeed, such as Florence, have in the course of many ages, and after the fall of the mother city, grown up to be considerable states. But the progress of no one of them seems ever to have been very rapid. They were all established in conquered provinces, which in most cases had been fully inhabited before. The quantity of land assigned to each colonist was seldom very considerable, and as the colony was not independent, they were not always at liberty to manage their own affairs in the way that they judged was most suitable to their own interest.

In the plenty of good land, the European colonies established in America and the West Indies resemble, and even greatly surpass, those of ancient Greece. In their dependency upon the mother state, they resemble those of ancient Rome; but their great distance from Europe has in all of them alleviated more or less the effects of this dependency. Their situation has placed them less in the view and less in the power of their mother country. In pursuing their interest their own way, their conduct has, upon many occasions, been overlooked, either because not known or not understood in Europe; and upon some occasions it has been fairly suffered and submitted to, because their distance rendered it difficult to restrain it. Even the violent and arbitrary government of Spain has, upon many occasions, been obliged to recall or soften the orders which had been given for the government of her colonies, for fear of a general insurrection. The progress of all the European colonies in wealth, population, and improvement has accordingly been very great.

The crown of Spain, by its share of the gold and silver, derived some revenue from its colonies from the moment of their first establishment. It was a revenue, too, of a nature to excite in human avidity the most extravagant expectations of still greater riches. The Spanish colonies, therefore, from the moment of their first establishment, attracted very much the attention of their mother country, while those of the other European nations were for a long time in a great measure neglected. The former did not, perhaps, thrive the better in consequence of this attention, nor the latter the worse in consequence of this neglect. In proportion to the extent of the country which they in some measure possess, the Spanish colonies are considered as less populous and thriving than those of almost any other European nation. The progress even of the Spanish colonies, however, in population and improvement, has certainly been very rapid and very great. The city of Lima, founded since the conquest, is represented by Ulloa as containing fifty thousand inhabitants nearly thirty years ago.[2] Quito, which had been but a miserable hamlet of Indians, is represented by the same author as in his time equally populous. Gemelli Carreri, a pretended traveler it is said, indeed, but who seems everywhere to have written upon extremely good information, represents the city of Mexico as containing a hundred thousand inhabitants;[3] a number which, in spite of all the exaggerations of the Spanish writers, is probably more than five times greater than what it contained in the time of Montezuma. These numbers exceed greatly those of Boston, New York, and Philadelphia, the three greatest cities of the English colonies. Before the conquest of the Spaniards there were no cattle fit for draft either in Mexico or Peru. The llama was their only beast of burden, and its strength seems to have been a good deal inferior to that of a common ass. The plow was unknown among them. They were ignorant of the use of iron. They had no coined money, nor any established instrument of commerce of any kind. Their commerce was carried on by barter. A sort of

[2] [Juan and Ulloa, *Voyage historique*, Vol. I, 229.—C.]

[3] [In Awnsham and John Churchill's *Collection of Voyages and Travels*, 1704, Vol. IV, 508.—C.]

wooden spade was their principal instrument of agriculture. Sharp stones served them for knives and hatchets to cut with, fish bones and the hard sinews of certain animals served them for needles to sew with, and these seem to have been their principal instruments of trade. In this state of things, it seems impossible that either of those empires could have been so much improved or so well cultivated as at present, when they are plentifully furnished with all sorts of European cattle, and when the use of iron, of the plow, and of many of the arts of Europe, has been introduced among them. But the populousness of every country must be in proportion to the degree of its improvement and cultivation. In spite of the cruel destruction of the natives which followed the conquest, these two great empires are, probably, more populous now than they ever were before: and the people are surely very different; for we must acknowledge, I apprehend, that the Spanish creoles are in many respects superior to the ancient Indians.

After the settlements of the Spaniards, that of the Portuguese in Brazil is the oldest of any European nation in America. But, as for a long time after the first discovery neither gold nor silver mines were found in it, and as it afforded, upon that account, little or no revenue to the crown, it was for a long time in a great measure neglected; and during this state of neglect, it grew up to be a great and powerful colony. While Portugal was under the dominion of Spain, Brazil was attacked by the Dutch, who got possession of seven of the fourteen provinces into which it is divided. They expected soon to conquer the other seven, when Portugal recovered its independency by the elevation of the family of Braganza to the throne. The Dutch then, as enemies to the Spaniards, became friends to the Portuguese, who were likewise the enemies of the Spaniards. They agreed, therefore, to leave that part of Brazil which they had not conquered to the king of Portugal, who agreed to leave that part which they had conquered to them, as a matter not worth disputing about with such good allies. But the Dutch government soon began to oppress the Portuguese colonists, who, instead of amusing themselves with complaints, took arms against their new masters, and by their own valor and resolution, with the connivance, indeed, but without any avowed assistance from the mother country, drove them out of Brazil. The Dutch, therefore, finding it impossible to keep any part of the country to themselves, were contented that it should be entirely restored to the crown of Portugal. In this colony there are said to be more than six hundred thousand people, either Portuguese or descended from Portuguese, creoles, mulattoes, and a mixed race between Portuguese and Brazilians. No one colony in America is supposed to contain so great a number of people of European extraction.

Toward the end of the fifteenth, and during the greater part of the sixteenth, century, Spain and Portugal were the two great naval powers upon the ocean, for though the commerce of Venice extended to every part of Europe, its fleets had scarcely ever sailed beyond the Mediterranean. The Spaniards, in virtue of the first discovery, claimed all America as their own; and though they could not hinder so great a naval power as that of Portugal from settling in Brazil, such was, at that time, the terror of their name, that the greater part of the other nations of Europe were afraid to establish themselves in any other part of that great continent. The French, who attempted to settle in Florida, were all murdered by the Spaniards. But the declension of the naval power of this latter nation, in consequence of the defeat or miscarriage of what they called their Invincible Armada, which happened toward the end of the sixteenth century, put it out of their power to obstruct any longer the settlements of the other European nations. In the course of the seventeenth century, therefore, the English, French, Dutch, Danes, and Swedes, all the great nations who had any ports upon the ocean, attempted to make some settlements in the New World.

The Swedes established themselves in New Jersey; and the number of Swedish families still to be found there sufficiently demonstrates that this colony was very likely to prosper had it been protected by the mother country. But being neglected

by Sweden it was soon swallowed up by the Dutch colony of
New York, which again, in 1674,[4] fell under the dominion of
the English.

The small islands of St. Thomas and Santa Cruz are the
only countries in the New World that have ever been possessed
by the Danes. These little settlements, too, were under the
government of an exclusive company, which had the sole right
both of purchasing the surplus produce of the colonists, and
of supplying them with such goods of other countries as they
wanted, and which, therefore, both in its purchases and sales,
had not only the power of oppressing them, but the greatest
temptation to do so. The government of an exclusive company
of merchants is, perhaps, the worst of all governments for any
country whatever. It was not, however, able to stop altogether
the progress of these colonies, though it rendered it more slow
and languid. The late king of Denmark dissolved this company, and since that time the prosperity of these colonies has
been very great.

The Dutch settlements in the West, as well as those in the
East Indies, were originally put under the government of an
exclusive company. The progress of some of them, therefore,
though it has been considerable, in comparison with that of
almost any country that has been long peopled and established,
has been languid and slow in comparison with that of the
greater part of new colonies. The colony of Surinam, though
very considerable, is still inferior to the greater part of the
sugar colonies of the other European nations. The colony of
Nova Belgia, now divided into the two provinces of New
York and New Jersey, would probably have soon become considerable too, even though it had remained under the government of the Dutch. The plenty and cheapness of good land
are such powerful causes of prosperity that the very worst
government is scarcely capable of checking altogether the
efficacy of their operation. The great distance, too, from the
mother country would enable the colonists to evade more or

4 [A mistake for 1664.—C.]

less, by smuggling, the monopoly which the company enjoyed against them. At present the company allows all Dutch ships to trade to Surinam upon paying two and a half per cent upon the value of their cargo for a license; and only reserves to itself exclusively the direct trade from Africa to America, which consists almost entirely in the slave trade. This relaxation in the exclusive privileges of the company is probably the principal cause of that degree of prosperity which that colony at present enjoys. Curaçao and Eustatia, the two principal islands belonging to the Dutch, are free ports open to the ships of all nations; and this freedom, in the midst of better colonies whose ports are open to those of one nation only, has been the great cause of the prosperity of those two barren islands.

The French colony of Canada was, during the greater part of the last century and some part of the present, under the government of an exclusive company. Under so unfavorable an administration its progress was necessarily very slow in comparison with that of other new colonies; but it became much more rapid when this company was dissolved after the fall of what is called the Mississippi scheme.[5] When the English got possession of this country, they found in it nearly double the number of inhabitants which Father Charlevoix had assigned to it between twenty and thirty years before.[6] That Jesuit had traveled over the whole country, and had no inclination to represent it as less considerable than it really was.

The French colony of St. Domingo was established by pirates and freebooters who, for a long time, neither required the protection, nor acknowledged the authority, of France;

[5] [The Mississippi scheme, largely the work of a Scotsman named John Law, was a gigantic stock speculation in France, based on expectations about colonial trade. When the bubble burst, a financial panic ensued. At about the same time, a similar speculative affair—the South Sea Bubble (1711-1721)—took place in England.—M.]

[6] [P. F. X. de Charlevoix, *Histoire et description générale de la Nouvelle France, avec le journal historique d'un voyage dans l'Amérique Septentrionnale,* 1744, tom. ii., p. 390.—C.]

and when that race of banditti became so far citizens as to acknowledge this authority, it was for a long time necessary to exercise it with very great gentleness. During this period the population and improvement of this colony increased very fast. Even the oppression of the exclusive company, to which it was for some time subjected with all the other colonies of France, though it no doubt retarded, had not been able to stop its progress altogether. The course of its prosperity returned as soon as it was relieved from that oppression. It is now the most important of the sugar colonies of the West Indies, and its produce is said to be greater than that of all the English sugar colonies put together. The other sugar colonies of France are in general all very thriving.

But there are no colonies of which the progress has been more rapid than that of the English in North America.

Plenty of good land, and liberty to manage their own affairs their own way, seem to be the two great causes of the prosperity of all new colonies.

In the plenty of good land the English colonies of North America, though, no doubt, very abundantly provided, are, however, inferior to those of the Spaniards and Portuguese and not superior to some of those possessed by the French before the late war. But the political institutions of the English colonies have been more favorable to the improvement and cultivation of this land than those of any of the other three nations.

First, the engrossing of uncultivated land, though it has by no means been prevented altogether, has been more restrained in the English colonies than in any other. The colony law which imposes upon every proprietor the obligation of improving and cultivating, within a limited time, a certain proportion of his lands, and which, in case of failure, declares those neglected lands grantable to any other person, though it has not, perhaps, been very strictly executed, has, however, had some effect.

Secondly, in Pennsylvania there is no right of primogeniture,[7] and lands, like movables, are divided equally among all the children of the family. In three of the provinces of New England the oldest has only a double share, as in the Mosaic law. Though in those provinces, therefore, too great a quantity of land should sometimes be engrossed by a particular individual, it is likely, in the course of a generation or two, to be sufficiently divided again. In the other English colonies, indeed, the right of primogeniture takes place, as in the law of England. But in all the English colonies the tenure of the lands, which are all held by free socage, facilitates alienation, and the grantee of any extensive tract of land generally finds it to his interest to alienate, as fast as he can, the greater part of it, reserving only a small quitrent. In the Spanish and Portuguese colonies, what is called the right of *majorazzo* [8] takes place in the succession of all those great estates to which any title of honor is annexed. Such estates go all to one person and are in effect entailed and unalienable. The French colonies, indeed, are subject to the custom of Paris, which, in the inheritance of land, is much more favorable to the younger children than the law of England. But, in the French colonies, if any part of an estate, held by the noble tenure of chivalry and homage, is alienated, it is, for a limited time, subject to the right of redemption, either by the heir of the superior or by the heir of the family; and all the largest estates of the country are held by such noble tenures, which necessarily embarrass alienation. But, in a new colony, a great uncultivated estate is likely to be much more speedily divided by alienation than by succession. The plenty and cheapness of good land, it has already been observed, are the principal causes of the rapid prosperity of new colonies. The engrossing of land, in effect, destroys this plenty and cheapness. The engrossing of

---

[7] ["Primogeniture" means the exclusive right of the first-born child to inherit all the property. In what follows, "socage" refers to a medieval form of holding land, and "entailed" means that the land is settled inalienably on a person and his descendants and therefore cannot be sold by them.—M.]

[8] *Jus majoratus.*

uncultivated land, besides, is the greatest obstruction to its improvement. But the labor that is employed in the improvement and cultivation of land affords the greatest and most valuable produce to the society. The produce of labor, in this case, pays not only its own wages and the profit of the stock which employs it, but the rent of the land, too, upon which it is employed. The labor of the English colonists, therefore, being more employed in the improvement and cultivation of land, is likely to afford a greater and more valuable produce than that of any of the other three nations, which, by the engrossing of land, is more or less diverted toward other employments.

Thirdly, the labor of the English colonists is not only likely to afford a greater and more valuable produce, but, in consequence of the moderation of their taxes, a greater proportion of this produce belongs to themselves, which they may store up and employ in putting into motion a still greater quantity of labor. The English colonists have never yet contributed anything toward the defense of the mother country or toward the support of its civil government. They themselves, on the contrary, have hitherto been defended almost entirely at the expense of the mother country. But the expense of fleets and armies is out of all proportion greater than the necessary expense of civil government. The expense of their own civil government has always been very moderate. It has generally been confined to what was necessary for paying competent salaries to the governor, to the judges, and to some other offices of police, and for maintaining a few of the most useful public works. The expense of the civil establishment of Massachusetts Bay, before the commencement of the present disturbances, used to be but about 18,000*l.* a year; that of New Hampshire and Rhode Island, 3,500*l.* each; that of Connecticut, 4,000*l.*; that of New York and Pennsylvania, 4,500*l.* each; that of New Jersey, 1,200*l.*; that of Virginia and South Carolina, 8,000*l.* each. The civil establishments of Nova Scotia and Georgia are partly supported by an annual grant of parliament. But Nova Scotia pays, besides, about 7,000*l.* a year towards the public expense of the colony, and Georgia about 2,500*l.* a year. All the different civil establishments in North America, in short, exclusive of those of Maryland and North Carolina, of which no exact account has been got, did not, before the commencement of the present disturbances, cost the inhabitants above 64,700*l.* a year—an ever-memorable example at how small an expense three millions of people may not only be governed, but well governed. The most important part of the expense of government, indeed, that of defense and protection, has constantly fallen upon the mother country. The ceremonial, too, of the civil government in the colonies, upon the reception of a new governor, upon the opening of a new assembly, etc., though sufficiently decent, is not accompanied with any expensive pomp or parade. Their ecclesiastical government is conducted upon a plan equally frugal. Tithes are unknown among them; and their clergy, who are far from being numerous, are maintained either by moderate stipends, or by the voluntary contributions of the people. The power of Spain and Portugal, on the contrary, derives some support from the taxes levied upon their colonies. France, indeed, has never drawn any considerable revenue from its colonies, the taxes which it levies upon them being generally spent among them. But the colony government of all these three nations is conducted upon a much more expensive plan, and is accompanied with a much more expensive ceremonial. The sums spent upon the reception of a new viceroy of Peru, for example, have frequently been enormous. Such ceremonials are not only real taxes paid by the rich colonists upon those particular occasions, but they serve to introduce among them the habit of vanity and expense upon all other occasions. They are not only very grievous occasional taxes, but they contribute to establish perpetual taxes of the same kind still more grievous: the ruinous taxes of private luxury and extravagance. In the colonies of all those three nations, too, the ecclesiastical government is extremely oppressive. Tithes take place in all of them, and are levied with the utmost rigor in those of Spain and Portugal. All of them besides are oppressed with a numerous race of mendicant friars, whose beggary, being not only licensed, but consecrated by religion, is a most grievous tax upon the poor people, who are most carefully taught that it is a duty to give, and a very great sin to refuse them their charity. Over and above all this, the clergy are, in all of them, the greatest engrossers of land.

Fourthly, in the disposal of their surplus produce, or of what is over and above their own consumption, the English colonies have been more favored, and have been allowed a more extensive market, than those of any other European nation. Every European nation has endeavored more or less to monopolize to itself the commerce of its colonies, and, upon that account, has prohibited the ships of foreign nations from trading to them, and has prohibited them from importing European goods from any foreign nation. But the manner in which this monopoly has been exercised in different nations has been very different.

Some nations have given up the whole commerce of their colonies to an exclusive company, of whom the colonies were obliged to buy all such European goods as they wanted, and to whom they were obliged to sell the whole of their own surplus produce. It was in the interest of the company, therefore, not only to sell the former as dear, and to buy the latter as cheap as possible, but to buy no more of the latter, even at this low price, than what they could dispose of for a very high price in Europe. It was in their interest not only to degrade in all cases the value of the surplus produce of the colony, but in many cases to discourage and keep down the natural increase of its quantity. Of all the expedients that can well be contrived to stunt the natural growth of a new colony, that of an exclusive company is undoubtedly the most effectual. This, however, has been the policy of Holland, though their company, in the course of the present century, has given up in many respects the exertion of their exclusive privilege. This, too, was the policy of Denmark till the reign of the late king. It has occasionally been the policy of France, and of late, since 1755, after it had been abandoned by all other nations

on account of its absurdity, it has become the policy of
Portugal with regard at least to two of the principal provinces
of Brazil, Fernambuco [Pernambuco], and Marannon [Ma-
ranhão].[9]

Other nations, without establishing an exclusive company,
have confined the whole commerce of their colonies to a
particular port of the mother country, from whence no ship
was allowed to sail, but either in a fleet and at a particular
season, or, if single, in consequence of a particular license,
which in most cases was very well paid for. This policy
opened, indeed, the trade of the colonies to all the natives of
the mother country, provided they traded from the proper
port, at the proper season, and in the proper vessels. But as
all the different merchants who joined their stocks in order
to fit out those licensed vessels would find it for their interest
to act in concert, the trade which was carried on in this
manner would necessarily be conducted very nearly upon the
same principles as that of an exclusive company. The profit of
those merchants would be almost equally exorbitant and oppressive. The colonies would be ill supplied, and would be
obliged both to buy very dear, and to sell very cheap. This,
however, till within these few years, had always been the
policy of Spain, and the price of all European goods, accordingly, is said to have been enormous in the Spanish West
Indies. At Quito, we are told by Ulloa, a pound of iron sold
for about four and sixpence, and a pound of steel for about
six and ninepence sterling.[10] But it is chiefly in order to purchase European goods that the colonies part with their own
produce. The more, therefore, they pay for the one, the less
they really get for the other, and the dearness of the one is
the same thing with the cheapness of the other. The policy of
Portugal is in this respect the same as the ancient policy of
Spain with regard to all its colonies except Fernambuco and

[9] [Marannon in 1755 and Fernambuco four years later.—Raynal, *Histoire
philosophique*, Amsterdam ed., 1773, tom. iii., p. 402.—C.]

[10] [Iron sometimes at 100 écus the quintal and steel at 150.—Juan and
Ulloa, *Voyage historique*, tom. i., p. 252.—C.]

Marannon, and with regard to these it has lately adopted a still worse.

Other nations leave the trade of their colonies free to all their subjects, who may carry it on from all the different ports of the mother country, and who have occasion for no other license than the common dispatches of the customhouse. In this case the number and dispersed situation of the different traders renders it impossible for them to enter into any general combination, and their competition is sufficient to hinder them from making very exorbitant profits. Under so liberal a policy the colonies are enabled both to sell their own produce and to buy the goods of Europe at a reasonable price. But since the dissolution of the Plymouth Company, when our colonies were but in their infancy, this has always been the policy of England. It has generally, too, been that of France, and has been uniformly so since the dissolution of what, in England, is commonly called their Mississippi Company. The profits of the trade, therefore, which France and England carry on with their colonies, though no doubt somewhat higher than if the competition was free to all other nations, are, however, by no means exorbitant; and the price of European goods accordingly is not extravagantly high in the greater part of the colonies of either of those nations.

In the exportation of their own surplus produce, too, it is only with regard to certain commodities that the colonies of Great Britain are confined to the market of the mother country. These commodities having been enumerated in the Act of Navigation and in some other subsequent acts, have upon that account been called *enumerated commodities*. The rest are called *non-enumerated*, and may be exported directly to other countries, provided it is in British or Plantation ships, of which the owners and three-fourths of the mariners are British subjects.

Among the non-enumerated commodities are some of the most important productions of America and the West Indies: grain of all sorts, lumber, salt provisions, fish, sugar, and rum.

Grain is naturally the first and principal object of the cul-

ture of all new colonies. By allowing them a very extensive
market for it, the law encourages them to extend this culture
much beyond the consumption of a thinly inhabited country,
and thus to provide beforehand an ample subsistence for a
continually increasing population.

In a country quite covered with wood, where timber consequently is of little or no value, the expense of clearing the
ground is the principal obstacle to improvement. By allowing
the colonies a very extensive market for their lumber, the
law endeavors to facilitate improvement by raising the price
of a commodity which would otherwise be of little value,
and thereby enabling them to make some profit of what
would otherwise be mere expense.

In a country neither half-peopled nor half-cultivated, cattle
naturally multiply beyond the consumption of the inhabitants,
and are often upon that account of little or no value. But it
is necessary, it has already been shown, that the price of cattle
should bear a certain proportion to that of corn before the
greater part of the lands of any country can be improved. By
allowing to American cattle, in all shapes, dead and alive, a
very extensive market, the law endeavors to raise the value of
a commodity of which the high price is so very essential to
improvement. The good effects of this liberty, however, must
be somewhat diminished by the 4th of George III c. 15, which
puts hides and skins among the enumerated commodities, and
thereby tends to reduce the value of American cattle.

To increase the shipping and naval power of Great Britain,
by the extension of the fisheries of our colonies, is an object
which the legislature seems to have had almost constantly in
view. Those fisheries, upon this account, have had all the
encouragement which freedom can give them, and they have
flourished accordingly. The New England fishery in particular
was, before the late disturbances, one of the most important,
perhaps, in the world. The whale fishery which, notwithstanding an extravagant bounty, is in Great Britain carried on
to so little purpose that in the opinion of many people
(which I do not, however, pretend to warrant) the whole

produce does not much exceed the value of the bounties which are annually paid for it, is in New England carried on without any bounty to a very great extent. Fish is one of the principal articles with which the North Americans trade to Spain, Portugal, and the Mediterranean.

Sugar was originally an enumerated commodity which could be exported only to Great Britain. But in 1731, upon a representation of the sugar planters, its exportation was permitted to all parts of the world.[11] The restrictions,[12] however, with which this liberty was granted, joined to the high price of sugar in Great Britain, have rendered it, in a great measure, ineffectual. Great Britain and her colonies still continue to be almost the sole market for all the sugar produced in the British plantations. Their consumption increases so fast that, though in consequence of the increasing improvement of Jamaica, as well as of the Ceded Islands, the importation of sugar has increased very greatly within these twenty years, the exportation to foreign countries is said to be not much greater than before.

Rum is a very important article in the trade which the Americans carry on to the coast of Africa, from which they bring back Negro slaves in return.

If the whole surplus produce of America in grain of all sorts, in salt provisions, and in fish, had been put into the enumeration, and thereby forced into the market of Great Britain, it would have interfered too much with the produce of the industry of our own people. It was probably not so much from any regard to the interest of America, as from a jealousy of this interference, that those important commodities have not only been kept out of the enumeration, but that the importation into Great Britain of all grain, except rice, and of salt provisions, has, in the ordinary state of the law, been prohibited.

[11] [There seems to be some mistake here. The true date is apparently 1739, under the Act 12 Geo. II, c. 30.—C.]

[12] [Ships not going to places south of Cape Finisterre were compelled to call at some port in Great Britain.—C.]

The non-enumerated commodities could originally be exported to all parts of the world. Lumber and rice, having been once put into the enumeration, when they were afterwards taken out of it, were confined, as to the European market, to the countries that lie south of Cape Finisterre. By the 6th of George III c. 52, all non-enumerated commodities were subjected to the like restriction. The parts of Europe which lie south of Cape Finisterre are not manufacturing countries, and we were less jealous of the colonial ships carrying home from them any manufactures which could interfere with our own.

The enumerated commodities are of two sorts: first, such as are either the peculiar produce of America, or as cannot be produced, or at least are not produced, in the mother country. Of this kind are molasses, coffee, cacao nuts, tobacco, pimento, ginger, whalefins, raw silk, cotton wool, beaver, and other peltry of America, indigo, fustic, and other dyeing woods; secondly, such as are not the peculiar produce of America, but which are and may be produced in the mother country, though not in such quantities as to supply the greater part of her demand, which is principally supplied from foreign countries. Of this kind are all naval stores, masts, yards, and bowsprits, tar, pitch, and turpentine, pig and bar iron, copper ore, hides and skins, pot and pearl ashes. The largest importation of commodities of the first kind could not discourage the growth or interfere with the sale of any part of the produce of the mother country. By confining them to the home market, our merchants, it was expected, would not only be enabled to buy them cheaper in the Plantations and consequently to sell them with a better profit at home, but to establish between the Plantations and foreign countries an advantageous carrying trade, of which Great Britain was necessarily to be the center or emporium, as the European country into which those commodities were first to be imported. The importation of commodities of the second kind might be so managed too, it was supposed, as to interfere, not with the sale of those of the same kind which were produced at home, but with that of those which were imported from foreign countries; because, by means of proper duties, they might be rendered always somewhat dearer than the former, and yet a good deal cheaper than the latter. By confining such commodities to the home market, therefore, it was proposed to discourage the produce, not of Great Britain, but of some foreign countries with which the balance of trade was believed to be unfavorable to Great Britain.

The prohibition of exporting from the colonies, to any other country but Great Britain, masts, yards, and bowsprits, tar, pitch, and turpentine, naturally tended to lower the price of timber in the colonies, and consequently to increase the expense of clearing their lands, the principal obstacle to their improvement. But about the beginning of the present century, in 1703, the pitch and tar company of Sweden endeavored to raise the price of their commodities to Great Britain by prohibiting their exportation, except in their own ships, at their own price, and in such quantities as they thought proper. In order to counteract this notable piece of mercantile policy, and to render herself as much as possible independent, not only of Sweden but of all the other northern powers, Great Britain gave a bounty upon the importation of naval stores from America, and the effect of this bounty was to raise the price of timber in America much more than the confinement to the home market could lower it; and as both regulations were enacted at the same time, their joint effect was rather to encourage than to discourage the clearing of land in America.

Though pig and bar iron too have been put among the enumerated commodities, yet as, when imported from America, they are exempted from considerable duties to which they are subject when imported from any other country, the one part of the regulation contributes more to encourage the erection of furnaces in America than the other to discourage it. There is no manufacture which occasions so great a consumption of wood as a furnace, or which can contribute so much to the clearing of a country overgrown with it.

The tendency of some of these regulations to raise the value

of timber in America, and thereby to facilitate the clearing of
the land, was neither, perhaps, intended nor understood by
the legislature. Though their beneficial effects, however, have
been in this respect accidental, they have not upon that account been less real.

The most perfect freedom of trade is permitted between
the British colonies of America and the West Indies, both in
the enumerated and in the non-enumerated commodities.
Those colonies are now become so populous and thriving,
that each of them finds in some of the others a great and extensive market for every part of its produce. All of them
taken together, they make a great internal market for the produce of one another.

The liberality of England, however, toward the trade of
her colonies has been confined chiefly to what concerns the
market for their produce, either in its rude state, or in what
may be called the very first stage of manufacture. The more
advanced or more refined manufactures, even of the colonial
produce, the merchants and manufacturers of Great Britain
choose to reserve to themselves, and have prevailed upon the
legislature to prevent their establishment in the colonies, sometimes by high duties, and sometimes by absolute prohibitions.

While, for example, Muskovado sugars from the British
plantations pay upon importation only 6s. 4d. the hundredweight, white sugars pay 1l. 1s. 1d., and refined, either double
or single, in loaves 4l. 2s. 5d. ⁸⁄₂₀. When those high duties were
imposed, Great Britain was the sole, and she still continues to
be the principal, market to which the sugars of the British
colonies could be exported. They amounted, therefore, to a
prohibition, at first of claying or refining sugar for any foreign
market, and at present of claying or refining it for the market,
which takes off, perhaps, more than nine-tenths of the whole
produce. The manufacture of claying or refining sugar, accordingly, though it has flourished in all the sugar colonies
of France, has been little cultivated in any of those of England, except for the market of the colonies themselves. While
Grenada was in the hands of the French, there was a refinery

of sugar, by claying at least, upon almost every plantation. Since it fell into those of the English, almost all works of this kind have been given up, and there are at present, October 1773, I am assured, not above two or three remaining in the island. At present, however, by an indulgence of the custom-house, clayed or refined sugar, if reduced from loaves into powder, is commonly imported as Muskovado.

While Great Britain encourages in America the manufactures of pig and bar iron by exempting them from duties to which the like commodities are subject when imported from any other country, she imposes an absolute prohibition upon the erection of steel furnaces and slit-mills in any of her American plantations. She will not suffer her colonists to work in those more refined manufactures even for their own consumption, but insists upon their purchasing of her merchants and manufacturers all goods of this kind which they have occasion for.

She prohibits the exportation from one province to another by water, and even the carriage by land upon horseback or in a cart, of hats, of wools and woolen goods, of the produce of America, a regulation which effectually prevents the establishment of any manufacture of such commodities for distant sale, and confines the industry of her colonists in this way to such coarse and household manufactures as a private family commonly makes for its own use, or for that of some of its neighbors in the same province.

To prohibit a great people, however, from making all that they can of every part of their own produce, or from employing their stock and industry in the way that they judge most advantageous to themselves, is a manifest violation of the most sacred rights of mankind. Unjust, however, as such prohibitions may be, they have not hitherto been very hurtful to the colonies. Land is still so cheap and, consequently, labor so dear among them that they can import from the mother country almost all the more refined or more advanced manufactures cheaper than they could make them for themselves. Though they had not, therefore, been prohibited from establishing such manufactures, yet in their present state of improvement a regard to their own interest would, probably, have prevented them from doing so. In their present state of improvement, those prohibitions, perhaps, without cramping their industry, or restraining it from any employment to which it would have gone of its own accord, are only impertinent badges of slavery imposed upon them, without any sufficient reason, by the groundless jealousy of the merchants and manufacturers of the mother country. In a more advanced state they might be really oppressive and insupportable.

Great Britain, too, as she confines to her own market some of the most important productions of the colonies, so in compensation she gives to some of them an advantage in that market, sometimes by imposing higher duties upon the like productions when imported from other countries, and sometimes by giving bounties upon their importation from the colonies. In the first way, she gives an advantage in the home market to the sugar, tobacco, and iron of her own colonies, and in the second, to their raw silk, to their hemp and flax, to their indigo, to their naval stores, and to their building timber. This second way of encouraging the colony produce by bounties upon importation is, so far as I have been able to learn, peculiar to Great Britain. The first is not. Portugal does not content herself with imposing higher duties upon the importation of tobacco from any other country, but prohibits it under the severest penalties.

With regard to the importation of goods from Europe, England has likewise dealt more liberally with her colonies than any other nation.

Great Britain allows a part, almost always the half, generally a larger portion, and sometimes the whole of the duty which is paid upon the importation of foreign goods, to be drawn back upon their exportation to any foreign country. No independent foreign country, it was easy to foresee, would receive them if they came to it loaded with the heavy duties to which almost all foreign goods are subjected on their importation into Great Britain. Unless, therefore, some part of those duties was drawn back upon exportation, there was an end of the carrying trade, a trade so much favored by the mercantile system.

Our colonies, however, are by no means independent foreign countries; and Great Britain, having assumed to herself the exclusive right of supplying them with all goods from Europe, might have forced them (in the same manner as other countries have done their colonies) to receive such goods, loaded with all the same duties which they paid in the mother country. But, on the contrary, till 1763, the same drawbacks were paid upon the exportation of the greater part of foreign goods to our colonies as to any independent foreign country. In 1763, indeed, by the 4th of Geo. III c. 15, this indulgence was a good deal abated, and it was enacted, "That no part of the duty called the old subsidy should be drawn back for any goods of the growth, production, or manufacture of Europe or the East Indies, which should be exported from this kingdom to any British colony or plantation in America; wines, white callicoes and muslins excepted." Before this law, many different sorts of foreign goods might have been bought cheaper in the plantations than in the mother country, and some may still.

Of the greater part of the regulations concerning the colonial trade, the merchants who carry it on, it must be observed, have been the principal advisers. We must not wonder, therefore, if, in the greater part of them, their interest has been more considered than either that of the colonies or that of the mother country. In their exclusive privilege of supplying the colonies with all the goods which they wanted from Europe, and of purchasing all such parts of their surplus produce as could not interfere with any of the trades which they themselves carried on at home, the interest of the colonies was sacrificed to the interest of those merchants. In allowing the same drawbacks upon the re-exportation of the greater part of European and East Indian goods to the colonies, as upon their re-exportation to any independent country, the interest of the mother country was sacrificed to it, even according to the mercantile ideas of that interest. It was for the interest of the merchants to pay as little as possible for the foreign goods which they sent to the colonies, and consequently, to get back as much as possible of the duties which they advanced upon their importation into Great Britain. They might thereby be enabled to sell in the colonies either the same quantity of goods with a greater profit, or a greater quantity with the same profit, and, consequently, to gain something either in the one way or the other. It was, likewise, for the interest of the colonies to get all such goods as cheaply and in as great abundance as possible. But this might not always be for the interest of the mother country. She might frequently suffer both in her revenue, by giving back a great part of the duties which had been paid upon the importation of such goods, and in her manufactures, by being undersold in the colonial market, in consequence of the easy terms upon which foreign manufactures could be carried thither by means of those drawbacks. The progress of the linen manufacture of Great Britain, it is commonly said, has been a good deal retarded by the drawbacks upon the re-exportation of German linen to the American colonies.

But though the policy of Great Britain with regard to the trade of her colonies has been dictated by the same mercantile spirit as that of other nations, it has, however, upon the whole, been less illiberal and oppressive than that of any of them.

In everything except their foreign trade, the liberty of the English colonists to manage their own affairs their own way is complete. It is in every respect equal to that of their fellow-citizens at home, and is secured in the same manner by an assembly of the representatives of the people, who claim the sole right of imposing taxes for the support of the colonial government. The authority of this assembly overawes the executive power, and neither the meanest nor the most obnoxious colonist, as long as he obeys the law, has anything to fear from the resentment either of the governor, or of any other civil or military officer in the province. The colonial assemblies, though, like the House of Commons in England, they are not always a very equal representation of the people, yet they approach more nearly to that character; and as the executive power either has not the means to corrupt them, or, on account of the support which it receives from the mother country, is not under the necessity of doing so, they are, perhaps, in general more influenced by the inclinations of their constituents. The councils, which, in the colonial legislatures, correspond to the House of Lords in Great Britain, are not composed of a hereditary nobility. In some of the colonies, as in three of the governments of New England, those councils are not appointed by the king, but chosen by the representatives of the people. In none of the English colonies is there any hereditary nobility. In all of them, indeed, as in all other free countries, the descendant of an old colonial family is more respected than an upstart of equal merit and fortune; but he is only more respected, and he has no privileges by which he can be troublesome to his neighbors. Before the commencement of the present disturbances, the colonial assemblies had not only the legislative, but a part of the executive power. In Connecticut and Rhode Island, they elected the governor. In the other colonies they appointed the revenue officers who collected the taxes imposed by those respective assemblies, to whom those officers were immediately responsible. There is more equality, therefore, among the English colonists than among the inhabitants of the mother country. Their manners are more republican, and their governments, those of three of the provinces of New England in particular, have hitherto been more republican too.

The absolute governments of Spain, Portugal, and France, on the contrary, take place in their colonies; and the discretionary powers which such governments commonly delegate to all their inferior officers are, on account of the great distance, naturally exercised there with more than ordinary violence. Under all absolute governments there is more liberty in the capital than in any other part of the country. The sovereign himself can never have either interest or inclination to pervert the order of justice, or to oppress the great body of the people.

In the capital his presence overawes more or less all his inferior officers, who in the remoter provinces, from whence the
complaints of the people are less likely to reach him, can exercise their tyranny with much more safety. But the European colonies in America are more remote than the most
distant provinces of the greatest empires which had ever been
known before. The government of the English colonies is perhaps the only one which, since the world began, could give
perfect security to the inhabitants of so very distant a province. The administration of the French colonies, however, has
always been conducted with more gentleness and moderation
than that of the Spanish and Portuguese. This superiority of
conduct is suitable both to the character of the French nation
and to what forms the character of every nation, the nature
of their government, which, though arbitrary and violent in
comparison with that of Great Britain, is legal and free in
comparison with those of Spain and Portugal.

It is in the progress of the North American colonies, however, that the superiority of the English policy chiefly appears.
The progress of the sugar colonies of France has been at least
equal, perhaps superior, to that of the greater part of those
of England; and yet the sugar colonies of England enjoy a free
government nearly of the same kind with that which takes
place in her colonies of North America. But the sugar colonies
of France are not discouraged, like those of England, from refining their own sugar; and, what is of still greater importance, the genius of their government naturally introduces a
better management of their Negro slaves.

In all European colonies the culture of the sugar cane is
carried on by Negro slaves. The constitution of those who
have been born in the temperate climate of Europe could not,
it is supposed, support the labor of digging the ground under
the burning sun of the West Indies; and the culture of the
sugar cane, as it is managed at present, is all hand labor,
though, in the opinion of many, the drill plow might be introduced into it with great advantage. But, as the profit and success of the cultivation which is carried on by means of cattle

depend very much upon the good management of those cattle, so the profit and success of that which is carried on by slaves must depend equally upon the good management of those slaves; and in the good management of their slaves the French planters, I think it is generally allowed, are superior to the English. The law, so far as it gives some weak protection to the slave against the violence of his master, is likely to be better executed in a colony where the government is in a great measure arbitrary, than in one where it is altogether free. In every country where the unfortunate law of slavery is established, the magistrate, when he protects the slave, intermeddles in some measure in the management of the private property of the master; and, in a free country, where the master is perhaps either a member of the colony assembly, or an elector of such a member, he dare not do this but with the greatest caution and circumspection. The respect which he is obliged to pay to the master renders it more difficult for him to protect the slave. But in a country where the government is in a great measure arbitrary, where it is usual for the magistrate to intermeddle even in the management of the private property of individuals, and to send them, perhaps, a *lettre de cachet* [13] if they do not manage it according to his liking, it is much easier for him to give some protection to the slave; and common humanity naturally disposes him to do so. The protection of the magistrate renders the slave less contemptible in the eyes of his master, who is thereby induced to consider him with more regard, and to treat him with more gentleness. Gentle usage renders the slave not only more faithful, but more intelligent, and therefore, upon a double account, more useful. He approaches more to the condition of a free servant, and may possess some degree of integrity and attachment to his master's interest, virtues which frequently belong to free servants, but which never can belong to a slave who is treated as slaves commonly are in countries where the master is perfectly free and secure.

[13] [A *lettre de cachet* was a sealed letter, especially from the king, and was often used to effect an arbitrary imprisonment.—M.]

That the condition of a slave is better under an arbitrary than under a free government is, I believe, supported by the history of all ages and nations. In the Roman history, the first time we read of the magistrate interposing to protect the slave from the violence of his master is under the emperors. When Vedius Pollio, in the presence of Augustus, ordered one of his slaves, who had committed a slight fault, to be cut into pieces and thrown into his fishpond in order to feed his fishes, the emperor commanded him, with indignation, to emancipate immediately not only that slave, but all the others that belonged to him.[14] Under the republic no magistrate could have had authority enough to protect the slave, much less to punish the master.

The stock, it is to be observed, which has improved the sugar colonies of France, particularly the great colony of St. Domingo, has been raised almost entirely from the gradual improvement and cultivation of those colonies. It has been almost altogether the produce of the soil and of the industry of the colonists, or, what comes to the same thing, the price of that produce gradually accumulated by good management and employed in raising a still greater produce. But the stock which has improved and cultivated the sugar colonies of England has, a great part of it, been sent out from England, and has by no means been altogether the produce of the soil and industry of the colonists.[15] The prosperity of the English sugar colonies has been, in a great measure, owing to the great riches of England, of which a part has overflowed, if one may say so, upon those colonies. But the prosperity of the sugar colonies of France has been entirely owing to the good conduct of the

---

[14] [The story is told in the same way in *Lectures*, p. 97, but Seneca, *De ira*, lib. iii., cap. 40, and Dio Cassius, *Hist.*, lib. liv., cap. 23, say, not that Augustus ordered all the slaves to be emancipated, but that he ordered all the goblets on the table to be broken. Seneca says the offending slave was emancipated. Dio does not mention emancipation.—C.]

[15] [The West Indian merchants and planters asserted, in 1775, that there was capital worth £60,000,000 in the sugar colonies and that half of this belonged to residents in Great Britain.—See the continuation of Anderson's *Commerce*, A.D. 1775.—C.]

colonists, which must therefore have had some superiority over that of the English; and this superiority has been remarked in nothing so much as in the good management of their slaves.

Such have been the general outlines of the policy of the different European nations with regard to their colonies.

The policy of Europe, therefore, has very little to boast of, either in the original establishment, or, so far as concerns their internal government, in the subsequent prosperity of the colonies of America.

Folly and injustice seem to have been the principles which presided over and directed the first project of establishing those colonies; the folly of hunting after gold and silver mines, and the injustice of coveting the possession of a country whose harmless natives, far from having ever injured the people of Europe, had received the first adventurers with every mark of kindness and hospitality.

The adventurers, indeed, who formed some of the latter establishments, joined, to the chimerical project of finding gold and silver mines, other motives more reasonable and more laudable; but even these motives do very little honor to the policy of Europe.

The English Puritans, restrained at home, fled for freedom to America, and established there the four governments of New England. The English Catholics, treated with much greater injustice, established that of Maryland; the Quakers, that of Pennsylvania. The Portuguese Jews, persecuted by the Inquisition, stripped of their fortunes and banished to Brazil, introduced, by their example, some sort of order and industry among the transported felons and strumpets, by whom that colony was originally peopled, and taught them the culture of the sugar cane. Upon all these different occasions it was not the wisdom and policy, but the disorder and injustice, of the European governments, which peopled and cultivated America.

In effectuating some of the most important of these establishments, the different governments of Europe had as little merit as in projecting them. The conquest of Mexico was the project, not of the council of Spain, but of a governor of Cuba; [16] and it was effectuated by the spirit of the bold adventurer [17] to whom it was entrusted, in spite of everything which that governor, who soon repented of having trusted such a person, could do to thwart it. The conquerors of Chile and Peru, and of almost all the other Spanish settlements upon the continent of America, carried out with them no other public encouragement but a general permission to make settlements and conquests in the name of the king of Spain. Those adventures were all at the private risk and expense of the adventurers. The government of Spain contributed scarcely anything to any of them. That of England contributed as little towards effectuating the establishment of some of its most important colonies in North America.

When those establishments were effectuated, and had become so considerable as to attract the attention of the mother country, the first regulations which she made with regard to them had always in view to secure to herself the monopoly of their commerce, to confine their market and to enlarge her own at their expense, and, consequently, rather to damp and discourage than to quicken and forward the course of their prosperity. In the different ways in which this monopoly has been exercised consists one of the most essential differences in the policy of the different European nations with regard to their colonies. The best of them all, that of England, is only somewhat less illiberal and oppressive than that of any of the rest.

In what way, therefore, has the policy of Europe contributed either to the first establishment, or to the present grandeur of the colonies of America? In one way, and in one way only, it has contributed a good deal. *Magna virûm Mater!* [18] It bred and formed the men who were capable of achieving

16 [Velasquez.—C.]

17 [Cortez.—C.]

18 ["Salve magna parens frugum, Saturnia tellus, Magna virum."—Virgil, *Georgics*, ii., 173-174. ("Hail, mighty mother of harvests, O land of Saturn, mighty of men."—J. W. Mackail.)—C.]

such great actions, and of laying the foundation of so great an empire; and there is no other quarter of the world of which the policy is capable of forming, or has ever actually and in fact formed, such men. The colonies owe to the policy of Europe the education and great views of their active and enterprising founders; and some of the greatest and most important of them, so far as concerns their internal government, owe to it scarcely anything else.

[CHAPTERS VII (PART III) AND VIII]

[Editor's Summary]

In Part III of Chapter VII, Smith deals with the advantages which Europe has derived from the discovery of America and of the passage through the Cape of Good Hope to India. He lists two: the increase of Europe's enjoyments and the augmentation of its industry. Smith contends, however, that a monopoly of the colony's trade by the mother country is not, as the mercantilists would have it, beneficial; a policy of colonial free trade would bring even greater benefits to Europe. Smith then makes various proposals, on the basis of the above principle, for settling the "present disturbances" between Great Britain and the American colonies. He also gives some suggestions about the East India Company.

Chapter VIII concludes Smith's formal attack on the mercantile system with more examples. Smith suggests that the mercantilists not only harm their own country but, unwittingly, contradict and injure themselves.

CHAPTER IX

OF THE AGRICULTURAL SYSTEMS, OR OF THOSE SYSTEMS OF POLITICAL ECONOMY WHICH REPRESENT THE PRODUCE OF LAND AS EITHER THE SOLE OR THE PRINCIPAL SOURCE OF THE REVENUE AND WEALTH OF EVERY COUNTRY

The agricultural systems of political economy will not require so long an explanation as that which I have thought it necessary to bestow upon the mercantile or commercial system.

That system which represents the produce of land as the sole source of the revenue and wealth of every country has, so far as I know, never been adopted by any nation, and it at present exists only in the speculations of a few men of great learning and ingenuity in France.[1] It would not, surely, be worthwhile to examine at great length the errors of a system which never had done, and probably never will do, any harm in any part of the world. I shall endeavor to explain, however, as distinctly as I can, the great outlines of this very ingenious system.

Mr. Colbert, the famous minister of Louis XIV, was a man of probity, of great industry and knowledge of detail, of great experience and acuteness in the examination of public accounts, and of abilities in short, every way fitted for introducing method and good order into the collection and expenditure of the public revenue. That minister had unfortunately embraced all the prejudices of the mercantile system, in its nature and essence a system of restraint and regulation, and such as could scarcely fail to be agreeable to a laborious and plodding man of business, who had been accustomed to

1 [Here, Smith is referring to the *Économistes* or Physiocrats, of whom the most important was Quesnay; others were Mirabeau, Mercier de la Rivière, and Du Pont de Nemours.—M.]

regulate the different departments of public offices and to
establish the necessary checks and controls for confining each
to its proper sphere. The industry and commerce of a great
country he endeavored to regulate upon the same model as
the departments of a public office; and instead of allowing
every man to pursue his own interest his own way, upon the
liberal plan of equality, liberty and justice, he bestowed upon
certain branches of industry extraordinary privileges, while
he laid others under as extraordinary restraints. He was not
only disposed, like other European ministers, to encourage
the industry of the towns more than that of the country, but,
in order to support the industry of the towns, he was willing
even to depress and keep down that of the country. In order
to render provisions cheap to the inhabitants of the towns,
and thereby to encourage manufactures and foreign commerce, he prohibited altogether the exportation of corn and
thus excluded the inhabitants of the country from every
foreign market for by far the most important part of the
produce of their industry. This prohibition, joined to the
restraints imposed by the ancient provincial laws of France
upon the transportation of corn from one province to another,
and to the arbitrary and degrading taxes which are levied
upon the cultivators in almost all the provinces, discouraged
and kept down the agriculture of that country very much below the state to which it would naturally have risen in so very
fertile a soil and so very happy a climate. This state of discouragement and depression was felt more or less in every
different part of the country, and many different inquiries
were set on foot concerning the causes of it. One of those
causes appeared to be the preference given by the institutions
of Mr. Colbert to the industry of the towns above that of the
country.

If the rod be bent too much one way, says the proverb, in
order to make it straight you must bend it as much the other.
The French philosophers, who have proposed the system which
represents agriculture as the sole source of the revenue and
wealth of every country, seem to have adopted this proverbial

maxim; and as in the plan of Mr. Colbert the industry of the towns was certainly overvalued in comparison with that of the country, so in their system it seems to be as certainly undervalued.

The different orders of people who have ever been supposed to contribute in any respect toward the annual produce of the land and labor of the country, they divide into three classes. The first is the class of the proprietors of land. The second is the class of the cultivators, of farmers and country laborers, whom they honor with the peculiar appellation of the productive class. The third is the class of artificers, manufacturers and merchants whom they endeavor to degrade by the humiliating appellation [2] of the barren or unproductive class.

The class of proprietors contributes to the annual produce by the expense which they may occasionally lay out upon the improvement of the land, upon the buildings, drains, enclosures, and other ameliorations which they may either make or maintain upon it, and by means of which the cultivators are enabled, with the same capital, to raise a greater produce, and consequently to pay a greater rent. This advanced rent may be considered as the interest or profit due to the proprietor upon the expense or capital which he thus employs in the improvement of his land. Such expenses are in this system called ground expenses (*dépenses foncières*).

The cultivators or farmers contribute to the annual produce by what are in this system called the original and annual expenses (*dépenses primitives et dépenses annuelles*) which they lay out upon the cultivation of the land. The original expenses consist in the instruments of husbandry, in the stock of

[2] [But, see below, pp. 225f., where the usefulness of the class is said to be admitted. In his exposition of physiocratic doctrine, Smith does not appear to follow any particular book closely. His library contained Du Pont's *Physiocratie, ou constitution naturelle du gouvernement le plus avantageux au genre humain*, 1768 (see Bonar, *Catalogue*, p. 92), and he refers lower down to La Rivière, *L'ordre naturel et essentiel des sociétés politiques*, 1767, but he probably relied largely on his recollection of conversations in Paris; see Rae, *Life of Adam Smith*, pp. 215-222.—C.]

cattle, in the seed, and in the maintenance of the farmer's family, servants, and cattle during at least a great part of the first year of his occupancy, or till he can receive some return from the land. The annual expenses consist in the seed, in the wear and tear of the instruments of husbandry, and in the annual maintenance of the farmer's servants and cattle, and of his family too, so far as any part of them can be considered as servants employed in cultivation. That part of the produce of the land which remains to him after paying the rent ought to be sufficient, first, to replace to him within a reasonable time, at least during the term of his occupancy, the whole of his original expenses, together with the ordinary profits of stock; and, secondly, to replace to him annually the whole of his annual expenses, together likewise with the ordinary profits of stock. Those two sorts of expenses are two capitals which the farmer employs in cultivation; and unless they are regularly restored to him, together with a reasonable profit, he cannot carry on his employment upon a level with other employments, but, from a regard to his own interest, must desert it as soon as possible, and seek some other. That part of the produce of the land which is thus necessary for enabling the farmer to continue his business ought to be considered as a fund sacred to cultivation which, if the landlord violates, he necessarily reduces the produce of his own land, and in a few years not only disables the farmer from paying this racked rent, but from paying the reasonable rent which he might otherwise have got for his land. The rent which properly belongs to the landlord is no more than the net [Original manuscript uses "neat" produce.] produce which remains after paying in the most complete manner all the necessary expenses which must be previously laid out in order to raise the gross, or the whole, produce. It is because the labor of the cultivators, over and above paying completely all those necessary expenses, affords a net produce of this kind, that this class of people are in this system peculiarly distinguished by the honorable appellation of the productive class. Their original and annual expenses are for the same reason called, in this system, productive expenses, because, over and above replacing their own value, they occasion the annual reproduction of this net produce.

The ground expenses, as they are called, or what the land-lord lays out upon the improvement of his land, are in this system too honored with the appellation of productive expenses. Till the whole of those expenses, together with the ordinary profits of stock, have been completely repaid to him by the advanced rent which he gets from his land, that advanced rent ought to be regarded as sacred and inviolable, both by the church and by the king, ought to be subject neither to tithe nor to taxation. If it is otherwise, by discouraging the improvement of land, the church discourages the future increase of her own tithes, and the king, the future increase of his own taxes. As in a well-ordered state of things, therefore, those ground expenses, over and above reproducing in the most complete manner their own value, occasion likewise after a certain time a reproduction of a net produce; they are in this system considered as productive expenses.

The ground expenses of the landlord, however, together with the original and the annual expenses of the farmer, are the only three sorts of expenses which in this system are considered as productive. All other expenses and all other orders of people, even those who in the common apprehensions of men are regarded as the most productive, are in this account of things represented as altogether barren and unproductive.

Artificers and manufacturers, in particular, whose industry, in the common apprehensions of men, increases so much the value of the rude produce of land, are in this system represented as a class of people altogether barren and unproductive. Their labor, it is said, replaces only the stock which employs them, together with its ordinary profits. That stock consists in the materials, tools, and wages, advanced to them by their employer, and is the fund destined for their employment and maintenance. Its profits are the fund destined for the maintenance of their employer. Their employer, as he advances to them the stock of materials, tools and wages necessary for their employment, so he advances to himself what is necessary for his own maintenance, and this maintenance he generally proportions to the profit which he expects to make by the price of their work. Unless its price repays to him the maintenance which he advances to himself, as well as the materials, tools and wages which he advances to his workmen, it evidently does not repay to him the whole expense which he lays out upon it. The profits of manufacturing stock, therefore, are not, like the rent of land, a net produce which remains after completely repaying the whole expense which must be laid out in order to obtain them. The stock of the farmer yields him a profit as well as that of the master manufacturer; and it yields a rent likewise to another person, which that of the master manufacturer does not. The expense, therefore, laid out in employing and maintaining artificers and manufacturers, does no more than continue, if one may say so, the existence of its own value, and does not produce any new value. It is therefore altogether a barren and unproductive expense. The expense, on the contrary, laid out in employing farmers and country laborers, over and above continuing the existence of its own value, produces a new value, the rent of the landlord. It is therefore a productive expense.

Mercantile stock is equally barren and unproductive with manufacturing stock. It only continues the existence of its own value, without producing any new value. Its profits are only the repayment of the maintenance which its employer advances to himself during the time that he employs it, or till he receives the returns of it. They are only the repayment of a part of the expense which must be laid out in employing it.

The labor of artificers and manufacturers never adds anything to the value of the whole annual amount of the rude produce of the land. It adds indeed greatly to the value of some particular parts of it. But the consumption which in the meantime it occasions of other parts is precisely equal to the value which it adds to those parts, so that the value of the whole amount is not, at any one moment of time, in the least augmented by it. The person who works the lace of a pair of

fine ruffles, for example, will sometimes raise the value of perhaps a pennyworth of flax to thirty pounds sterling. But
though at first sight he appears thereby to multiply the value
of a part of the rude produce about seven thousand two
hundred times, he in reality adds nothing to the value of the
whole annual amount of the rude produce. The working of
that lace costs him perhaps two years labor. The thirty pounds
which he gets for it when it is finished is no more than the
repayment of the subsistence which he advances to himself
during the two years that he is employed about it. The value
which, by every day's, month's, or year's labor he adds to the
flax, does no more than replace the value of his own consumption during that day, month, or year. At no moment of
time, therefore, does he add anything to the value of the whole
annual amount of the rude produce of the land, the portion
of that produce which he is continually consuming being always equal to the value which he is continually producing.
The extreme poverty of the greater part of the persons employed in this expensive, though trifling, manufacture, may
satisfy us that the price of their work does not in ordinary
cases exceed the value of their subsistence. It is otherwise with
the work of farmers and country laborers. The rent of the
landlord is a value, which, in ordinary cases, it is continually
producing, over and above replacing, in the most complete
manner, the whole consumption, the whole expense laid out
upon the employment and maintenance both of the workmen
and of their employer.

Artificers, manufacturers, and merchants can augment the
revenue and wealth of their society by parsimony only; or, as
it is expressed in this system, by privation, that is, by de-
priving themselves of a part of the funds destined for their
own subsistence. They annually reproduce nothing but those
funds. Unless, therefore, they annually save some part of them,
unless they annually deprive themselves of the enjoyment of
some part of them, the revenue and wealth of their society can
never be in the smallest degree augmented by means of their
industry. Farmers and country laborers, on the contrary, may

enjoy completely the whole funds destined for their own sub-sistence, and yet augment at the same time the revenue and wealth of their society. Over and above what is destined for their own subsistence, their industry annually affords a net produce, of which the augmentation necessarily augments the revenue and wealth of their society. Nations, therefore, which, like France or England, consist in a great measure of proprie-tors and cultivators, can be enriched by industry and enjoy-ment. Nations, on the contrary, which, like Holland and Hamburg, are composed chiefly of merchants, artificers and manufacturers, can grow rich only through parsimony and privation. As the interest of nations so differently circum-stanced is very different, so is likewise the common character of the people. In those of the former kind, liberality, frank-ness, and good fellowship naturally make a part of that com-mon character. In the latter, narrowness, meanness, and a selfish disposition averse to all social pleasure and enjoyment.

The unproductive class, that of merchants, artificers and manufacturers, is maintained and employed altogether at the expense of the two other classes, of that of proprietors, and of that of cultivators. They furnish it both with the materials of its work and with the fund of its subsistence, with the corn and cattle which it consumes while it is employed about that work. The proprietors and cultivators finally pay both the wages of all the workmen of the unproductive class, and the profits of all their employers. Those workmen and their em-ployers are properly the servants of the proprietors and culti-vators. They are only servants who work without doors, as menial servants work within. Both the one and the other, how-ever, are equally maintained at the expense of the same mas-ters. The labor of both is equally unproductive. It adds noth-ing to the value of the sum total of the rude produce of the land. Instead of increasing the value of that sum total, it is a charge and expense which must be paid out of it.

The unproductive class, however, is not only useful, but greatly useful to the other two classes. By means of the indus-try of merchants, artificers and manufacturers, the proprietors and cultivators can purchase both the foreign goods and the manufactured produce of their own country for which they have occasion with the produce of a much smaller quantity of their own labor, than what they would be obliged to employ if they were to attempt, in an awkward and unskillful manner, either to import the one, or to make the other for their own use. By means of the unproductive class, the cultivators are delivered from many cares which would otherwise distract their attention from the cultivation of land. The superiority of produce, which, in consequence of this undivided attention, they are enabled to raise, is fully sufficient to pay the whole expense which the maintenance and employment of the unproductive class costs either the proprietors or themselves. The industry of merchants, artificers and manufacturers, though in its own nature altogether unproductive, yet contributes in this manner indirectly to increase the produce of the land. It increases the productive powers of productive labor by leaving it at liberty to confine itself to its proper employment, the cultivation of land; and the plow goes frequently the easier and the better by means of the labor of the man whose business is most remote from the plow.

It can never be the interest of the proprietors and cultivators to restrain or to discourage in any respect the industry of merchants, artificers and manufacturers. The greater the liberty which this unproductive class enjoys, the greater will be the competition in all the different trades which compose it, and the cheaper will the other two classes be supplied, both with foreign goods and with the manufactured produce of their own country.

It can never be the interest of the unproductive class to oppress the other two classes. It is the surplus produce of the land, or what remains after deducting the maintenance, first, of the cultivators, and afterwards, of the proprietors, that maintains and employs the unproductive class. The greater this surplus, the greater must likewise be the maintenance and employment of that class. The establishment of perfect justice, of perfect liberty, and of perfect equality is the very simple secret which most effectually secures the highest degree of prosperity to all the three classes.

The merchants, artificers and manufacturers of those mercantile states which, like Holland and Hamburg, consist chiefly of this unproductive class are in the same manner maintained and employed altogether at the expense of the proprietors and cultivators of land. The only difference is that those proprietors and cultivators are, the greater part of them, placed at a most inconvenient distance from the merchants, artificers and manufacturers whom they supply with the materials of their work and the fund of their subsistence, are the inhabitants of other countries, and the subjects of other governments.

Such mercantile states, however, are not only useful, but greatly useful to the inhabitants of those other countries. They fill up, in some measure, a very important void, and supply the place of the merchants, artificers and manufacturers, whom the inhabitants of those countries ought to find at home, but whom, from some defect in their policy, they do not find at home.

It can never be the interest of those landed nations, if I may call them so, to discourage or distress the industry of such mercantile states by imposing high duties upon their trade or upon the commodities which they furnish. Such duties, by rendering those commodities dearer, could serve only to sink the real value of the surplus produce of their own land, with which, or, what comes to the same thing, with the price of which, those commodities are purchased. Such duties could serve only to discourage the increase of that surplus produce, and consequently the improvement and cultivation of their own land. The most effectual expedient, on the contrary, for raising the value of that surplus produce, for encouraging its increase, and consequently the improvement and cultivation of their own land, would be to allow the most perfect freedom to the trade of all such mercantile nations.

This perfect freedom of trade would even be the most effectual expedient for supplying them, in due time, with all the artificers, manufacturers and merchants whom they wanted at home, and for filling up in the most proper and advantageous manner that very important void which they felt there.

The continual increase of the surplus produce of their land would, in due time, create a greater capital than what could be employed with the ordinary rate of profit in the improvement and cultivation of land; and the surplus part of it would naturally turn itself to the employment of artificers and manufacturers at home. But those artificers and manufacturers, finding at home both the materials of their work and the fund of their subsistence, might immediately, even with much less art and skill, be able to work as cheaply as the like artificers and manufacturers of such mercantile states who had both to bring from a great distance. Even though, from want of art and skill, they might not for some time be able to work as cheaply, yet, finding a market at home, they might be able to sell their work there as cheaply as that of the artificers and manufacturers of such mercantile states, which could not be brought to that market but from so great a distance; and as their art and skill improved, they would soon be able to sell it cheaper. The artificers and manufacturers of such mercantile states, therefore, would immediately be rivalled in the market of those landed nations, and soon after undersold and jostled out of it altogether. The cheapness of the manufactures of those landed nations, in consequence of the gradual improvements of art and skill, would, in due time, extend their sale beyond the home market, and carry them to many foreign markets, from which they would in the same manner gradually jostle out many of the manufactures of such mercantile nations.

This continual increase both of the rude and manufactured produce of those landed nations would in due time create a greater capital than could, with the ordinary rate of profit, be employed either in agriculture or in manufactures. The surplus of this capital would naturally turn itself to foreign trade, and be employed in exporting, to foreign countries, such parts of the rude and manufactured produce of its own country as exceeded the demand of the home market. In the exportation of the produce of their own country, the merchants of a landed nation would have an advantage of the same kind over those of mercantile nations, which its artificers and manufacturers had over the artificers and manufacturers of such nations—the advantage of finding at home that cargo, and those stores and provisions, which the others were obliged to seek for at a distance. With inferior art and skill in navigation, therefore, they would be able to sell that cargo as cheaply in foreign markets as the merchants of such mercantile nations; and with equal art and skill they would be able to sell it cheaper. They would soon, therefore, rival those mercantile nations in this branch of foreign trade, and in due time would jostle them out of it altogether.

According to this liberal and generous system, therefore, the most advantageous method in which a landed nation can raise up artificers, manufacturers, and merchants of its own, is to grant the most perfect freedom of trade to the artificers, manufacturers, and merchants of all other nations. It thereby raises the value of the surplus produce of its own land, of which the continual increase gradually establishes a fund, which in due time necessarily raises up all the artificers, manufacturers, and merchants whom it has occasion for.

When a landed nation, on the contrary, oppresses either by high duties or by prohibitions the trade of foreign nations, it necessarily hurts its own interest in two different ways. First, by raising the price of all foreign goods and of all sorts of manufactures, it necessarily sinks the real value of the surplus produce of its own land, with which, or, what comes to the same thing, with the price of which, it purchases those foreign goods and manufactures. Secondly, by giving a sort of monopoly of the home market to its own merchants, artificers, and manufacturers, it raises the rate of mercantile and manufacturing profit in proportion to that of agricultural profit, and consequently either draws from agriculture a part of the capital which had before been employed in it, or hinders from going to it a part of what would otherwise have gone to it. This policy, therefore, discourages agriculture in two different ways: first, by sinking the real value of its produce, and thereby lowering the rate of its profit, and, secondly, by raising the rate of profit in all other employments. Agriculture is rendered less advantageous, and trade and manufactures more advantageous, than they otherwise would be; and every man is tempted by his own interest to turn, as much as he can, both his capital and his industry from the former to the latter employments.

Though, by this oppressive policy, a landed nation should be able to raise up artificers, manufacturers, and merchants of its own somewhat sooner than it could do by the freedom of trade, a matter, however, which is not a little doubtful; yet it would raise them up, if one may say so, prematurely, and before it was perfectly ripe for them. By raising up too hastily one species of industry, it would depress another more valuable species of industry. By raising up too hastily a species of industry which only replaces the stock which employs it, together with the ordinary profit, it would depress a species of industry which, over and above replacing that stock with its profit, affords likewise a net produce, a free rent to the landlord. It would depress productive labor by encouraging too hastily that labor which is altogether barren and unproductive.

In what manner, according to this system, the sum total of the annual produce of the land is distributed among the three classes above mentioned, and in what manner the labor of the unproductive class does no more than replace the value of its own consumption, without increasing in any respect the value of that sum total, is represented by Mr. Quesnay, the very ingenious and profound author of this system, in some arithmetical formularies. The first of these formularies, which by way of eminence he peculiarly distinguishes by the name of the Economical Table,[3] represents the manner in which he

3 [See François Quesnay (also Quesnai), *Tableau Œconomique*, 1758.—C.]

supposes this distribution takes place, in a state of the most perfect liberty, and therefore of the highest prosperity, in a state where the annual produce is such as to afford the greatest possible net produce, and where each class enjoys its proper share of the whole annual produce. Some subsequent formularies represent the manner in which he supposes this distribution is made in different states of restraint and regulation; in which either the class of proprietors, or the barren and unproductive class, is more favored than the class of cultivators, and in which either the one or the other encroaches more or less upon the share which ought properly to belong to this productive class. Every such encroachment, every violation of that natural distribution, which the most perfect liberty would establish, must, according to this system, necessarily degrade more or less, from one year to another, the value and sum total of the annual produce and must necessarily occasion a gradual declension in the real wealth and revenue of the society—a declension of which the progress must be quicker or slower, according to the degree of this encroachment, according as that natural distribution, which the most perfect liberty would establish, is more or less violated. Those subsequent formularies represent the different degrees of declension which, according to this system, correspond to the different degrees in which this natural distribution of things is violated.

Some speculative physicians seem to have imagined that the health of the human body could be preserved only by a certain precise regimen of diet and exercise, of which every, even the smallest, violation necessarily occasioned some degree of disease or disorder proportioned to the degree of the violation. Experience, however, would seem to show that the human body frequently preserves, to all appearance at least, the most perfect state of health under a vast variety of different regimens, even under some which are generally believed to be very far from being perfectly wholesome. But the healthful state of the human body, it would seem, contains in itself some unknown principle of preservation, capable either of preventing or of correcting, in many respects, the bad effects even of a very faulty regimen. Mr. Quesnay, who was himself a physician, and a very speculative physician, seems to have entertained a notion of the same kind concerning the political body, and to have imagined that it would thrive and prosper only under a certain precise regimen, the exact regimen of perfect liberty and perfect justice. He seems not to have considered that in the political body the natural effort which every man is continually making to better his own condition is a principle of preservation capable of preventing and correcting, in many respects, the bad effects of a political economy, in some degree both partial and oppressive. Such a political economy, though it no doubt retards more or less, is not always capable of stopping altogether the natural progress of a nation toward wealth and prosperity, and still less of making it go backward. If a nation could not prosper without the enjoyment of perfect liberty and perfect justice, there is not in the world a nation which could ever have prospered. In the political body, however, the wisdom of nature has fortunately made ample provision for remedying many of the bad effects of the folly and injustice of man, in the same manner as it has done in the natural body, for remedying those of his sloth and intemperance.

The capital error of this system, however, seems to lie in its representing the class of artificers, manufacturers, and merchants as altogether barren and unproductive. The following observations may serve to show the impropriety of this representation.

First, this class, it is acknowledged, reproduces annually the value of its own annual consumption, and continues, at least, the existence of the stock or capital which maintains and employs it. But upon this account alone the denomination of barren or unproductive should seem to be very improperly applied to it. We should not call a marriage barren or unproductive, though it produced only a son and a daughter to replace the father and mother, and though it did not increase the number of the human species, but only continued it as it was before. Farmers and country laborers, indeed, over and above the stock which maintains and employs them, reproduce annually a net produce, a free rent to the landlord. As a marriage which affords three children is certainly more productive than one which affords only two, so the labor of farmers and country laborers is certainly more productive than that of merchants, artificers, and manufacturers. The superior produce of the one class, however, does not render the other barren or unproductive.

Secondly, it seems, upon this account, altogether improper to consider artificers, manufacturers, and merchants in the same light as menial servants. The labor of menial servants does not continue the existence of the fund which maintains and employs them. Their maintenance and employment is altogether at the expense of their masters, and the work which they perform is not of a nature to repay that expense. That work consists in services which perish generally in the very instant of their performance, and does not fix or realize itself in any vendible commodity which can replace the value of their wages and maintenance. The labor, on the contrary, of artificers, manufacturers, and merchants naturally does fix and realize itself in some such vendible commodity. It is upon this account that, in the chapter in which I treat of productive and unproductive labor,[4] I have classed artificers, manufacturers, and merchants among the productive laborers, and menial servants among the barren or unproductive.

Thirdly, it seems, upon every supposition, improper to say that the labor of artificers, manufacturers, and merchants does not increase the real revenue of the society. Though we should suppose, for example, as it seems to be supposed in this system, that the value of the daily, monthly, and yearly consumption of this class was exactly equal to that of its daily, monthly, and yearly production; yet it would not from thence follow that its labor added nothing to the real revenue, to the real value of the annual produce of the land and labor of the society. An artificer, for example, who in the first six months

4 [See Book II, Chapter III, pp. 111-34.]

after harvest executes ten pounds worth of work, though he should in the same time consume ten pounds worth of corn and other necessities, yet really adds the value of ten pounds to the annual produce of the land and labor of the society. While he has been consuming a half-yearly revenue of ten pounds worth of corn and other necessities, he has produced an equal value of work capable of purchasing, either to himself or to some other person, an equal half-yearly revenue. The value, therefore, of what has been consumed and produced during these six months is equal, not to ten, but to twenty pounds. It is possible, indeed, that no more than ten pounds worth of this value may ever have existed at any one moment of time. But if the ten pounds worth of corn and other necessities, which were consumed by the artificer, had been consumed by a soldier or by a menial servant, the value of that part of the annual produce which existed at the end of the six months would have been ten pounds less than it actually is in consequence of the labor of the artificer. Though the value of what the artificer produces, therefore, should not at any one moment of time be supposed greater than the value he consumes, yet at every moment of time the actually existing value of goods in the market is, in consequence of what he produces, greater than it otherwise would be.

When the patrons of this system assert that the consumption of artificers, manufacturers, and merchants is equal to the value of what they produce, they probably mean no more than that their revenue, or the fund destined for their consumption, is equal to it. But if they had expressed themselves more accurately, and only asserted that the revenue of this class was equal to the value of what they produced, it might readily have occurred to the reader that what would naturally be saved out of this revenue must necessarily increase more or less the real wealth of the society. In order, therefore, to make out something like an argument, it was necessary that they should express themselves as they have done; and this argument, even supposing things actually were as it seems to presume them to be, turns out to be a very inconclusive one.

Fourthly, farmers and country laborers can no more augment, without parsimony, the real revenue, the annual produce of the land and labor of their society, than artificers, manufacturers, and merchants. The annual produce of the land and labor of any society can be augmented only in two ways: either, first, by some improvement in the productive powers of the useful labor actually maintained within it, or, secondly, by some increase in the quantity of that labor.

The improvement in the productive powers of useful labor depends, first, upon the improvement in the ability of the workman, and, secondly, upon that of the machinery with which he works. But the labor of artificers and manufacturers, as it is capable of being more subdivided, and the labor of each workman reduced to a greater simplicity of operation than that of farmers and country laborers, so it is likewise capable of both these sorts of improvement in a much higher degree.[5] In this respect, therefore, the class of cultivators can have no sort of advantage over that of artificers and manufacturers.

The increase in the quantity of useful labor actually employed within any society must depend altogether upon the increase of the capital which employs it; and the increase of that capital again must be exactly equal to the amount of the savings from the revenue, either of the particular persons who manage and direct the employment of that capital, or of some other persons who lend it to them. If merchants, artificers, and manufacturers are, as this system seems to suppose, naturally more inclined to parsimony and saving than proprietors and cultivators, they are, so far, more likely to augment the quantity of useful labor employed within their society, and consequently to increase its real revenue, the annual produce of its land and labor.

Fifthly and lastly, though the revenue of the inhabitants of every country was supposed to consist altogether, as this system seems to suppose, in the quantity of subsistence which their

[5] [See Book I, Chapter I, pp. 4-7.]

industry could procure to them; yet even upon this supposition, the revenue of a trading and manufacturing country must, other things being equal, always be much greater than that of one without trade or manufactures. By means of trade and manufactures, a greater quantity of subsistence can be annually imported into a particular country than what its own lands, in the actual state of their cultivation, could afford. The inhabitants of a town, though they frequently possess no lands of their own, yet draw to themselves by their industry such a quantity of the rude produce of the lands of other people as supplies them, not only with the materials of their work, but with the fund of their subsistence. What a town always is with regard to the country in its neighborhood, one independent state or country may frequently be with regard to other independent states or countries. It is thus that Holland draws a great part of its subsistence from other countries: live cattle from Holstein and Jutland, and corn from almost all the different countries of Europe. A small quantity of manufactured produce purchases a great quantity of rude produce. A trading and manufacturing country, therefore, naturally purchases with a small part of its manufactured produce a great part of the rude produce of other countries; while, on the contrary, a country without trade and manufactures is generally obliged to purchase, at the expense of a great part of its rude produce, a very small part of the manufactured produce of other countries. The one exports what can subsist and accommodate but a very few, and imports the subsistence and accommodation of a great number. The other exports the accommodation and subsistence of a great number, and imports that of a very few only. The inhabitants of the one must always enjoy a much greater quantity of subsistence than what their own lands, in the actual state of their cultivation, could afford. The inhabitants of the other must always enjoy a much smaller quantity.

This system, however, with all its imperfections, is, perhaps, the nearest approximation to the truth that has yet been published upon the subject of political economy, and is upon that account well worth the consideration of every man who wishes to examine with attention the principles of that very important science. Though in representing the labor which is employed upon land as the only productive labor, the notions which it inculcates are perhaps too narrow and confined; yet in representing the wealth of nations as consisting, not in the unconsumable riches of money, but in the consumable goods annually reproduced by the labor of the society, and in representing perfect liberty as the only effectual expedient for rendering this annual reproduction the greatest possible, its doctrine seems to be in every respect as just as it is generous and liberal. Its followers are very numerous; and as men are fond of paradoxes and of appearing to understand what surpasses the comprehension of ordinary people, the paradox which it maintains, concerning the unproductive nature of manufacturing labor, has not perhaps contributed a little to increase the number of its admirers. They have for some years past made a pretty considerable sect, distinguished in the French republic of letters by the name of the Economists. Their works have certainly been of some service to their country, not only by bringing into general discussion many subjects which had never been well examined before, but by influencing in some measure the public administration in favor of agriculture. It has been in consequence of their representations, accordingly, that the agriculture of France has been delivered from several of the oppressions which it before labored under. The term during which such a lease can be granted, as will be valid against every future purchaser or proprietor of the land, has been prolonged from nine to twenty-seven years. The ancient provincial restraints upon the transportation of corn from one province of the kingdom to another have been entirely taken away, and the liberty of exporting it to all foreign countries has been established as the common law of the kingdom in all ordinary cases. This sect, in their works, which are very numerous, and which treat not only of what is properly called Political Economy, or of the nature and causes of the wealth of nations, but of every other branch of the system of civil government, all follow implicitly, and without any sensible variation, the doctrine of Mr. Quesnai. There is upon this account little variety in the greater part of their works. The most distinct and best connected account of this doctrine is to be found in a little book written by Mr. Mercier de la Rivière, sometime Intendant of Martinique entitled, *The natural and essential Order of Political Societies.*[6] The admiration of this whole sect for their master, who was himself a man of the greatest modesty and simplicity, is not inferior to that of any of the ancient philosophers for the founders of their respective systems. "There have been, since the world began," says a very diligent and respectable author, the Marquis de Mirabeau, "three great inventions which have principally given stability to political societies, independent of many other inventions which have enriched and adorned them. The first is the invention of writing, which alone gives human nature the power of transmitting, without alteration, its laws, its contracts, its annals, and its discoveries. The second is the invention of money, which binds together all the relations between civilized societies. The third is the Economical Table, the result of the other two, which completes them both by perfecting their object, the great discovery of our age, but of which our posterity will reap the benefit."[7]

As the political economy of the nations of modern Europe has been more favorable to manufactures and foreign trade, the industry of the towns, than to agriculture, the industry of the country; so that of other nations has followed a different plan, and has been more favorable to agriculture than to manufactures and foreign trade.

The policy of China favors agriculture more than all other employments. In China, the condition of a laborer is said to be as much superior to that of an artificer as in most parts of

[6] [This work was published in 1767.—M.]

[7] [*Philosophie Rurale ou économie générale et politique de l'agriculture, pour servir de suite à l'Ami des Hommes,* Amsterdam, 1766, tom. i, pp. 52, 53.—C.]

Europe that of an artificer is to that of a laborer. In China, the great ambition of every man is to get possession of some little bit of land, either in property or in lease; and leases are there said to be granted upon very moderate terms, and to be sufficiently secured to the lessees. The Chinese have little respect for foreign trade. Your beggarly commerce! was the language in which the mandarins of Peking used to talk to Mr. de Lange,[8] the Russian envoy, concerning it. Except with Japan, the Chinese carry on, themselves, and in their own bottoms, little or no foreign trade, and it is only into one or two ports of their kingdom that they even admit the ships of foreign nations. Foreign trade, therefore, is in China every way confined within a much narrower circle than that to which it would naturally extend itself, if more freedom was allowed to it, either in their own ships, or in those of foreign nations.

Manufactures, as in a small bulk they frequently contain a great value, and can upon that account be transported at less expense from one country to another than most parts of rude produce, are, in almost all countries, the principal support of foreign trade. In countries, besides, less extensive and less favorably circumstanced for interior commerce than China, they generally require the support of foreign trade. Without an extensive foreign market, they could not well flourish, either in countries so moderately extensive as to afford but a narrow home market, or in countries where the communication between one province and another was so difficult as to render it impossible for the goods of any particular place to enjoy the whole of that home market which the country could afford. The perfection of manufacturing industry, it must be remembered, depends altogether upon the division of labor; and the degree to which the division of labor

---

[8] See the Journal of Mr. de Lange in Bell's Travels, vol. ii., pp. 258, 276 and 293. [*Travels from St. Petersburg in Russia to Diverse Parts of Asia*, by John Bell of Antermony, Glasgow, 1763. The mandarins requested the Russians to cease "from importuning the council about their beggarly commerce," p. 293. Smith was a subscriber to this book.—C.]

can be introduced into any manufacture is necessarily regulated, it has already been shown,[9] by the extent of the market. But the great extent of the empire of China, the vast multitude of its inhabitants, the variety of climate, and consequently of productions in its different provinces, and the easy communication by means of water carriage between the greater part of them, render the home market of that country of so great extent as to be alone sufficient to support very great manufacturers and to admit of very considerable subdivisions of labor. The home market of China is, perhaps, in extent, not much inferior to the market of all the different countries of Europe put together. A more extensive foreign trade, however, which to this great home market added the foreign market of all the rest of the world, especially if any considerable part of this trade was carried on in Chinese ships, could scarcely fail to increase very much the manufactures of China, and to improve very much the productive powers of its manufacturing industry. By a more extensive navigation, the Chinese would naturally learn the art of using and constructing themselves all the different machines made use of in other countries, as well as the other improvements of art and industry which are practiced in all the different parts of the world. Upon their present plan they have little opportunity of improving themselves by the example of any other nation, except that of the Japanese.

The policy of ancient Egypt too, and that of the Gentoo [Hindu] government of Indostan [India], seem to have favored agriculture more than all other employments.

Both in ancient Egypt and Indostan, the whole body of the people was divided into different castes or tribes, each of which was confined, from father to son, to a particular employment or class of employments. The son of a priest was necessarily a priest; the son of a soldier, a soldier; the son of a laborer, a laborer; the son of a weaver, a weaver; the son of a tailor, a tailor, etc. In both countries, the caste of the priests

[9] [See pp. 18-25.]

held the highest rank, and that of the soldiers the next; and in both countries, the caste of the farmers and laborers was superior to the castes of merchants and manufacturers.

The government of both countries was particularly attentive to the interest of agriculture. The works constructed by the ancient sovereigns of Egypt for the proper distribution of the waters of the Nile were famous in antiquity, and the ruined remains of some of them are still the admiration of travellers. Those of the same kind which were constructed by the ancient sovereigns of Indostan, for the proper distribution of the waters of the Ganges as well as of many other rivers, though they have been less celebrated, seem to have been equally great. Both countries, accordingly, though subject occasionally to dearths, have been famous for their great fertility. Though both were extremely populous, yet, in years of moderate plenty, they were both able to export great quantities of grain to their neighbors.

The ancient Egyptians had a superstitious aversion to the sea; and as the Gentoo religion does not permit its followers to light a fire, nor consequently to dress any victuals upon the water, it in effect prohibits them from all distant sea voyages. Both the Egyptians and Indians must have depended almost altogether upon the navigation of other nations for the exportation of their surplus produce; and this dependency, as it must have confined the market, so it must have discouraged the increase of this surplus produce. It must have discouraged, too, the increase of the manufactured produce more than that of the rude produce. Manufactures require a much more extensive market than the most important parts of the rude produce of the land. A single shoemaker will make more than three hundred pairs of shoes in the year, and his own family will not perhaps wear out six pairs. Unless, therefore, he has the custom of at least fifty such families as his own, he cannot dispose of the whole produce of his own labor. The most numerous class of artificers will seldom, in a large country, make more than one in fifty or one in a hundred of the whole number of families contained in it. But in such large countries as France and England, the number of people employed in agriculture has by some authors been computed at a half, by others at a third, and by no author that I know of at less than a fifth of the whole inhabitants of the country. But as the produce of the agriculture of both France and England is, the far greater part of it, consumed at home, each person employed in it must, according to these computations, require little more than the custom of one, two, or at most, of four such families as his own, in order to dispose of the whole produce of his own labor. Agriculture, therefore, can support itself under the discouragement of a confined market much better than manufactures. In both ancient Egypt and Indostan, indeed, the confinement of the foreign market was in some measure compensated by the convenience of many inland navigations, which opened, in the most advantageous manner, the whole extent of the home market to every part of the produce of every different district of those countries. The great extent of Indostan, too, rendered the home market of that country very great, and sufficient to support a great variety of manufactures. But the small extent of ancient Egypt, which was never equal to England, must at all times have rendered the home market of that country too narrow for supporting any great variety of manufactures. Bengal, accordingly, the province of Indostan which commonly exports the greatest quantity of rice, has always been more remarkable for the exportation of a great variety of manufactures than for that of its grain. Ancient Egypt, on the contrary, though it exported some manufactures, fine linen in particular, as well as some other goods, was always most distinguished for its great exportation of grain. It was long the granary of the Roman Empire.

The sovereigns of China, of ancient Egypt, and of the different kingdoms into which Indostan has at different times been divided have always derived the whole, or by far the most considerable part, of their revenue from some sort of land tax or land rent. This land tax or land rent, like the tithe in Europe, consisted in a certain proportion, a fifth, it is said, of the produce of the land, which was either delivered in kind or paid in money, according to a certain valuation, and which therefore varied from year to year according to all the variations of the produce. It was natural, therefore, that the sovereigns of those countries should be particularly attentive to the interests of agriculture, upon the prosperity or declension of which immediately depended the yearly increase or diminution of their own revenue.

The policy of the ancient republics of Greece, and that of Rome, though it honored agriculture more than manufactures or foreign trade, yet seems rather to have discouraged the latter employments than to have given any direct or intentional encouragement to the former. In several of the ancient states of Greece foreign trade was prohibited altogether; and in several others the employments of artificers and manufacturers were considered as hurtful to the strength and agility of the human body, as rendering it incapable of those habits which their military and gymnastic exercises endeavored to form in it, and as thereby disqualifying it more or less for undergoing the fatigues and encountering the dangers of war. Such occupations were considered as fit only for slaves, and the free citizens of the state were prohibited from exercising them.[10] Even in those states where no such prohibition took place, as in Rome and Athens, the great body of the people were in effect excluded from all the trades which are now commonly exercised by the lower sort of the inhabitants of towns. Such trades were, at Athens and Rome, all occupied by the slaves of the rich, who exercised them for the benefit of their masters, whose wealth, power, and protection made it almost impossible for a poor freeman to find a market for his work when it came into competition with that of the slaves of the rich. Slaves, however, are very seldom inventive; and all the most important improvements, either in machinery, or in the arrangement and distribution of work which facilitate and abridge labor, have been the discoveries of freemen.

---

[10] Montesquieu, *Esprit des lois*, liv. iv., chap. 8.

Should a slave propose any improvement of this kind, his master would be very apt to consider the proposal as the suggestion of laziness and of a desire to save his own labor at the master's expense. The poor slave, instead of reward, would probably meet with much abuse, perhaps with some punishment. In the manufactures carried on by slaves, therefore, more labor must generally have been employed to execute the same quantity of work, than in those carried on by freemen. The work of the former must, upon that account, generally have been dearer than that of the latter. The Hungarian mines, it is remarked by Mr. Montesquieu, though not richer, have always been wrought with less expense, and therefore with more profit, than the Turkish mines in their neighborhood. The Turkish mines are wrought by slaves; and the arms of those slaves are the only machines which the Turks have ever thought of employing. The Hungarian mines are wrought by freemen who employ a great deal of machinery by which they facilitate and abridge their own labor. From the very little that is known about the price of manufactures in the times of the Greeks and Romans, it would appear that those of the finer sort were excessively dear. Silk sold for its weight in gold. It was not, indeed, in those times a European manufacture; and as it was all brought from the East Indies, the distance of the carriage may in some measure account for the greatness of the price. The price, however, which a lady, it is said, would sometimes pay for a piece of very fine linen, seems to have been equally extravagant; and as linen was always either a European, or, at farthest, an Egyptian manufacture, this high price can be accounted for only by the great expense of the labor which must have been employed about it, and the expense of this labor again could arise from nothing but the awkwardness of the machinery which it made use of. The price of fine woolens, too, though not quite so extravagant, seems however to have been much above that of the present times. Some cloths, we are told by Pliny, dyed in a particular manner, cost a hundred denarii, or three pounds six shillings

and eight pence the pound weight.[11] Others dyed in another
manner cost a thousand denarii the pound weight, or thirty-
three pounds six shillings and eight pence. The Roman
pound, it must be remembered, contained only twelve of our
avoirdupois ounces. This high price, indeed, seems to have
been principally owing to the dye. But had not the cloths
themselves been much dearer than any which are made in the
present times, so very expensive a dye would not probably
have been bestowed upon them. The disproportion would
have been too great between the value of the accessory and
that of the principal. The price mentioned by the same [12] author of some *triclinaria* [*tricliniaria*], a sort of woolen pillows
or cushions made use of to lean upon as they reclined upon
their couches at table, passes all credibility; some of them being said to have cost more than thirty thousand, others more
than three hundred thousand pounds. This high price, too, is
not said to have arisen from the dye. In the dress of the people
of fashion of both sexes, there seems to have been much less
variety, it is observed by Dr. Arbuthnot, in ancient than in
modern times; and the very little variety which we find in that
of the ancient statues confirms his observation. He infers from
this that their dress must upon the whole have been cheaper
than ours, but the conclusion does not seem to follow. When
the expense of fashionable dress is very great, the variety must
be very small. But when, by the improvements in the productive powers of manufacturing art and industry, the expense
of any one dress comes to be very moderate, the variety will
naturally be very great. The rich, not being able to distinguish themselves by the expense of any one dress, will naturally endeavor to do so by the multitude and variety of their
dresses.

The greatest and most important branch of the commerce
of every nation, it has already been observed,[13] is that which

11 Pliny, l. ix. c. 39.
12 Pliny, l. viii. c. 48.
13 [See p. 137.]

is carried on between the inhabitants of the town and those of the country. The inhabitants of the town draw from the country the rude produce which constitutes both the materials of their work and the fund of their subsistence; and they pay for this rude produce by sending back to the country a certain portion of it manufactured and prepared for immediate use. The trade which is carried on between those two different sets of people consists ultimately in a certain quantity of rude produce exchanged for a certain quantity of manufactured produce. The dearer the latter, therefore, the cheaper the former; and whatever tends in any country to raise the price of manufactured produce tends to lower that of the rude produce of the land, and thereby to discourage agriculture. The smaller the quantity of manufactured produce which any given quantity of rude produce, or, which comes to the same thing, which the price of any given quantity of rude produce is capable of purchasing, the smaller the exchangeable value of that given quantity of rude produce, and the smaller the encouragement which either the landlord has to increase its quantity by improving, or the farmer by cultivating, the land. Whatever, besides, tends to diminish in any country the number of artificers and manufacturers tends to diminish the home market, the most important of all markets for the rude produce of the land, and thereby still further to discourage agriculture.

Those systems, therefore, which, preferring agriculture to all other employments, in order to promote it, impose restraints upon manufactures and foreign trade, act contrary to the very end which they propose, and indirectly discourage that very species of industry which they mean to promote. They are so far, perhaps, more inconsistent than even the mercantile system. That system, by encouraging manufactures and foreign trade more than agriculture, turns a certain portion of the capital of the society from supporting a more advantageous, to support a less advantageous, species of industry. But still it really and in the end encourages that species of industry which it means to promote. Those agricultural systems, on the contrary, really and in the end discourage their own favorite species of industry.

It is thus that every system which endeavors, either by extraordinary encouragements to draw towards a particular species of industry a greater share of the capital of the society than what would naturally go to it, or by extraordinary restraints to force from a particular species of industry some share of the capital which would otherwise be employed in it, is in reality subversive of the great purpose which it means to promote. It retards, instead of accelerating, the progress of the society toward real wealth and greatness, and diminishes, instead of increasing, the real value of the annual produce of its land and labor.

All systems either of preference or of restraint, therefore, being thus completely taken away, the obvious and simple system of natural liberty establishes itself of its own accord. Every man, as long as he does not violate the laws of justice, is left perfectly free to pursue his own interest his own way, and to bring both his industry and capital into competition with those of any other man, or order of men. The sovereign is completely discharged from a duty, in the attempting to perform which he must always be exposed to innumerable delusions, and for the proper performance of which no human wisdom or knowledge could ever be sufficient: the duty of superintending the industry of private people, and of directing it toward the employments most suitable to the interest of the society. According to the system of natural liberty, the sovereign has only three duties to attend to, three duties of great importance, indeed, but plain and intelligible to common understandings: first, the duty of protecting the society from the violence and invasion of other independent societies; secondly, the duty of protecting, as far as possible, every member of the society from the injustice or oppression of every other member of it, or the duty of establishing an exact administration of justice; and, thirdly, the duty of erecting and maintaining certain public works and certain public institutions, which it can never be for the interest of any individual,

or small number of individuals, to erect and maintain, because
the profit could never repay the expense to any individual or
small number of individuals, though it may frequently do
much more than repay it to a great society.

The proper performance of those several duties of the
sovereign necessarily supposes a certain expense; and this expense again necessarily requires a certain revenue to support
it. In the following book, therefore, I shall endeavor to explain first, what are the necessary expenses of the sovereign or
commonwealth; and which of those expenses ought to be defrayed by the general contribution of the whole society; and
which of them, by that of some particular part only, or of
some particular members of the society; secondly, what are
the different methods in which the whole society may be made
to contribute toward defraying the expenses incumbent on
the whole society, and what are the principal advantages and
inconveniences of each of those methods; and, thirdly, what
are the reasons and causes which have induced almost all
modern governments to mortgage some part of this revenue,
or to contract debts, and what have been the effects of those
debts upon the real wealth, the annual produce of the land,
and labor of the society. The following book, therefore, will
naturally be divided into three chapters.

BOOK FIVE

OF THE REVENUE OF THE SOVEREIGN OR COMMONWEALTH

CHAPTER I

OF THE EXPENSES OF THE SOVEREIGN OR COMMONWEALTH

[Editor's Summary]

As Smith has promised, Book V treats "Of the Revenue of the Sovereign or Commonwealth." Under this heading, Chapter I deals with the expenses of the sovereign power. It is divided into four parts, of which Part I relates to the expenses of defense. Smith deals with the problem as it exists in different stages of society, i.e., among nations of hunters, shepherds, and among advanced states. In reference to the latter stage, he examines the pros and cons of a militia versus a standing army. In a very brief compass, he offers a history of military organization from primitive forms through to the invention of firearms. At times facile in its causal analysis, the material once again shows Smith's great breadth of interest and of information. Part II, which we reprint, takes up the expense of justice.

PART II

Of the Expense of Justice

The second duty of the sovereign, that of protecting, as far as possible, every member of the society from the injustice or oppression of every other member of it, or the duty of establishing an exact administration of justice requires two very different degrees of expense in the different periods of society.

Among nations of hunters, as there is scarcely any property, or at least none that exceeds the value of two or three days' labor, so there is seldom any established magistrate or any regular administration of justice. Men who have no property can injure one another only in their persons or reputations.

But when one man kills, wounds, beats, or defames another, though he to whom the injury is done suffers, he who does it receives no benefit. It is otherwise with the injuries to property. The benefit of the person who does the injury is often equal to the loss of him who suffers it. Envy, malice, or resentment are the only passions which can prompt one man to injure another in his person or reputation. But the greater part of men are not very frequently under the influence of those passions; and the very worst men are so only occasionally. As their gratification, too, howsoever agreeable it may be to certain characters, is not attended with any real or permanent advantage, it is in the greater part of men commonly restrained by prudential considerations. Men may live together in society with some tolerable degree of security, though there is no civil magistrate to protect them from the injustice of those passions. But avarice and ambition in the rich, in the poor the hatred of labor and the love of present ease and enjoyment, are the passions which prompt to invade property, passions much more steady in their operation, and much more universal in their influence. Wherever there is great property, there is great inequality. For one very rich man, there must be at least five hundred poor, and the affluence of the few supposes the indigence of the many. The affluence of the rich excites the indignation of the poor, who are often both driven by want and prompted by envy to invade his possessions. It is only under the shelter of the civil magistrate that the owner of that valuable property, which is acquired by the labor of many years, or perhaps of many successive generations, can sleep a single night in security. He is at all times surrounded by unknown enemies, whom, though he never provoked, he can never appease, and from whose injustice he can be protected only by the powerful arm of the civil magistrate continually held up to chastise it. The acquisition of valuable and extensive property, therefore, necessarily requires the establishment of civil government. Where there is no property, or at least none that exceeds the value of two or three days' labor, civil government is not so necessary.

Civil government supposes a certain subordination. But, as the necessity of civil government gradually grows up with the acquisition of valuable property, so the principal causes which naturally introduce subordination gradually grow up with the growth of that valuable property.

The causes or circumstances which naturally introduce subordination, or which naturally, and antecedent to any civil institution, give some men some superiority over the greater part of their brethren, seem to be four in number.

The first of those causes or circumstances is the superiority of personal qualifications, of strength, beauty, and agility of body; of wisdom, and virtue, of prudence, justice, fortitude, and moderation of mind. The qualifications of the body, unless supported by those of the mind, can give little authority in any period of society. He is a very strong man who, by mere strength of body, can force two weak ones to obey him. The qualifications of the mind can alone give very great authority. They are, however, invisible qualities, always disputable, and generally disputed. No society, whether barbarous or civilized, has ever found it convenient to settle the rules of precedency of rank and subordination according to those invisible qualities, but according to something that is more plain and palpable.

The second of those causes or circumstances is the superiority of age. An old man, provided his age is not so far advanced as to give suspicion of dotage, is everywhere more respected than a young man of equal rank, fortune, and abilities. Among nations of hunters, such as the native tribes of North America, age is the sole foundation of rank and precedency. Among them, father is the appellation of a superior; brother, of an equal; and son, of an inferior. In the most opulent and civilized nations, age regulates rank among those who are in every other respect equal and among whom, therefore, there is nothing else to regulate it. Among brothers and among sisters, the eldest always take place; and in the succession of the paternal estate everything which cannot be divided, but must go entirely to one person, such as a title of honor, is in most cases given to the eldest. Age is a plain and palpable quality which admits of no dispute.

The third of those causes or circumstances is the superiority of fortune. The authority of riches, however, though great in every age of society, is perhaps greatest in the rudest age of society which admits of any considerable inequality of fortune. A Tartar chief, the increase of whose herds and flocks is sufficient to maintain a thousand men, cannot well employ that increase in any other way than in maintaining a thousand men. The rude state of his society does not afford him any manufactured produce, any trinkets or baubles of any kind, for which he can exchange that part of his rude produce which is over and above his own consumption. The thousand men whom he thus maintains, depending entirely upon him for their subsistence, must both obey his orders in war, and submit to his jurisdiction in peace. He is necessarily both their general and their judge, and his chieftainship is the necessary effect of the superiority of his fortune. In an opulent and civilized society a man may possess a much greater fortune, and yet not be able to command a dozen of people. Though the produce of his estate may be sufficient to maintain, and may perhaps actually maintain, more than a thousand people, yet as those people pay for everything which they get from him, as he gives scarcely anything to anybody but in exchange for an equivalent, there is scarcely anybody who considers himself as entirely dependent upon him, and his authority extends only over a few menial servants. The authority of fortune, however, is very great even in an opulent and civilized society. That it is much greater than that either of age or of personal qualities has been the constant complaint of every period of society which admitted of any considerable inequality of fortune. The first period of society, that of hunters, admits of no such inequality. Universal poverty establishes there universal equality, and the superiority either of age or of personal qualities are the feeble, but the sole, foundations of authority and subordination. There is therefore little or no authority or subordination in this period of society. The second period of society, that of shepherds, admits of very great inequalities of fortune, and there is no period in which the superiority of fortune gives so great authority to those who possess it. There is no period, accordingly, in which authority and subordination are more perfectly established. The authority of an Arabian sherif is very great; that of a Tartar khan altogether despotical.

The fourth of those causes or circumstances is the superiority of birth. Superiority of birth supposes an ancient superiority of fortune in the family of the person who claims it. All families are equally ancient, and the ancestors of the prince, though they may be better known, cannot well be more numerous than those of the beggar. Antiquity of family means everywhere the antiquity either of wealth, or of that greatness which is commonly either founded upon wealth, or accompanied with it. Upstart greatness is everywhere less respected than ancient greatness.[1] The hatred of usurpers, the love of the family of an ancient monarch, are, in a great measure, founded upon the contempt which men naturally have for the former, and upon their veneration for the latter. As a military officer submits without reluctance to the authority of a superior by whom he has always been commanded, but cannot bear that his inferior should be set over his head, so men easily submit to a family to whom they and their ancestors have always submitted; but are fired with indignation when another family, in whom they had never acknowledged any such superiority, assumes a dominion over them.

The distinction of birth, being subsequent to the inequality of fortune, can have no place in nations of hunters, among whom all men, being equal in fortune, must likewise be very nearly equal in birth. The son of a wise and brave man may, indeed, even among them, be somewhat more respected than a man of equal merit who has the misfortune to be the son of a fool or a coward. The difference, however, will not be very great; and there never was, I believe, a great family in the

---

[1] [*Lectures*, p. 10.—C.]

world whose illustration was entirely derived from the inheritance of wisdom and virtue.

The distinction of birth not only may, but always does take place among nations of shepherds Such nations are always strangers to every sort of luxury, and great wealth can scarcely ever be dissipated among them by improvident profusion. There are no nations, accordingly, who abound more in families revered and honored on account of their descent from a long race of great and illustrious ancestors, because there are no nations among whom wealth is likely to continue longer in the same families.

Birth and fortune are evidently the two circumstances which principally set one man above another. They are the two great sources of personal distinction, and are therefore the principal causes which naturally establish authority and subordination among men. Among nations of shepherds both those causes operate with their full force. The great shepherd or herdsman, respected on account of his great wealth, and of the great number of those who depend upon him for subsistence, and revered on account of the nobleness of his birth and of the immemorial antiquity of his illustrious family, has a natural authority over all the inferior shepherds or herdsmen of his horde or clan. He can command the united force of a greater number of people than any of them. His military power is greater than that of any of them. In time of war they are all of them naturally disposed to muster themselves under his banner, rather than under that of any other person, and his birth and fortune thus naturally procure to him some sort of executive power. By commanding, too, the united force of a greater number of people than any of them, he is best able to compel any one of them who may have injured another to compensate the wrong. He is the person, therefore, to whom all those who are too weak to defend themselves naturally look up for protection. It is to him that they naturally complain of the injuries which they imagine have been done to them, and his interposition in such cases is more easily submitted to, even by the person complained of, than that of any other person would be. His birth and fortune thus naturally procure him some sort of judicial authority.

It is in the age of shepherds, in the second period of society, that the inequality of fortune first begins to take place, and introduces among men a degree of authority and subordination which could not possibly exist before. It thereby introduces some degree of that civil government which is indispensably necessary for its own preservation, and it seems to do this naturally, and even independent of the consideration of that necessity. The consideration of that necessity comes no doubt afterwards to contribute very much to maintain and secure that authority and subordination. The rich, in particular, are necessarily interested to support that order of things which can alone secure them in the possession of their own advantages. Men of inferior wealth combine to defend those of superior wealth in the possession of their property, in order that men of superior wealth may combine to defend them in the possession of theirs. All the inferior shepherds and herdsmen feel that the security of their own herds and flocks depends upon the security of those of the great shepherd or herdsman, that the maintenance of their lesser authority depends upon that of his greater authority, and that upon their subordination to him depends his power of keeping their inferiors in subordination to them. They constitute a sort of little nobility, who feel themselves interested to defend the property and to support the authority of their own little sovereign, in order that he may be able to defend their property and to support their authority. Civil government, so far as it is instituted for the security of property, is in reality instituted for the defense of the rich against the poor, or of those who have some property against those who have none at all.[2]

The judicial authority of such a sovereign, however, far

2 [*Lectures*, p. 15: "Till there be property there can be no government, the very end of which is to secure wealth and to defend the rich from the poor." Cf. Locke, *Civil Government*, § 94, "government has no other end but the preservation of property."—C.]

from being a cause of expense, was for a long time a source of revenue to him. The persons who applied to him for justice were always willing to pay for it, and a present never failed to accompany a petition. After the authority of the sovereign, too, was thoroughly established, the person found guilty, over and above the satisfaction which he was obliged to make to the party, was likewise forced to pay an amercement to the sovereign. He had given trouble, he had disturbed, he had broken the peace of his lord the king, and for those offenses an amercement was thought due. In the Tartar governments of Asia, in the governments of Europe which were founded by the German and Scythian nations who overturned the Roman Empire, the administration of justice was a considerable source of revenue, both to the sovereign, and to all the lesser chiefs or lords who exercised under him any particular jurisdiction, either over some particular tribe or clan, or over some particular territory or district. Originally both the sovereign and the inferior chiefs used to exercise this jurisdiction in their own persons. Afterwards they universally found it convenient to delegate it to some substitute, bailiff, or judge. This substitute, however, was still obliged to account to his principal or constituent for the profits of the jurisdiction. Whoever reads the instructions which were given to the judges of the circuit in the time of Henry II will see clearly that those judges were a sort of itinerant factors, sent round the country for the purpose of levying certain branches of the king's revenue. In those days the administration of justice not only afforded a certain revenue to the sovereign, but to procure this revenue seems to have been one of the principal advantages which he proposed to obtain by the administration of justice.

This scheme of making the administration of justice subservient to the purposes of revenue could scarcely fail to be productive of several very gross abuses. The person who applied for justice with a large present in his hand was likely to get something more than justice; while he who applied for it with a small one was likely to get something less. Justice, too, might frequently be delayed, in order that this present might be repeated. The amercement, besides, of the person complained of might frequently suggest a very strong reason for finding him in the wrong, even when he had not really been so. That such abuses were far from being uncommon, the ancient history of every country in Europe bears witness.

When the sovereign or chief exercised his judicial authority in his own person, howsoever much he might abuse it, it must have been scarcely possible to get any redress, because there could seldom be anybody powerful enough to call him to account. When he exercised it by a bailiff, indeed, redress might sometimes be had. If it was for his own benefit only that the bailiff had been guilty of any act of injustice, the sovereign himself might not always be unwilling to punish him, or to oblige him to repair the wrong. But if it was for the benefit of his sovereign, if it was in order to make court to the person who appointed him and who might prefer him that he had committed any act of oppression, redress would upon most occasions be as impossible as if the sovereign had committed it himself. In all barbarous governments, accordingly, in all those ancient governments of Europe in particular which were founded upon the ruins of the Roman Empire, the administration of justice appears for a long time to have been extremely corrupt; far from being quite equal and impartial even under the best monarchs, and altogether profligate under the worst.

Among nations of shepherds, where the sovereign or chief is only the greatest shepherd or herdsman of the horde or clan, he is maintained in the same manner as any of his vassals or subjects, by the increase of his own herds or flocks. Among those nations of husbandmen who are but just come out of the shepherd state, and who are not much advanced beyond that state, such as the Greek tribes appear to have been about the time of the Trojan War and our German and Scythian ancestors when they first settled upon the ruins of the western empire, the sovereign or chief is, in the same manner, only the greatest landlord of the country and is maintained in the same manner as any other landlord by a revenue derived from his own private estate, or from what, in modern Europe, was called the demesne of the crown. His subjects, upon ordinary occasions, contribute nothing to his support, except when, in order to protect them from the oppression of some of their fellow subjects, they stand in need of his authority. The presents which they make him upon such occasions constitute the whole ordinary revenue, the whole of the emoluments which, except perhaps upon some very extraordinary emergencies, he derives from his dominion over them. When Agamemnon, in Homer, offers to Achilles for his friendship the sovereignty of seven Greek cities, the sole advantage which he mentions as likely to be derived from it was that the people would honor him with presents.[3] As long as such presents, as long as the emoluments of justice, or what may be called the fees of court, constituted in this manner the whole ordinary revenue which the sovereign derived from his sovereignty, it could not well be expected, it could not even decently be proposed, that he should give them up altogether. It might, and it frequently was proposed, that he should regulate and ascertain them. But after they had been so regulated and ascertained, how to hinder a person who was all-powerful from extending them beyond those regulations was still very difficult, not to say impossible. During the continuance of this state of things, therefore, the corruption of justice, naturally resulting from the arbitrary and uncertain nature of those presents, scarcely admitted of any effectual remedy.

But when from different causes, chiefly from the continually increasing expense of defending the nation against the invasion of other nations, the private estate of the sovereign had become altogether insufficient for defraying the expense of the sovereignty; and when it had become necessary that the people should, for their own security, contribute toward this expense by taxes of different kinds, it seems to have been very commonly stipulated that no present for the administration

[3] [*Iliad*, ix., 149-156, but the presents are not the "sole advantage" mentioned.—C.]

of justice should, under any pretense, be accepted either by the sovereign, or by his bailiffs and substitutes, the judges. Those presents, it seems to have been supposed, could more easily be abolished altogether than effectually regulated and ascertained. Fixed salaries were appointed to the judges, which were supposed to compensate to them the loss of whatever might have been their share of the ancient emoluments of justice, as the taxes more than compensated to the sovereign the loss of his. Justice was then said to be administered gratis.

Justice, however, never was in reality administered gratis in any country. Lawyers and attorneys, at least, must always be paid by the parties; and, if they were not, they would perform their duty still worse than they actually perform it. The fees annually paid to lawyers and attorneys amount, in every court, to a much greater sum than the salaries of the judges. The circumstance of those salaries being paid by the crown can nowhere much diminish the necessary expense of a lawsuit. But it was not so much to diminish the expense, as to prevent the corruption of justice, that the judges were prohibited from receiving any present or fee from the parties.

The office of judge is in itself so very honorable that men are willing to accept of it, though accompanied with very small emoluments. The inferior office of justice of peace, though attended with a good deal of trouble, and in most cases with no emoluments at all, is an object of ambition to the greater part of our country gentlemen. The salaries of all the different judges, high and low, together with the whole expense of the administration and execution of justice, even where it is not managed with very good economy, makes, in any civilized country, but a very inconsiderable part of the whole expense of government.

The whole expense of justice, too, might easily be defrayed by the fees of court; and, without exposing the administration of justice to any real hazard of corruption, the public revenue might thus be entirely discharged from a certain, though, perhaps, but a small, encumbrance. It is difficult to regulate the fees of court effectually where a person so powerful as the

sovereign is to share in them, and to derive any considerable
part of his revenue from them. It is very easy where the judge
is the principal person who can reap any benefit from them.
The law can very easily oblige the judge to respect the regulation, though it might not always be able to make the sovereign respect it. Where the fees of court are precisely regulated and ascertained, where they are paid all at once, at a
certain period of every process, into the hands of a cashier or
receiver, to be by him distributed in certain known proportions among the different judges after the process is decided,
and not till it is decided, there seems to be no more danger of
corruption than where such fees are prohibited altogether.
Those fees, without occasioning any considerable increase in
the expense of a lawsuit, might be rendered fully sufficient
for defraying the whole expense of justice. By not being paid
to the judges till the process was determined, they might be
some incitement to the diligence of the court in examining
and deciding it. In courts which consisted of a considerable
number of judges, by proportioning the share of each judge
to the number of hours and days which he had employed in
examining the process, either in the court or in a committee
by order of the court, those fees might give some encouragement to the diligence of each particular judge. Public services
are never better performed than when their reward comes
only in consequence of their being performed and is proportioned to the diligence employed in performing them. In
the different parliaments of France, the fees of court (called
Epicès and *vacations*) constitute the far greater part of the
emoluments of the judges. After all deductions are made, the
net salary paid by the crown to a counselor or judge in the
parliament of Toulouse, in rank and dignity the second parliament of the kingdom, amounts only to a hundred and
fifty livres, about six pounds eleven shillings sterling a year.
About seven years ago [4] that sum was in the same place the
ordinary yearly wages of a common footman. The distribution

---

[4] [Smith was in Toulouse from February or March, 1764, to August,
1765.—Rae, *Life of Adam Smith*, pp. 174, 175, 188.—C.]

of those *Epicès* too is according to the diligence of the judges. A diligent judge gains a comfortable, though moderate, revenue by his office; an idle one gets little more than his salary. Those parliaments are perhaps, in many respects, not very convenient courts of justice; but they have never been accused, they seem never even to have been suspected, of corruption.

The fees of court seem originally to have been the principal support of the different courts of justice in England. Each court endeavored to draw to itself as much business as it could, and was, upon that account, willing to take cognizance of many suits which were not originally intended to fall under its jurisdiction. The Court of King's Bench, instituted for the trial of criminal causes only, took cognizance of civil suits, the plaintiff pretending that the defendant, in not doing him justice, had been guilty of some trespass or misdemeanor. The Court of Exchequer, instituted for the levying of the king's revenue, and for enforcing the payment of such debts only as were due to the king, took cognizance of all other contract debts, the plaintiff alleging that he could not pay the king because the defendant would not pay him. In consequence of such fictions it came, in many cases, to depend altogether upon the parties before what court they would choose to have their cause tried; and each court endeavored, by superior dispatch and impartiality, to draw to itself as many causes as it could. The present admirable constitution of the courts of justice in England was, perhaps, originally in a great measure formed by this emulation, which anciently took place between their respective judges, each judge endeavoring to give, in his own court, the speediest and most effectual remedy which the law would admit for every sort of injustice. Originally the courts of law gave damages only for breach of contract. The Court of Chancery, as a court of conscience, first took upon itself to enforce the specific performance of agreements. When the breach of contract consisted in the nonpayment of money, the damage sustained could be compensated in no other way than by ordering payment, which was equivalent to a specific performance of the agreement. In such cases, therefore, the remedy of the courts of law was sufficient. It was not so in others. When the tenant sued his lord for having unjustly outed him of his lease, the damages which he recovered were by no means equivalent to the possession of the land. Such causes, therefore, for some time, went all to the Court of Chancery, to the no small loss of the courts of law. It was to draw back such causes to themselves that the courts of law are said to have invented the artificial and fictitious writ of eject-ment, the most effectual remedy for an unjust outer or dis-possession of land.[5]

A stamp duty upon the law proceedings of each particular court, to be levied by that court, and applied towards the maintenance of the judges and other officers belonging to it, might, in the same manner, afford a revenue sufficient for de-fraying the expense of the administration of justice without bringing any burden upon the general revenue of the society. The judges indeed might, in this case, be under the tempta-tion of multiplying unnecessarily the proceedings upon every cause, in order to increase as much as possible the produce of such a stamp duty. It has been the custom in modern Europe to regulate, upon most occasions, the payment of the attorneys and clerks of court, according to the number of pages which they had occasion to write, the court, however, requiring that each page should contain so many lines, and each line so many words. In order to increase their payment, the attorneys and clerks have contrived to multiply words beyond all neces-sity, to the corruption of the law language of, I believe, every court of justice in Europe. A like temptation might perhaps occasion a like corruption in the form of law proceedings.

But whether the administration of justice be so contrived as to defray its own expense, or whether the judges be main-tained by fixed salaries paid to them from some other fund, it does not seem necessary that the person or persons entrusted with the executive power should be charged with the manage-ment of that fund, or with the payment of those salaries. That

[5] [*Lectures*, p. 49. See also Book III, Chapter II (not included in this edition).]

fund might arise from the rent of landed estates, the management of each estate being entrusted to the particular court
which was to be maintained by it. That fund might arise
even from the interest of a sum of money, the lending out of
which might, in the same manner, be entrusted to the court
which was to be maintained by it. A part, though indeed but
a small part, of the salary of the judges of the Court of Session
in Scotland arises from the interest of a sum of money. The
necessary instability of such a fund seems, however, to render
it an improper one for the maintenance of an institution
which ought to last forever.

The separation of the judicial from the executive power
seems originally to have arisen from the increasing business
of the society in consequence of its increasing improvement.
The administration of justice became so laborious and so
complicated a duty as to require the undivided attention of
the persons to whom it was entrusted. The person entrusted
with the executive power not having leisure to attend to the
decision of private causes himself, a deputy was appointed to
decide them in his stead. In the progress of the Roman greatness, the consul was too much occupied with the political
affairs of the state to attend to the administration of justice.
A praetor, therefore, was appointed to administer it in his
stead. In the progress of the European monarchies which were
founded upon the ruins of the Roman Empire, the sovereigns
and the great lords came universally to consider the administration of justice as an office both too laborious and too ig-
noble for them to execute in their own persons. They universally, therefore, discharged themselves of it by appointing
a deputy, bailiff, or judge.

When the judicial is united to the executive power, it is
scarcely possible that justice should not frequently be sacrificed
to what is vulgarly called politics. The persons entrusted with
the great interests of the state may, even without any corrupt
views, sometimes imagine it necessary to sacrifice to those
interests the rights of a private man. But upon the impartial
administration of justice depends the liberty of every in-

dividual, the sense which he has of his own security. In order to make every individual feel himself perfectly secure in the possession of every right which belongs to him, it is not only necessary that the judicial should be separated from the executive power, but that it should be rendered as much as possible independent of that power. The judge should not be liable to be removed from his office according to the caprice of that power. The regular payment of his salary should not depend upon the good will, or even upon the good economy of that power.

[PARTS III AND IV]

[Editor's Summary]

In Part III, Smith concerns himself with the expense of public works and public institutions. Article I takes up the question as to what public works and institutions facilitate the commerce of society: public highways, bridges, canals, and turnpikes are discussed, and the question of tolls is investigated. In the second part of Article I, Smith discusses the public works and institutions necessary for facilitating particular branches of commerce. Under this heading, he deals with ambassadors, forts, and the usefulness of promoting joint-stock companies. It is interesting to note that Smith was not in favor of the joint-stock company—the forerunner of the modern corporation—in such fields as copper mining, lead smelting and glass grinding.

In Article II, Smith deals with the "Expense of the Institutions for the Education of Youth." In this section, too, Smith pursues his belief in free enterprise. He deplores public endowments of schools and colleges, as diminishing "the necessity of application in the teachers," who would work harder, he believes, if dependent on students' fees. In general, Smith regards the universities as monopolistic corporations, originating in the Middle Ages as training grounds for ecclesiastics and now (in the eighteenth century) restrictive and outdated. Like his friend, David Hume, Smith scoffs at metaphysics as incapable of improvement, and appeals for more experiment and observation in moral subjects. He also advocates government support—public education—for the training of the common people to read and write: it is, he contends, an essential part of a free government, which depends for its safety on the judgment of the people. In sum, Smith's treatment of education illustrates the broad range of his interests as well as his general philosophic position.

In Article III, Smith continues his discussion of the expenses of the sovereign power, this time in relation to the institutions for the instruction of people of any age. Under this heading, he considers the problem of religious instruction. He discusses the merits of an established church versus the existence of numerous sects, especially in relation to the security and well-being of the sovereign state. In the course of his remarks, he offers a brief historical disquisition on the Catholic and Presbyterian churches.

Part IV hardly deserves the appellation of a separate part; it deals with the expense of supporting the dignity of the sovereign in less than half a page.

Smith's Conclusion to Chapter I suggests that contributions from the general public are proper for either the whole or part of the following expenses: the expense of defending the society, supporting the dignity of the chief magistrate, of administrating justice, of maintaining good roads and communications, and of supporting the institutions for education and religious instruction. All of the matters enumerated are beneficial to the whole society.

[CHAPTERS II AND III]

[Editor's Summary]

After having discussed expenses, Smith turns in Chapter II to the sources of revenue for the society. He takes up, initially, the sources of revenue which may belong particularly to the sovereign power, such as public banks, the post office, and public or crown lands. Next, in the course of his lengthy chapter, he lays down broad principles with regard to taxes in general. Then he considers the respective merits of taxes upon rent, rent of land, produce of land, profit, capital value of land, houses and stock, wages of labor, and so forth. It is a fairly technical discussion. At the very end of the chapter, Smith offers an interesting comparison of the French system of taxation with that of the English.

Proceeding thence to Chapter III, Smith takes up what is really another, though peculiar, source of revenue: public debts. He discusses the dangers of rising public debts and analyzes the problem of taxation in wartime. The latter discussion leads him to the question of the British system of taxation as extended to the provinces of the empire; among these, he pays special attention to the American colonies. Thereby, he links his treatment of colonies and of public debts and taxes into one coherent whole, as well as contributing to the debate surrounding the events of the American Revolution. It is, in fact, on this note that he ends his book.

Except for a few minor deletions, we reprint the whole of the chapter.

CHAPTER III

OF PUBLIC DEBTS

In that rude state of society which precedes the extension of commerce and the improvement of manufactures, when those expensive luxuries which commerce and manufactures can alone introduce are altogether unknown, the person who possesses a large revenue, I have endeavored to show in the third book of this inquiry,[1] can spend or enjoy that revenue in no other way than by maintaining nearly as many people as it can maintain. A large revenue may at all times be said to consist in the command of a large quantity of the necessities of life. In that rude state of things it is commonly paid in a large quantity of those necessities, in the materials of plain

1 [See pp. 144-46.]

food and coarse clothing, in corn and cattle, in wool and raw hides. When neither commerce nor manufactures furnish anything for which the owner can exchange the greater part of those materials which are over and above his own consumption, he can do nothing with the surplus but feed and clothe nearly as many people as it will feed and clothe. A hospitality in which there is no luxury, and a liberality in which there is no ostentation, occasion, in this situation of things, the principal expenses of the rich and the great. But these, I have likewise endeavored to show in the same book,[2] are expenses by which people are not very apt to ruin themselves. There is not, perhaps, any selfish pleasure so frivolous, of which the pursuit has not sometimes ruined even sensible men. A passion for cockfighting has ruined many. But the instances, I believe, are not very numerous of people who have been ruined by a hospitality or liberality of this kind, though the hospitality of luxury and the liberality of ostentation have ruined many. Among our feudal ancestors, the long time during which estates used to continue in the same family sufficiently demonstrates the general disposition of people to live within their income. Though the rustic hospitality, constantly exercised by the great landholders, may not, to us in the present times, seem consistent with that order which we are apt to consider as inseparably connected with good economy, yet we must certainly allow them to have been at least so far frugal as not commonly to have spent their whole income. A part of their wool and raw hides they had generally an opportunity of selling for money. Some part of this money, perhaps, they spent in purchasing the few objects of vanity and luxury with which the circumstances of the times could furnish them; but some part of it they seem commonly to have hoarded. They could not well indeed do anything else but hoard whatever money they saved. To trade was disgraceful to a gentleman, and to lend money at interest, which at that time was considered as usury and prohibited by law, would have been still more so.

[2] [See pp. 151-53.]

In those times of violence and disorder, besides, it was convenient to have a hoard of money at hand, that in case they should be driven from their own home, they might have something of known value to carry with them to some place of safety. The same violence which made it convenient to hoard made it equally convenient to conceal the hoard. The frequency of treasure-trove, or of treasure found of which no owner was known, sufficiently demonstrates the frequency in those times both of hoarding and of concealing the hoard. Treasure-trove was then considered as an important branch of the revenue of the sovereign. All the treasure-trove of the kingdom would scarcely perhaps in the present times make an important branch of the revenue of a private gentleman of a good estate.

The same disposition to save and to hoard prevailed in the sovereign as well as in the subjects. Among nations to whom commerce and manufactures are little known, the sovereign, it has already been observed in the fourth book, is in a situation which naturally disposes him to the parsimony requisite for accumulation. In that situation the expense even of a sovereign cannot be directed by that vanity which delights in the gaudy finery of a court. The ignorance of the times affords but few of the trinkets in which that finery consists. Standing armies are not then necessary, so that the expense even of a sovereign, like that of any other great lord, can be employed in scarcely anything but bounty to his tenants and hospitality to his retainers. But bounty and hospitality very seldom lead to extravagance; though vanity almost always does. All the ancient sovereigns of Europe accordingly, it has already been observed, had treasures. Every Tartar chief in the present times is said to have one.

In a commercial country abounding with every sort of expensive luxury, the sovereign, in the same manner as almost all the great proprietors in his dominions, naturally spends a great part of his revenue in purchasing those luxuries. His own and the neighboring countries supply him abundantly with all the costly trinkets which compose the splendid, but insignificant, pageantry of a court. For the sake of an inferior pageantry of the same kind, his nobles dismiss their retainers, make their tenants independent, and become gradually themselves as insignificant as the greater part of the wealthy burghers in his dominions. The same frivolous passions which influence their conduct influence his. How can it be supposed that he should be the only rich man in his dominions who is insensible to pleasures of this kind? If he does not, what he is very likely to do, spend upon those pleasures so great a part of his revenue as to debilitate very much the defensive power of the state, it cannot well be expected that he should not spend upon them all that part of it which is over and above what is necessary for supporting that defensive power. His ordinary expense becomes equal to his ordinary revenue, and it is well if it does not frequently exceed it. The amassing of treasure can no longer be expected; and when extraordinary exigencies require extraordinary expenses, he must necessarily call upon his subjects for an extraordinary aid. The present and the late kings of Prussia [3] are the only great princes of Europe who, since the death of Henry IV of France in 1610, are supposed to have amassed any considerable treasure. The parsimony which leads to accumulation has become almost as rare in republican as in monarchical governments. The Italian republics, the United Provinces of the Netherlands, are all in debt. The canton of Berne is the single republic in Europe which has amassed any considerable treasure. The other Swiss republics have not. The taste for some sort of pageantry, for splendid buildings, at least, and other public ornaments, frequently prevails as much in the apparently sober senatehouse of a little republic as in the dissipated court of the greatest king.

The want of parsimony in time of peace imposes the necessity of contracting debt in time of war. When war comes, there is no money in the treasury but what is necessary for carrying on the ordinary expense of the peace establishment. In war an

---

[3] [Smith here refers to Frederick II, "The Great," (1740-1786) and his father, Frederick William I (1713-1740).—M.]

establishment of three or four times that expense becomes necessary for the defense of the state, and consequently a revenue three or four times greater than the peace revenue. Supposing that the sovereign should have, what he scarcely ever has, the immediate means of augmenting his revenue in proportion to the augmentation of his expense, yet still the produce of the taxes, from which this increase of revenue must be drawn, will not begin to come into the treasury till perhaps ten or twelve months after they are imposed. But the moment in which war begins, or rather the moment in which it appears likely to begin, the army must be augmented, the fleet must be fitted out, the garrisoned towns must be put into a posture of defense; that army, that fleet, those garrisoned towns must be furnished with arms, ammunition, and provisions. An immediate and great expense must be incurred in that moment of immediate danger, which will not wait for the gradual and slow returns of the new taxes. In this exigency government can have no other resource but in borrowing.

The same commercial state of society which, by the operation of moral causes, brings government in this manner into the necessity of borrowing, produces in the subjects both an ability and an inclination to lend. If it commonly brings along with it the necessity of borrowing, it likewise brings along with it the facility of doing so.

A country abounding with merchants and manufacturers necessarily abounds with a set of people through whose hands not only their own capitals, but the capitals of all those who either lend them money or trust them with goods pass as frequently, or more frequently, than the revenue of a private man who, without trade or business, lives upon his income, passes through his hands. The revenue of such a man can regularly pass through his hands only once in a year. But the whole amount of the capital and credit of a merchant, who deals in a trade of which the returns are very quick, may sometimes pass through his hands two, three, or four times in a year. A country abounding with merchants and manufacturers, therefore, necessarily abounds with a set of people who have it at all times in their power to advance, if they choose to do so, a very large sum of money to government. Hence the ability in the subjects of a commercial state to lend.

Commerce and manufactures can seldom flourish long in any state which does not enjoy a regular administration of justice, in which the people do not feel themselves secure in the possession of their property, in which the faith of contracts is not supported by law, and in which the authority of the state is not supposed to be regularly employed in enforcing the payment of debts from all those who are able to pay. Commerce and manufactures, in short, can seldom flourish in any state in which there is not a certain degree of confidence in the justice of government. The same confidence which disposes great merchants and manufacturers, upon ordinary occasions, to trust their property to the protection of a particular government disposes them, upon extraordinary occasions, to trust that government with the use of their property. By lending money to government, they do not even for a moment diminish their ability to carry on their trade and manufactures. On the contrary, they commonly augment it. The necessities of the state render government upon most occasions willing to borrow upon terms extremely advantageous to the lender. The security which it grants to the original creditor is made transferable to any other creditor and, from the universal confidence in the justice of the state, generally sells in the market for more than was originally paid for it. The merchant or moneyed man makes money by lending money to government, and instead of diminishing, increases his trading capital. He generally considers it as a favor, therefore, when the administration admits him to a share in the first subscription for a new loan. Hence the inclination or willingness in the subjects of a commercial state to lend.

The government of such a state is very apt to repose itself upon this ability and willingness of its subjects to lend it their money on extraordinary occasions. It foresees the facility of borrowing, and therefore dispenses itself from the duty of saving.

In a rude state of society there are no great mercantile or manufacturing capitals. The individuals who hoard whatever money they can save, and who conceal their hoard, do so from a distrust of the justice of government, from a fear that if it was known that they had a hoard, and where that hoard was to be found, they would quickly be plundered. In such a state of things few people would be able, and nobody would be willing, to lend their money to government on extraordinary exigencies. The sovereign feels that he must provide for such exigencies by saving, because he foresees the absolute impossibility of borrowing. This foresight increases still further his natural disposition to save.

The progress of the enormous debts which at present oppress, and will in the long run probably ruin, all the great nations of Europe, has been pretty uniform.[4] Nations, like private men, have generally begun to borrow upon what may be called personal credit, without assigning or mortgaging any particular fund for the payment of the debt; and when this resource has failed them, they have gone on to borrow upon assignments or mortgages of particular funds.

What is called the unfunded debt of Great Britain is contracted in the former of those two ways. It consists partly in a debt which bears, or is supposed to bear, no interest, and which resembles the debts that a private man contracts upon account, and partly in a debt which bears interest, and which resembles what a private man contracts upon his bill or promissory note. The debts which are due either for extraordinary services, or for services either not provided for, or not paid at the time when they are performed, part of the extraordinaries of the army, navy, and ordnance, the arrears of subsidies to foreign princes, those of seamen's wages, etc.,

---

[4] [That Smith was not being merely fanciful about the problem of public debts—a problem which is, indeed, still with us—was proven by the example of Spain in the seventeenth century. Cf. Richard Ehrenberg, *Capitalism and Finance in the Age of the Renaissance,* tr. from the German (London, 1928).—M.]

usually constitute a debt of the first kind. Navy and Exchequer bills, which are issued sometimes in payment of a part of such debts and sometimes for other purposes, constitute a debt of the second kind, Exchequer bills bearing interest from the day on which they are issued, and navy bills six months after they are issued. The Bank of England, either by voluntarily discounting those bills at their current value, or by agreeing with government for certain considerations to circulate Exchequer bills, that is, to receive them at par, paying the interest which happens to be due upon them, keeps up their value and facilitates their circulation, and thereby frequently enables government to contract a very large debt of this kind. In France, where there is no bank, the state bills (*billets d'état* [5]) have sometimes sold at sixty and seventy per cent discount. During the great recoinage in King William's time, when the Bank of England thought proper to put a stop to its usual transactions, Exchequer bills and tallies are said to have sold from twenty-five to sixty per cent discount; owing partly, no doubt, to the supposed instability of the new government established by the Revolution, but partly, too, to the want of the support of the Bank of England.

When this resource is exhausted and it becomes necessary, in order to raise money, to assign or mortgage some particular branch of the public revenue for the payment of the debt, government has upon different occasions done this in two different ways. Sometimes it has made this assignment or mortgage for a short period of time only, a year, or a few years, for example, and sometimes for perpetuity. In the one case, the fund was supposed sufficient to pay, within the limited time, both principal and interest of the money borrowed. In the other, it was supposed sufficient to pay the interest only, or a perpetual annuity equivalent to the interest, government being at liberty to redeem at any time this annuity, upon paying

[5] See Examen des Réflexions politiques sur les Finances. [P. J. Duverney. *Examen du livre intitulé Réflexions politiques sur les finances et le commerce* (by Du Tot), tom. i., p. 225.–C.]

back the principal sum borrowed. When money was raised in the one way, it was said to be raised by anticipation; when in the other, by perpetual funding, or, more shortly, by funding.

In Great Britain the annual land and malt taxes are regularly anticipated every year, by virtue of a borrowing clause constantly inserted into the acts which impose them. The Bank of England generally advances at an interest, which since the Revolution has varied from eight to three per cent, the sums for which those taxes are granted, and receives payment as their produce gradually comes in. If there is a deficiency, which there always is, it is provided for in the supplies of the ensuing year. The only considerable branch of the public revenue which yet remains unmortgaged is thus regularly spent before it comes in. Like an improvident spendthrift whose pressing occasions will not allow him to wait for the regular payment of his revenue, the state is in the constant practice of borrowing of its own factors and agents and of paying interest for the use of its own money.

[We eliminate here a few pages dealing with the particular duties and annuities of eighteenth-century England, wherein Smith once again exhibits his knowledge of the details of his subject.]

The ordinary expense of the greater part of modern governments in time of peace being equal or nearly equal to their ordinary revenue, when war comes, they are both unwilling and unable to increase their revenue in proportion to the increase of their expense. They are unwilling, for fear of offending the people, who by so great and so sudden an increase of taxes would soon be disgusted with the war; and they are unable, from not well knowing what taxes would be sufficient to produce the revenue wanted. The facility of borrowing delivers them from the embarrassment which this fear and inability would otherwise occasion. By means of borrowing they are enabled, with a very moderate increase of taxes, to raise, from year to year, money sufficient for carrying on the

war, and by the practice of perpetual funding they are enabled, with the smallest possible increase of taxes, to raise
annually the largest possible sum of money. In great empires
the people who live in the capital, and in the provinces remote
from the scene of action, feel, many of them, scarcely any inconvenience from the war, but enjoy, at their ease, the amusement of reading in the newspapers the exploits of their own
fleets and armies. To them this amusement compensates the
small difference between the taxes which they pay on account
of the war, and those which they had been accustomed to pay
in time of peace. They are commonly dissatisfied with the return of peace, which puts an end to their amusement and to
a thousand visionary hopes of conquest and national glory
from a longer continuance of the war.

The return of peace, indeed, seldom relieves them from the
greater part of the taxes imposed during the war. These are
mortgaged for the interest of the debt contracted in order to
carry it on. If, over and above paying the interest of this debt
and defraying the ordinary expense of government, the old
revenue together with the new taxes produce some surplus
revenue, it may perhaps be converted into a sinking fund for
paying off the debt. But, in the first place, this sinking fund,
even supposing it should be applied to no other purpose, is
generally altogether inadequate for paying, in the course of
any period during which it can reasonably be expected that
peace should continue, the whole debt contracted during the
war; and, in the second place, this fund is almost always applied to other purposes.

The new taxes were imposed for the sole purpose of paying
the interest of the money borrowed upon them. If they produce more, it is generally something which was neither intended nor expected, and is therefore seldom very considerable. Sinking funds have generally arisen not so much from
any surplus of the taxes which was over and above what was
necessary for paying the interest or annuity originally charged
upon them, as from a subsequent reduction of that interest.
That of Holland in 1655, and that of the Ecclesiastical State in

1685, were both formed in this manner. Hence the usual insufficiency of such funds.

During the most profound peace, various events occur which require an extraordinary expense, and government finds it always more convenient to defray this expense by misapplying the sinking fund than by imposing a new tax. Every new tax is immediately felt more or less by the people. It occasions always some murmur, and meets with some opposition. The more taxes may have been multiplied, the higher they may have been raised upon every different subject of taxation; the more loudly the people complain of every new tax, the more difficult it becomes either to find out new subjects of taxation, or to raise much higher the taxes already imposed upon the old. A momentary suspension of the payment of debt is not immediately felt by the people, and occasions neither murmur nor complaint. To borrow of the sinking fund is always an obvious and easy expedient for getting out of the present difficulty. The more the public debts may have been accumulated, the more necessary it may have become to study to reduce them; the more dangerous, the more ruinous it may be to misapply any part of the sinking fund, the less likely is the public debt to be reduced to any considerable degree; the more likely, the more certainly is the sinking fund to be misapplied toward defraying all the extraordinary expenses which occur in time of peace. When a nation is already overburdened with taxes, nothing but the necessities of a new war, nothing but either the animosity of national vengeance, or the anxiety for national security, can induce the people to submit with tolerable patience to a new tax. Hence the usual misapplication of the sinking fund.

In Great Britain, from the time that we had first recourse to the ruinous expedient of perpetual funding, the reduction of the public debt in time of peace has never borne any proportion to its accumulation in time of war. It was in the war which began in 1688, and was concluded by the treaty of Ryswick in 1697, that the foundation of the present enormous debt of Great Britain was first laid.

[Here again, we eliminate a few pages of particular details]

The public funds of the different indebted nations of
Europe, particularly those of England, have by one author
been represented as the accumulation of a great capital super-
added to the other capital of the country, by means of which
its trade is extended, its manufactures multiplied, and its
lands cultivated and improved much beyond what they could
have been by means of that other capital only.[6] He does not
consider that the capital which the first creditors of the public advanced to government was, from the moment in which
they advanced it, a certain portion of the annual produce
turned away from serving in the function of a capital, to serve
in that of a revenue; from maintaining productive laborers to
maintain unproductive ones, and to be spent and wasted, generally in the course of the year, without even the hope of any
future reproduction. In return for the capital which they advanced they obtained, indeed, an annuity in the public funds
in most cases of more than equal value. This annuity, no
doubt, replaced to them their capital and enabled them to
carry on their trade and business to the same or perhaps to a
greater extent than before; that is, they were enabled either
to borrow of other people a new capital upon the credit of
this annuity, or by selling it to get from other people a new
capital of their own, equal or superior to that which they
had advanced to government. This new capital, however,
which they in this manner either bought or borrowed of other
people, must have existed in the country before, and must
have been employed as all capitals are, in maintaining productive labor. When it came into the hands of those who had ad-

---

[6] [Garnier's note, *Recherches etc.*, tom. iv., p. 501, is "Pinto: *Traité de la
Circulation et du Crédit*," a work published in 1771 ("Amsterdam"), "par
l'auteur de l'essai sur le luxe," of which see esp. pp. 44, 45, 209-211. But
an English essay of 1731 to the same effect is quoted by Melon, *Essai
Politique sur le Commerce*, chap. xxiii., ed. of 1761, p. 296, and Melon
seems to be referred to below, pp. 281f. Cf. *Lectures*, p. 210.—C.]

vanced their money to government, though it was in some
respects a new capital to them, it was not so to the country,
but was only a capital withdrawn from certain employments
in order to be turned toward others. Though it replaced to
them what they had advanced to government, it did not replace it to the country. Had they not advanced this capital
to government, there would have been in the country two
capitals, two portions of the annual produce, instead of one,
employed in maintaining productive labor.

When for defraying the expense of government a revenue
is raised within the year from the produce of free or unmortgaged taxes, a certain portion of the revenue of private
people is only turned away from maintaining one species of
unproductive labor, toward maintaining another. Some part
of what they pay in those taxes might no doubt have been
accumulated into capital, and consequently employed in maintaining productive labor, but the greater part would probably
have been spent and consequently employed in maintaining
unproductive labor. The public expense, however, when defrayed in this manner, no doubt hinders more or less the
further accumulation of new capital; but it does not necessarily occasion the destruction of any actually existing capital.

When the public expense is defrayed by funding, it is defrayed by the annual destruction of some capital which had
before existed in the country, by the perversion of some portion of the annual produce which had before been destined
for the maintenance of productive labor, toward that of unproductive labor. As in this case, however, the taxes are lighter
than they would have been, had a revenue sufficient for defraying the same expense been raised within the year; the
private revenue of individuals is necessarily less burdened,
and consequently their ability to save and accumulate some
part of that revenue into capital is a good deal less impaired.
If the method of funding destroys more old capital, it at the
same time hinders less the accumulation or acquisition of new
capital than that of defraying the public expense by a revenue
raised within the year. Under the system of funding, the

frugality and industry of private people can more easily repair the breaches which the waste and extravagance of government may occasionally make in the general capital of the society.

It is only during the continuance of war, however, that the system of funding has this advantage over the other system. Were the expense of war to be defrayed always by a revenue raised within the year, the taxes from which that extraordinary revenue was drawn would last no longer than the year. The ability of private people to accumulate, though less during the war, would have been greater during the peace than under the system of funding. War would not necessarily have occasioned the destruction of any old capitals, and peace would have occasioned the accumulation of many more new. Wars would in general be more speedily concluded, and less wantonly undertaken. The people feeling, during the continuance of the war, the complete burden of it, would soon grow weary of it, and government, in order to humor them, would not be under the necessity of carrying it on longer than it was necessary to do so. The foresight of the heavy and unavoidable burdens of war would hinder the people from wantonly calling for it when there was no real or solid interest to fight for. The seasons during which the ability of private people to accumulate was somewhat impaired would occur more rarely, and be of shorter continuance. Those, on the contrary, during which that ability was in the highest vigor, would be of much longer duration than they can well be under the system of funding.

When funding, besides, has made a certain progress, the multiplication of taxes which it brings along with it sometimes impairs as much the ability of private people to accumulate even in time of peace, as the other system would in time of war. The peace revenue of Great Britain amounts at present to more than ten millions a year. If free and unmortgaged, it might be sufficient, with proper management and without contracting a shilling of new debt, to carry on the most vigorous war. The private revenue of the inhabitants of Great Britain is at present as much encumbered in time of peace, their ability to accumulate is as much impaired as it would have been in the time of the most expensive war, had the pernicious system of funding never been adopted.

In the payment of the interest of the public debt, it has been said, it is the right hand which pays the left. The money does not go out of the country. It is only a part of the revenue of one set of the inhabitants which is transferred to another, and the nation is not a farthing the poorer. This apology is founded altogether in the sophistry of the mercantile system, and after the long examination which I have already bestowed upon that system, it may perhaps be unnecessary to say anything further about it. It supposes, besides, that the whole public debt is owing to the inhabitants of the country, which happens not to be true; the Dutch, as well as several other foreign nations, having a very considerable share in our public funds. But though the whole debt were owing to the inhabitants of the country, it would not upon that account be less pernicious.

Land and capital stock are the two original sources of all revenue, both private and public. Capital stock pays the wages of productive labor, whether employed in agriculture, manufactures, or commerce. The management of those two original sources of revenue belongs to two different sets of people: the proprietors of land, and the owners or employers of capital stock.

The proprietor of land is interested for the sake of his own revenue to keep his estate in as good condition as he can, by building and repairing his tenants' houses, by making and maintaining the necessary drains and enclosures, and all those other expensive improvements which it properly belongs to the landlord to make and maintain. But by different land taxes the revenue of the landlord may be so much diminished; and by different duties upon the necessities and conveniences of life, that diminished revenue may be rendered of so little real value that he may find himself altogether unable to make or maintain those expensive improvements. When the landlord, however, ceases to do his part, it is altogether impossible that the tenant should continue to do his. As the distress of the landlord increases, the agriculture of the country must necessarily decline.

When, by different taxes upon the necessities and conveniences of life, the owners and employers of capital stock find that whatever revenue they derive from it will not, in a particular country, purchase the same quantity of those necessities and conveniences which an equal revenue would in almost any other, they will be disposed to remove to some other. And when, in order to raise those taxes, all or the greater part of merchants and manufacturers, that is, all or the greater part of the employers of great capitals, come to be continually exposed to the mortifying and vexatious visits of the taxgatherers, this disposition to remove will soon be changed into an actual removal. The industry of the country will necessarily fall with the removal of the capital which supported it, and the ruin of trade and manufactures will follow the declension of agriculture.

To transfer from the owners of those two great sources of revenue, land and capital stock, from the persons immediately interested in the good condition of every particular portion of land, and in the good management of every particular portion of capital stock, to another set of persons (the creditors of the public, who have no such particular interest), the greater part of the revenue arising from either must, in the long run, occasion both the neglect of land, and the waste or removal of capital stock. A creditor of the public has no doubt a general interest in the prosperity of the agriculture, manufactures, and commerce of the country, and consequently in the good condition of its lands and in the good management of its capital stock. Should there be any general failure or declension in any of these things, the produce of the different taxes might no longer be sufficient to pay him the annuity or interest which is due to him. But a creditor of the public, considered merely as such, has no interest in the good condition of any particular portion of land, or in the good management of any particular portion of capital stock. As a creditor of the public

he has no knowledge of any such particula. portion. He has
no inspection of it. He can have no care about it. Its ruin may
in some cases be unknown to him, and cannot directly affect
him.

The practice of funding has gradually enfeebled every state
which has adopted it. The Italian republics seem to have begun it. Genoa and Venice, the only two remaining which can
pretend to an independent existence, have both been enfeebled by it. Spain seems to have learned the practice from
the Italian republics, and (its taxes being probably less judicious than theirs) it has, in proportion to its natural strength,
been still more enfeebled. The debts of Spain are of very old
standing. It was deeply in debt before the end of the sixteenth
century, about a hundred years before England owed a shilling. France, notwithstanding all its natural resources, lan-
guishes under an oppressive load of the same kind. The republic of the United Provinces is as much enfeebled by its debts
as either Genoa or Venice. Is it likely that in Great Britain
alone a practice which has brought either weakness or desola-
tion into every other country should prove altogether innocent?

The system of taxation established in those different countries, it may be said, is inferior to that of England. I believe it
is so. But it ought to be remembered that when the wisest
government has exhausted all the proper subjects of taxation,
it must, in cases of urgent necessity, have recourse to improper
ones. The wise republic of Holland has upon some occasions
been obliged to have recourse to taxes as inconvenient as the
greater part of those of Spain. Another war begun before any
considerable liberation of the public revenue had been
brought about, and growing in its progress as expensive as
the last war, may, from irresistible necessity, render the British
system of taxation as oppressive as that of Holland, or even
as that of Spain. To the honor of our present system of taxation, indeed, it has hitherto given so little embarrassment to
industry that, during the course even of the most expensive
wars, the frugality and good conduct of individuals seem to

have been able, by saving and accumulation, to repair all the breaches which the waste and extravagance of government had made in the general capital of the society. At the conclusion of the late war, the most expensive that Great Britain ever waged, her agriculture was as flourishing, her manufacturers as numerous and as fully employed, and her commerce as extensive, as they had ever been before. The capital, therefore, which supported all those different branches of industry, must have been equal to what it had ever been before. Since the peace, agriculture has been still further improved, the rents of houses have risen in every town and village of the country, a proof of the increasing wealth and revenue of the people; and the annual amount of the greater part of the old taxes, of the principal branches of the excise and customs in particular, has been continually increasing—an equally clear proof of an increasing consumption, and consequently of an increasing produce which could alone support that consumption. Great Britain seems to support with ease a burden which, half a century ago, nobody believed her capable of supporting. Let us not, however, upon this account, rashly conclude that she is capable of supporting any burden; nor even be too confident that she could support, without great distress, a burden a little greater than what has already been laid upon her.

When national debts have once been accumulated to a certain degree, there is scarcely, I believe, a single instance of their having been fairly and completely paid. The liberation of the public revenue, if it has ever been brought about at all, has always been brought about by a bankruptcy; sometimes by an avowed one, but always by a real one, though frequently by a pretended payment.

The raising of the denomination of the coin has been the most usual expedient by which a real public bankruptcy has been disguised under the appearance of a pretended payment. If a sixpence, for example, should either by act of Parliament or royal proclamation be raised to the denomination of a shilling, and twenty sixpences to that of a pound sterling, the person who under the old denomination had borrowed twenty shillings, or near four ounces of silver, would, under the new, pay with twenty sixpences, or with something less than two ounces. A national debt of about a hundred and twenty-eight millions, nearly the capital of the funded and unfunded debt of Great Britain, might in this manner be paid with about sixty-four millions of our present money. It would indeed be a pretended payment only, and the creditors of the public would really be defrauded of ten shillings in the pound of what was due to them. The calamity, too, would extend much further than to the creditors of the public, and those of every private person would suffer a proportionable loss; and this without any advantage, but in most cases with a great additional loss to the creditors of the public. If the creditors of the public indeed were generally much in debt to other people, they might in some measure compensate their loss by paying their creditors in the same coin in which the public had paid them. But in most countries the creditors of the public are, the greater part of them, wealthy people, who stand more in the relation of creditors than in that of debtors toward the rest of their fellow citizens. A pretended payment of this kind, therefore, instead of alleviating, aggravates in most cases the loss of the creditors of the public; and, without any advantage to the public, extends the calamity to a great number of other innocent people. It occasions a general and most pernicious subversion of the fortunes of private people, enriching in most cases the idle and profuse debtor at the expense of the industrious and frugal creditor, and transporting a great part of the national capital from the hands which were likely to increase and improve it to those which are likely to dissipate and destroy it. When it becomes necessary for a state to declare itself bankrupt, in the same manner as when it becomes necessary for an individual to do so, a fair, open, and avowed bankruptcy is always the measure which is both least dishonorable to the debtor, and least hurtful to the creditor. The honor of a state is surely very poorly provided for when, in order to cover the disgrace of a real bankruptcy, it has recourse to a juggling trick of this kind, so easily seen through, and at the same time so extremely pernicious.

Almost all states, however, ancient as well as modern, when reduced to this necessity, have, upon some occasions, played this very juggling trick. The Romans, at the end of the first Punic war, reduced the *as,* the coin or denomination by which they computed the value of all their other coins, from containing twelve ounces of copper to contain only two ounces, that is, they raised two ounces of copper to a denomination which had always before expressed the value of twelve ounces. The republic was, in this manner, enabled to pay the great debts which it had contracted with the sixth part of what it really owed. So sudden and so great a bankruptcy, we should in the present times be apt to imagine, must have occasioned a very violent popular clamor. It does not appear to have occasioned any. The law which enacted it was, like all other laws relating to the coin, introduced and carried through the assembly of the people by a tribune, and was probably a very popular law. In Rome, as in all the other ancient republics, the poor people were constantly in debt to the rich and the great, who, in order to secure their votes at the annual elections, used to lend them money at exorbitant interest, which, being never paid, soon accumulated into a sum too great either for the debtor to pay, or for anybody else to pay for him. The debtor, for fear of a very severe execution, was obliged, without any further gratuity, to vote for the candidate whom the creditor recommended. In spite of all the laws against bribery and corruption, the bounty of the candidates, together with the occasional distributions of corn which were ordered by the senate, were the principal funds from which, during the latter times of the Roman republic, the poorer citizens derived their subsistence. To deliver themselves from this subjection to their creditors, the poorer citizens were continually calling out either for an entire abolition of debts, or for what they called "New Tables," that is, for a law which should entitle them to a complete acquittance, upon paying only a certain proportion of their accumulated debts. The law which reduced the coin of all denominations to a sixth part of its former value, as it enabled them to pay their debts with a sixth part of what they really owed, was equivalent to the most advantageous new tables. In order to satisfy the people, the rich and the great were, upon several different occasions, obliged to consent to laws both for abolishing debts, and for introducing new tables; and they probably were induced to consent to this law, partly for the same reason, and partly that, by liberating the public revenue, they might restore vigor to that government of which they themselves had the principal direction. An operation of this kind would at once reduce a debt of a hundred and twenty-eight millions to twenty-one millions three hundred and thirty-three thousand three hundred and thirty-three pounds six shillings and eightpence. In the course of the second Punic war the *as* was still further reduced, first, from two ounces of copper to one ounce; and afterwards from one ounce to half an ounce, that is, to the twenty-fourth part of its original value.[7] By combining the three Roman operations into one, a debt of a hundred and twenty-eight millions of our present money might in this manner be reduced all at once to a debt of five millions three hundred and thirty-three thousand three hundred and thirty-three pounds six shillings and eightpence. Even the enormous debt of Great Britain might in this manner soon be paid.

By means of such expedients the coin of, I believe, all nations has been gradually reduced more and more below its original value, and the same nominal sum has been gradually brought to contain a smaller and a smaller quantity of silver.

Nations have sometimes, for the same purpose, adulterated the standard of their coin, that is, have mixed a greater quantity of alloy in it. If in the pound weight of our silver coin, for example, instead of eighteen pennyweight, according to the present standard, there was mixed eight ounces of alloy; a pound sterling, or twenty shillings of such coin, would be

[7] [This chapter of Roman history is based on a few sentences in Pliny, *H.N.*, lib. xxxiii., cap. iii. Modern criticism has discovered the facts to be not nearly so simple as they are represented in the text.—C.]

worth little more than six shillings and eightpence of our present money. The quantity of silver contained in six shillings and eightpence of our present money would thus be raised very nearly to the denomination of a pound sterling. The adulteration of the standard has exactly the same effect with what the French call an augmentation, or a direct raising of the denomination of the coin.

An augmentation, or a direct raising of the denomination of the coin, always is, and from its nature must be, an open and avowed operation. By means of it pieces of a smaller weight and bulk are called by the same name which had before been given to pieces of a greater weight and bulk. The adulteration of the standard, on the contrary, has generally been a concealed operation. By means of it pieces were issued from the mint of the same denominations, and, as nearly as could be contrived, of the same weight, bulk, and appearance, with pieces which had been current before of much greater value. When King John of France, in order to pay his debts, adulterated his coin, all the officers of his mint were sworn to secrecy. Both operations are unjust. But a simple augmentation is an injustice of open violence; whereas an adulteration is an injustice of treacherous fraud. This latter operation, therefore, as soon as it has been discovered, and it could never be concealed very long, has always excited much greater indignation than the former. The coin after any considerable augmentation has very seldom been brought back to its former weight; but after the greatest adulterations it has almost always been brought back to its former fineness. It has scarcely ever happened that the fury and indignation of the people could otherwise be appeased.

In the end of the reign of Henry VIII and in the beginning of that of Edward VI, the English coin was not only raised in its denomination, but adulterated in its standard. The like frauds were practiced in Scotland during the minority of James VI. They have occasionally been practiced in most other countries.

That the public revenue of Great Britain can ever be completely liberated, or even that any considerable progress can ever be made toward that liberation, while the surplus of that revenue, or what is over and above defraying the annual expense of the peace establishment, is so very small, it seems altogether in vain to expect. That liberation, it is evident, can never be brought about without either some very considerable augmentation of the public revenue, or some equally considerable reduction of the public expense.

A more equal land tax, a more equal tax upon the rent of houses, and such alterations in the present system of customs and excise as those which have been mentioned in the foregoing chapter might, perhaps, without increasing the burden of the greater part of the people, but only distributing the weight of it more equally upon the whole, produce a considerable augmentation of revenue. The most sanguine projector, however, could scarcely flatter himself that any augmentation of this kind would be such as could give any reasonable hopes, either of liberating the public revenue altogether, or even of making such progress toward that liberation in time of peace, as either to prevent or to compensate the further accumulation of the public debt in the next war.

By extending the British system of taxation to all the different provinces of the Empire inhabited by people of either British or European extraction, a much greater augmentation of revenue might be expected. This, however, could scarcely, perhaps, be done consistently with the principles of the British constitution, without admitting into the British Parliament, or, if you will, into the states-general of the British Empire, a fair and equal representation of all those different provinces, that of each province bearing the same proportion to the produce of its taxes as the representation of Great Britain might bear to the produce of the taxes levied upon Great Britain. The private interest of many powerful individuals, the confirmed prejudices of great bodies of people seem, indeed, at present, to oppose to so great a change such obstacles as it may be very difficult, perhaps altogether impossible, to surmount. Without, however, pretending to determine whether such a union be practicable or impracticable, it may not, perhaps, be improper in a speculative work of this kind, to consider how far the British system of taxation might be applicable to all the different provinces of the empire; what revenue might be expected from it if so applied, and in what manner a general union of this kind might be likely to affect the happiness and prosperity of the different provinces comprehended within it. Such a speculation can at worst be regarded but as a new Utopia, less amusing certainly, but not more useless and chimerical than the old one.

The land tax, the stamp duties, and the different duties of customs and excise constitute the four principal branches of the British taxes.

Ireland is certainly as able, and our American and West Indian plantations more able, to pay a land tax than Great Britain. Where the landlord is subject neither to tithe nor poors rate, he must certainly be more able to pay such a tax, than where he is subject to both those other burdens. The tithe, where there is no modus and where it is levied in kind, diminishes more what would otherwise be the rent of the landlord than a land tax which really amounted to five shillings in the pound. Such a tithe will be found in most cases to amount to more than a fourth part of the real rent of the land, or of what remains after replacing completely the capital of the farmer, together with his reasonable profit. If all moduses and all impropriations [8] were taken away, the complete church tithe of Great Britain and Ireland could not well be estimated at less than six or seven millions. If there was no tithe either in Great Britain or Ireland, the landlords could afford to pay six or seven millions additional land tax without being more burdened than a very great part of them are at present. America pays no tithe, and could therefore very well afford to pay a land tax. The lands in America and the

8 ["Impropriation" is a term in English ecclesiastical law, referring to a right to tithes owned by a layman. "Modus" refers to a peculiar manner of tithing, growing out of custom, which involves a reduction of the tithe.—M.]

West Indies, indeed, are in general not tenanted nor leased out to farmers. They could not therefore be assessed according to any rent-roll. But neither were the lands of Great Britain, in the 4th of William and Mary, assessed according to any rent-roll, but according to a very loose and inaccurate estimation. The lands in America might be assessed either in the same manner, or according to an equitable valuation in consequence of an accurate survey, like that which was lately made in the Milanese, and in the dominions of Austria, Prussia, and Sardinia.

Stamp duties, it is evident, might be levied without any variation in all countries where the forms of law process, and the deeds by which property both real and personal is transferred, are the same or nearly the same.

The extension of the customhouse laws of Great Britain to Ireland and the plantations, provided it was accompanied, as in justice it ought to be, with an extension of the freedom of trade, would be in the highest degree advantageous to both. All the invidious restraints which at present oppress the trade of Ireland, the distinction between the enumerated and non-enumerated commodities of America, would be entirely at an end. The countries north of Cape Finisterre would be as open to every part of the produce of America as those south of that Cape are to some parts of that produce at present. The trade between all the different parts of the British empire would, in consequence of this uniformity in the customhouse laws, be as free as the coasting trade of Great Britain is at present. The British empire would thus afford within itself an immense internal market for every part of the produce of all its different provinces. So great an extension of market would soon compensate both to Ireland and the plantations all that they could suffer from the increase of the duties of customs.

The excise is the only part of the British system of taxation which would require to be varied in any respect according as it was applied to the different provinces of the empire. It might be applied to Ireland without any variation, the produce and consumption of that kingdom being exactly of the same nature with those of Great Britain. In its application to America and the West Indies, of which the produce and consumption are so very different from those of Great Britain, some modification might be necessary, in the same manner as in its application to the cider and beer counties of England.

A fermented liquor, for example, which is called beer, but which, as it is made of molasses, bears very little resemblance to our beer, makes a considerable part of the common drink of the people in America. This liquor, as it can be kept only for a few days, cannot, like our beer, be prepared and stored up for sale in great breweries; but every private family must brew it for their own use, in the same manner as they cook their victuals. But to subject every private family to the odious visits and examination of the taxgatherers, in the same manner as we subject the keepers of alehouses and the brewers for public sale, would be altogether inconsistent with liberty. If for the sake of equality it was thought necessary to lay a tax upon this liquor, it might be taxed by taxing the material of which it is made, either at the place of manufacture, or, if the circumstances of the trade rendered such an excise improper, by laying a duty upon its importation into the colony in which it was to be consumed. Besides the duty of one penny a gallon imposed by the British Parliament upon the importation of molasses into America, there is a provincial tax of this kind upon their importation into Massachusetts Bay, in ships belonging to any other colony, of eightpence the hogshead; and another upon their importation from the northern colonies into South Carolina, of fivepence the gallon. Or if neither of these methods was found convenient, each family might compound for its consumption of this liquor, either according to the number of persons of which it consisted, in the same manner as private families compound for the malt tax in England; or according to the different ages and sexes of those persons, in the same manner as several different taxes are levied in Holland; or nearly as Sir Matthew Decker proposes that all taxes upon consumable commodities should be levied in England. This mode of taxation, it has already been observed, when applied to objects of a speedy consumption, is not a very convenient one. It might be adopted, however, in cases where no better could be done.

Sugar, rum, and tobacco are commodities which are nowhere necessities of life, which have become objects of almost universal consumption, and which are therefore extremely proper subjects of taxation. If a union with the colonies were to take place, those commodities might be taxed either before they go out of the hands of the manufacturer or grower, or, if this mode of taxation did not suit the circumstances of those persons, they might be deposited in public warehouses both at the place of manufacture, and at all the different ports of the empire to which they might afterwards be transported, to remain there, under the joint custody of the owner and the revenue officer, till such time as they should be delivered out either to the consumer, to the merchant retailer for home consumption, or to the merchant exporter, the tax not to be advanced till such delivery. When delivered out for exportation, to go duty free, upon proper security being given that they should really be exported out of the empire. These are perhaps the principal commodities with regard to which a union with the colonies might require some considerable change in the present system of British taxation.

What might be the amount of the revenue which this system of taxation extended to all the different provinces of the empire might produce, it must, no doubt, be altogether impossible to ascertain with tolerable exactness. By means of this system there is annually levied in Great Britain, upon less than eight millions of people, more than ten millions of revenue. Ireland contains more than two millions of people, and according to the accounts laid before the congress, the twelve associated provinces of America contain more than three. Those accounts, however, may have been exaggerated, in order, perhaps, either to encourage their own people, or to intimidate those of this country, and we shall suppose therefore that our North American and West Indian colonies taken together contain no more than three millions, or that the whole British empire, in Europe and America, contains no more than thirteen millions of inhabitants. If upon less than eight millions of inhabitants this system of taxation raises a revenue of more than ten millions sterling, it ought upon thirteen millions of inhabitants to raise a revenue of more than sixteen millions two hundred and fifty thousand pounds sterling. From this revenue, supposing that this system could produce it, must be deducted the revenue usually raised in Ireland and the plantations for defraying the expense of their respective civil governments. The expense of the civil and military establishment of Ireland, together with the interest of the public debt, amounts, at a medium of the two years which ended March 1775, to something less than seven hundred and fifty thousand pounds a year. By a very exact account of the revenue of the principal colonies of America and the West Indies, it amounted, before the commencement of the present disturbances, to a hundred and forty-one thousand eight hundred pounds. In this account, however, the revenue of Maryland, of North Carolina, and of all our late acquisitions both upon the continent and in the islands is omitted, which may perhaps make a difference of thirty or forty thousand pounds. For the sake of even numbers therefore, let us suppose that the revenue necessary for supporting the civil government of Ireland and the plantations may amount to a million. There would remain consequently a revenue of fifteen millions two hundred and fifty thousand pounds, to be applied toward defraying the general expense of the empire, and toward paying the public debt. But if from the present revenue of Great Britain a million could in peaceable times be spared toward the payment of that debt, six millions two hundred and fifty thousand pounds could very well be spared from this improved revenue. This great sinking fund, too, might be augmented every year by the interest of the debt which had been discharged the year before, and might in this manner increase so very rapidly as to be sufficient in a few years to discharge the whole debt, and thus to restore completely the at present debilitated and languishing vigor of the empire. In the meantime the people might be relieved from some of the most burdensome taxes, from those which are imposed either upon the necessities of life, or upon the materials of manufacture. The laboring poor would thus be enabled to live better, to work cheaper, and to send their goods cheaper to market. The cheapness of their goods would increase the demand for them, and consequently for the labor of those who produced them. This increase in the demand for labor would both increase the numbers and improve the circumstances of the laboring poor. Their consumption would increase, and together with it the revenue arising from all those articles of their consumption upon which the taxes might be allowed to remain.

The revenue arising from this system of taxation, however, might not immediately increase in proportion to the number of people who were subjected to it. Great indulgence would for some time be due to those provinces of the empire which were thus subjected to burdens to which they had not before been accustomed, and even when the same taxes came to be levied everywhere as exactly as possible, they would not everywhere produce a revenue proportioned to the numbers of the people. In a poor country the consumption of the principal commodities subject to the duties of customs and excise is very small, and in a thinly inhabited country the opportunities of smuggling are very great. The consumption of malt liquors among the inferior ranks of people in Scotland is very small, and the excise upon malt, beer, and ale produces less there than in England in proportion to the numbers of the people and the rate of the duties, which upon malt is different on account of a supposed difference of quality. In these particular branches of the excise, there is not, I apprehend, much more smuggling in the one country than in the other. The duties upon the distillery, and the greater part of the duties of customs, in proportion to the numbers of people in the respective countries, produce less in Scotland than in England, not only on account of the smaller consumption of the taxed commodities, but of the much greater facility of smuggling. In Ireland, the inferior ranks of people are still poorer than in Scotland, and many parts of the country are almost as thinly inhabited. In Ireland, therefore, the consumption of the taxed commodities might, in proportion to the number of the people, be still less than in Scotland, and the facility of smuggling nearly the same. In America and the West Indies the white people even of the lowest rank are in much better circumstances than those of the same rank in England, and their consumption of all the luxuries in which they usually indulge themselves is probably much greater. The blacks, indeed, who make the greater part of the inhabitants both of the southern colonies upon the continent and of the West Indian islands, as they are in a state of slavery, are, no doubt, in a worse condition than the poorest people either in Scotland or Ireland. We must not, however, upon that account, imagine that they are worse fed, or that their consumption of articles which might be subjected to moderate duties is less than that even of the lower ranks of people in England. In order that they may work well, it is the interest of their master that they should be fed well and kept in good heart, in the same manner as it is his interest that his working cattle should be so. The blacks accordingly have almost everywhere their allowance of rum and of molasses or spruce beer, in the same manner as the white servants; and this allowance would not probably be withdrawn, though those articles should be subjected to moderate duties. The consumption of the taxed commodities, therefore, in proportion to the number of inhabitants, would probably be as great in America and the West Indies as in any part of the British empire. The opportunities of smuggling, indeed, would be much greater; America, in proportion to the extent of the country, being much more thinly inhabited than either Scotland or Ireland. If the revenue, however, which is at present raised by the different duties upon malt and malt liquors, were to be levied by a single duty upon malt, the opportunity of smuggling in the most important branch of the excise would be almost entirely taken away: And if the duties of customs, instead of being imposed upon almost all the different articles of importation, were confined to a few of the most general use and consumption, and if the levying of those duties were subjected to the excise laws, the opportunity of smuggling, though not so entirely taken away, would be very much diminished. In consequence of those two apparently very simple and easy alterations, the duties of customs and excise might probably produce a revenue as great in proportion to the consumption of the most thinly inhabited province as they do at present in proportion to that of the most populous.

The Americans, it has been said, indeed, have no gold or silver money, the interior commerce of the country being carried on by a paper currency, and the gold and silver which occasionally come among them being all sent to Great Britain in return for the commodities which they receive from us. But without gold and silver, it is added, there is no possibility of paying taxes. We already get all the gold and silver which they have. How is it possible to draw from them what they have not?

The present scarcity of gold and silver money in America is not the effect of the poverty of that country, or of the inability of the people there to purchase those metals. In a country where the wages of labor are so much higher, and the price of provisions so much lower, than in England, the greater part of the people must surely have wherewithal to purchase a greater quantity, if it were either necessary or convenient for them to do so. The scarcity of those metals, therefore, must be the effect of choice, and not of necessity.

It is for transacting either domestic or foreign business that gold and silver money is either necessary or convenient.

The domestic business of every country, it has been shown in the second book of this *Inquiry*, may, at least in peaceable times, be transacted by means of a paper currency, with nearly the same degree of convenience as by gold and silver money. It is convenient for the Americans, who could always employ with profit in the improvement of their lands a greater stock than they can easily get, to save as much as possible the expense of so costly an instrument of commerce as gold and silver, and rather to employ that part of their surplus produce which would be necessary for purchasing those metals, in purchasing the instruments of trade, the materials of clothing, several parts of household furniture, and the ironwork necessary for building and extending their settlements and plantations; in purchasing, not dead stock, but active and productive stock. The colony governments find it for their interest to supply the people with such a quantity of paper money as is fully sufficient and generally more than sufficient for transacting their domestic business. Some of those governments, that of Pennsylvania particularly, derive a revenue from lending this paper money to their subjects at an interest of so much per cent. Others, like that of Massachusetts Bay, advance upon extraordinary emergencies a paper money of this kind for defraying the public expense, and afterwards, when it suits the convenience of the colony, redeem it at the depreciated value to which it gradually falls. In 1747 [9] that colony paid, in this manner, the greater part of its public debts, with the tenth part of the money for which its bills had been granted. It suits the convenience of the planters to save the expense of employing gold and silver money in their domestic transactions; and it suits the convenience of the colonial governments to supply them with a medium which, though attended with some very considerable disadvantages, enables them to save that expense. The redundancy of paper money necessarily banishes gold and silver from the domestic transactions of the colonies, for the same reason that it has banished those metals from the greater part of the domestic transactions in Scotland; and in both countries it is not the poverty, but the enterprising and projecting spirit of the people, their desire of employing all the stock which they can get as active and productive stock which has occasioned this redundancy of paper money.

[9] See Hutchinson's Hist. of Massachusett's Bay, Vol. II., page 436 & seq. [*History of the Colony of Massachusetts Bay*, 2nd ed., 1765-8.—C.]

In the exterior commerce which the different colonies carry on with Great Britain, gold and silver are more or less employed exactly in proportion as they are more or less necessary. Where those metals are not necessary, they seldom appear. Where they are necessary, they are generally found.

In the commerce between Great Britain and the tobacco colonies, the British goods are generally advanced to the colonists at a pretty long credit, and are afterwards paid for in tobacco, rated at a certain price. It is more convenient for the colonists to pay in tobacco than in gold and silver. It would be more convenient for any merchant to pay for the goods which his correspondents had sold to him in some other sort of goods which he might happen to deal in, than in money. Such a merchant would have no occasion to keep any part of his stock by him unemployed and in ready money for answering occasional demands. He could have, at all times, a larger quantity of goods in his shop or warehouse, and he could deal to a greater extent. But it seldom happens to be convenient for all the correspondents of a merchant to receive payment for the goods which they sell to him, in goods of some other kind which he happens to deal in. The British merchants who trade to Virginia and Maryland happen to be a particular set of correspondents, to whom it is more convenient to receive payment for the goods which they sell to those colonies in tobacco than in gold and silver. They expect to make a profit by the sale of the tobacco. They could make none by that of the gold and silver. Gold and silver, therefore, very seldom appear in the commerce between Great Britain and the tobacco colonies. Maryland and Virginia have as little occasion for those metals in their foreign as in their domestic commerce. They are said, accordingly, to have less gold and silver money than any other colonies in America. They are reckoned, however, as thriving, and consequently as rich as any of their neighbors.

In the northern colonies, Pennsylvania, New York, New Jersey, the four governments of New England, etc., the value of their own produce which they export to Great Britain is not equal to that of the manufactures which they import for their own use, and for that of some of the other colonies to which they are the carriers. A balance, therefore, must be paid to the mother country in gold and silver, and this balance they generally find.

In the sugar colonies the value of the produce annually exported to Great Britain is much greater than that of all the goods imported from thence. If the sugar and rum annually sent to the mother country were paid for in those colonies, Great Britain would be obliged to send out every year a very large balance in money, and the trade to the West Indies would, by a certain species of politicians, be considered as extremely disadvantageous. But it so happens that many of the principal proprietors of the sugar plantations reside in Great Britain. Their rents are remitted to them in sugar and rum, the produce of their estates. The sugar and rum which the West Indian merchants purchase in those colonies upon their own account, are not equal in value to the goods which they annually sell there. A balance therefore must necessarily be paid to them in gold and silver, and this balance too is generally found.

The difficulty and irregularity of payment from the different colonies to Great Britain have not been at all in proportion to the greatness or smallness of the balances which were respectively due from them. Payments have in general been more regular from the northern than from the tobacco colonies, though the former have generally paid a pretty large balance in money, while the latter have either paid no balance, or a much smaller one. The difficulty of getting payment from our different sugar colonies has been greater or less in proportion, not so much to the extent of the balances respectively due from them, as to the quantity of uncultivated land which they contained; that is, to the greater or smaller temptation which the planters have been under of overtrading, or of undertaking the settlement and plantation of greater quantities of wasteland than suited the extent of their capitals. The returns from the great island of Jamaica, where there is still much uncultivated land, have, upon this account, been in general more irregular and uncertain than those from the smaller islands of Barbados, Antigua, and St. Christopher, which have for these many years been completely cultivated, and have, upon that account, afforded less field for the speculations of the planter. The new acquisitions of Grenada, Tobago, St. Vincent, and Dominica have opened a new field for speculations of this kind; and the returns from those islands have of late been as irregular and uncertain as those from the great island of Jamaica.

It is not, therefore, the poverty of the colonies which occasions, in the greater part of them, the present scarcity of gold and silver money. Their great demand for active and productive stock makes it convenient for them to have as little dead stock as possible, and disposes them upon that account to content themselves with a cheaper, though less commodious, instrument of commerce than gold and silver. They are thereby enabled to convert the value of that gold and silver into the instruments of trade, into the materials of clothing, into household furniture, and into the iron work necessary for building and extending their settlements and plantations. In those branches of business which cannot be transacted without gold and silver money, it appears that they can always find the necessary quantity of those metals; and if they frequently do not find it, their failure is generally the effect, not of their necessary poverty, but of their unnecessary and excessive enterprise. It is not because they are poor that their payments are irregular and uncertain, but because they are too eager to become excessively rich. Though all that part of the produce of the colonial taxes, which was over and above what was necessary for defraying the expense of their own civil and military establishments, were to be remitted to Great Britain in gold and silver, the colonies have abundantly wherewithal to purchase the requisite quantity of those metals. They would in this case be obliged, indeed, to exchange a part of their surplus produce, with which they now purchase active and productive stock, for dead stock. In transacting their domestic business they would be obliged to employ a costly instead of a cheap instrument of commerce; and the expense of purchasing this costly instrument might damp somewhat the vivacity and ardor of their excessive enterprise in the improvement of land. It might not, however, be necessary to remit any part of the American revenue in gold and silver. It might be remitted in bills drawn upon and accepted by particular merchants or companies in Great Britain, to whom a part of the surplus produce of America has been consigned, who would pay into the treasury the American revenue in money, after having themselves received the value of it in goods; and the whole business might frequently be transacted without exporting a single ounce of gold or silver from America.

It is not contrary to justice that both Ireland and America should contribute toward the discharge of the public debt of Great Britain. That debt has been contracted in support of the government established by the Revolution,[10] a government to which the Protestants of Ireland owe, not only the whole authority which they at present enjoy in their own country, but every security which they possess for their liberty, their property, and their religion; a government to which several of the colonies of America owe their present charters, and consequently their present constitution, and to which all the colonies of America owe the liberty, security, and property which they have ever since enjoyed. That public debt has been contracted in the defense, not of Great Britain alone, but of all the different provinces of the empire; the immense debt contracted in the late war in particular, and a great part of that contracted in the war before, were both properly contracted in defense of America.

By a union with Great Britain, Ireland would gain, besides the freedom of trade, other advantages much more important, and which would much more than compensate any increase of taxes that might accompany that union. By the union with

10 [Smith is referring here to the English Revolution of 1688-89, the "Glorious Revolution."—M.]

England, the middling and inferior ranks of people in Scotland gained a complete deliverance from the power of an aristocracy which had always before oppressed them. By a union with Great Britain, the greater part of the people of all ranks in Ireland would gain an equally complete deliverance from a much more oppressive aristocracy—an aristocracy not founded, like that of Scotland, in the natural and respectable distinctions of birth and fortune, but in the most odious of all distinctions, those of religious and political prejudices, distinctions which, more than any other, animate both the insolence of the oppressors and the hatred and indignation of the oppressed, and which commonly render the inhabitants of the same country more hostile to one another than those of different countries ever are. Without a union with Great Britain, the inhabitants of Ireland are not likely for many ages to consider themselves as one people.

No oppressive aristocracy has ever prevailed in the colonies. Even they, however, would, in point of happiness and tranquillity, gain considerably by a union with Great Britain. It would, at least, deliver them from those rancorous and virulent factions which are inseparable from small democracies, and which have so frequently divided the affections of their people and disturbed the tranquillity of their governments, in their form so nearly democratical. In the case of a total separation from Great Britain, which, unless prevented by a union of this kind, seems very likely to take place, those factions would be ten times more virulent than ever. Before the commencement of the present disturbances, the coercive power of the mother country had always been able to restrain those factions from breaking out into anything worse than gross brutality and insult. If that coercive power were entirely taken away, they would probably soon break out into open violence and bloodshed. In all great countries which are united under one uniform government, the spirit of party commonly prevails less in the remote provinces than in the center of the empire. The distance of those provinces from the capital, from the principal seat of the great scramble of faction and ambition, makes them enter less into the views of any of the contending parties, and renders them more indifferent and impartial spectators of the conduct of all. The spirit of party prevails less in Scotland than in England. In the case of a union it would probably prevail less in Ireland than in Scotland, and the colonies would probably soon enjoy a degree of concord and unanimity at present unknown in any part of the British empire. Both Ireland and the colonies, indeed, would be subjected to heavier taxes than any which they at present pay. In consequence, however, of a diligent and faithful application of the public revenue toward the discharge of the national debt, the greater part of those taxes might not be of long continuance, and the public revenue of Great Britain might soon be reduced to what was necessary for maintaining a moderate peace establishment.

The territorial acquisitions of the East India Company, the undoubted right of the crown, that is, of the state and people of Great Britain, might be rendered another source of revenue more abundant, perhaps, than all those already mentioned. Those countries are represented as more fertile, more extensive, and, in proportion to their extent, much richer and more populous than Great Britain. In order to draw a great revenue from them, it would not probably be necessary to introduce any new system of taxation into countries which are already sufficiently and more than sufficiently taxed. It might, perhaps, be more proper to lighten, than to aggravate, the burden of those unfortunate countries, and to endeavor to draw a revenue from them, not by imposing new taxes, but by preventing the embezzlement and misapplication of the greater part of those which they already pay.

If it should be found impracticable for Great Britain to draw any considerable augmentation of revenue from any of the resources above mentioned, the only resource which can remain to her is a diminution of her expense. In the mode of collecting, and in that of expending, the public revenue, though in both there may be still room for improvement, Great Britain seems to be at least as economical as any of her neighbors. The military establishment which she maintains for her own defense in time of peace is more moderate than that of any European state which can pretend to rival her either in wealth or in power. None of those articles, therefore, seem to admit of any considerable reduction of expense. The expense of the peace establishment of the colonies was, before the commencement of the present disturbances, very considerable, and is an expense which may, and if no revenue can be drawn from them, ought certainly to be saved altogether. This constant expense in time of peace, though very great, is insignificant in comparison with what the defense of the colonies has cost us in time of war. The last war, which was undertaken altogether on account of the colonies, cost Great Britain, it has already been observed, upwards of ninety millions. The Spanish war of 1739 was principally undertaken on their account, in which, and in the French war that was the consequence of it, Great Britain spent upwards of forty millions, a great part of which ought justly to be charged to the colonies. In those two wars the colonies cost Great Britain much more than double the sum which the national debt amounted to before the commencement of the first of them. Had it not been for those wars that debt might, and probably would by this time, have been completely paid; and had it ot been for the colonies, the former of those wars might not, and the latter certainly would not, have been undertaken. It was because the colonies were supposed to be provinces of the British empire that this expense was laid out upon them. But countries which contribute neither revenue nor military force towards the support of the empire cannot be considered as provinces. They may perhaps be considered as appendages, as a sort of splendid and showy equipage of the empire. But if the empire can no longer support the expense of keeping up this equipage, it ought certainly to lay it down; and if it cannot raise its revenue in proportion to its expense, it ought, at least, to accommodate its expense to its revenue. If the colonies, notwithstanding their refusal to submit to British taxes, are still to be considered as provinces of the British empire, their defense in some future war may cost Great Britain as great an expense as it ever has done in any former war. The rulers of Great Britain have, for more than a century past, amused the people with the imagination that they possessed a great empire on the west side of the Atlantic. This empire, however, has hitherto existed in imagination only. It has hitherto been not an empire, but the project of an empire; not a gold mine, but the project of a gold mine—a project which has cost, which continues to cost, and which, if pursued in the same way as it has been hitherto, is likely to cost immense expense, without being likely to bring any profit; for the effects of the monopoly of the colonial trade, it has been shown, are, to the great body of the people, mere loss instead of profit. It is surely now time that our rulers should either realize this golden dream in which they have been indulging themselves, perhaps, as well as the people, or, that they should awake from it themselves, and endeavor to awaken the people. If the project cannot be completed, it ought to be given up. If any of the provinces of the British empire cannot be made to contribute toward the support of the whole empire, it is surely time that Great Britain should free herself from the expense of defending those provinces in time of war, and of supporting any part of their civil or military establishments in time of peace, and endeavor to accommodate her future views and designs to the real mediocrity of her circumstances.

BIOGRAPHICAL INDEX

ARBUTHNOT, JOHN (1667-1735): British physician and writer, a friend of Swift and Pope. He wrote on mathematical subjects and contributed to the writings of the Scriblerus Club.

BLACK, JOSEPH (1728-1799): British chemist who discovered the principle of latent heat, thereby probably affecting James Watt's work on the steam engine.

BLACKSTONE, SIR WILLIAM (1723-1780): Famous English jurist. His *Commentaries on the Laws of England* were influential in both British and American thought.

CANTILLON, RICHARD (c. 1680-1734): Banker and economist; born in Ireland and died in England. His most noted work was *Essay on the Nature of Commerce in General*.

COLBERT, JEAN BAPTISTE (1619-1683): French statesman who served as finance minister under Louis XIV. A Mercantilist in his thinking.

DAVENANT, CHARLES (1656-1714): English economist who wrote numerous essays dealing with money, public revenues, and the balance of trade.

DU PONT DE NEMOURS, PIERRE SAMUEL (1739-1817): A mem-

ber of the Physiocratic School. His book, called *Physiocratie*, gave the sect its name, i.e., "government by nature." During the French Revolution, he emigrated to the United States, where his descendants today are prominent in industry.

GIBBON, EDWARD (1737-1794): British historian who wrote the famous *History of the Decline and Fall of the Roman Empire*.

GUICCIARDINI, FRANCESCO (1483-1540): Italian historian and statesman, contemporary with Machiavelli. His masterpiece was his book, *The History of Italy*.

HOBBES, THOMAS (1588-1679): English philosopher of the materialist school. Best known for his book, *Leviathan*.

HUME, DAVID (1711-1776): British philosopher, historian, and political economist. His major philosophical works were *The Treatise of Human Nature, An Inquiry Concerning Human Nature, An Inquiry Concerning the Principles of Morals,* and *Dialogues Concerning Natural Religion*. Like Smith, his close friend, Hume came from Scotland.

HUTTON, JAMES (1726-1797): Scottish geologist whose paper *The-*

309

ory of the Earth is one of the first efforts to establish a scientific basis for geology.

KING, GREGORY (1648-1712): English statistician who did valuable work on population figures.

MANDEVILLE, BERNARD DE (1670?-1733): English thinker and satirist, born in the Netherlands. Famous for his *Fable of the Bees: or, Private Vices, Public Benefits.*

MERCIER DE LA RIVIÈRE, PIERRE-PAUL (1720-1793): French Physiocrat; his most important work was *The Natural and Essential Order of Political Societies.*

MIRABEAU, MARQUIS VICTOR DE (1715-1789): A member of the Physiocratic School, who wrote *Philosophie Rurale.* His son, Compte Honoré Gabriel de Mirabeau (1749-1791), was an important figure in the French Revolution.

MONTESQUIEU, BARON CHARLES SECONDAT DE (1689-1775): French political philosopher and author; especially noted for his satiric *Persian Letters, The Considerations on the Grandeur and Decadence of the Romans,* and *The Spirit of Laws.* The latter work had an enormous influence on all subsequent political speculation.

PETTY, SIR WILLIAM (1623-1687): An early Fellow of the Royal Society who was a pioneer in statistical methods. Wrote a *Treatise on Taxes and Contributions* and was wrongly supposed to have written *Observations on the Bills of Mortality of the City of London.* Important in the development of "political arithmetic."

POCOCKE, RICHARD (1704-1765): English traveler whose book, *A Description of the East,* became celebrated.

QUESNAY, FRANÇOIS (1684-1774): French physician and economist. The founder of the Physiocratic School of economics which had an important influence on Smith. Quesnay's most important work is called *Tableau économique.*

STEIN, BARON HEINRICH FRIEDRICH KARL VOM UND ZUM (1757-1831): German statesman who took over Prussian policy at the time of Napoleon and made extensive reforms in the Prussian state. He was strongly influenced by the *Wealth of Nations.*

A CATALOG OF SELECTED
DOVER BOOKS
IN ALL FIELDS OF INTEREST

A CATALOG OF SELECTED DOVER
BOOKS IN ALL FIELDS OF INTEREST

CONCERNING THE SPIRITUAL IN ART, Wassily Kandinsky. Pioneering work by father of abstract art. Thoughts on color theory, nature of art. Analysis of earlier masters. 12 illustrations. 80pp. of text. 5⅜ x 8½.   23411-8

ANIMALS: 1,419 Copyright-Free Illustrations of Mammals, Birds, Fish, Insects, etc., Jim Harter (ed.). Clear wood engravings present, in extremely lifelike poses, over 1,000 species of animals. One of the most extensive pictorial sourcebooks of its kind. Captions. Index. 284pp. 9 x 12.   23766-4

CELTIC ART: The Methods of Construction, George Bain. Simple geometric techniques for making Celtic interlacements, spirals, Kells-type initials, animals, humans, etc. Over 500 illustrations. 160pp. 9 x 12. (Available in U.S. only.)   22923-8

AN ATLAS OF ANATOMY FOR ARTISTS, Fritz Schider. Most thorough reference work on art anatomy in the world. Hundreds of illustrations, including selections from works by Vesalius, Leonardo, Goya, Ingres, Michelangelo, others. 593 illustrations. 192pp. 7⅛ x 10¼.   20241-0

CELTIC HAND STROKE-BY-STROKE (Irish Half-Uncial from "The Book of Kells"): An Arthur Baker Calligraphy Manual, Arthur Baker. Complete guide to creating each letter of the alphabet in distinctive Celtic manner. Covers hand position, strokes, pens, inks, paper, more. Illustrated. 48pp. 8¼ x 11.   24336-2

EASY ORIGAMI, John Montroll. Charming collection of 32 projects (hat, cup, pelican, piano, swan, many more) specially designed for the novice origami hobbyist. Clearly illustrated easy-to-follow instructions insure that even beginning papercrafters will achieve successful results. 48pp. 8¼ x 11.   27298-2

THE COMPLETE BOOK OF BIRDHOUSE CONSTRUCTION FOR WOODWORKERS, Scott D. Campbell. Detailed instructions, illustrations, tables. Also data on bird habitat and instinct patterns. Bibliography. 3 tables. 63 illustrations in 15 figures. 48pp. 5¼ x 8½.   24407-5

BLOOMINGDALE'S ILLUSTRATED 1886 CATALOG: Fashions, Dry Goods and Housewares, Bloomingdale Brothers. Famed merchants' extremely rare catalog depicting about 1,700 products: clothing, housewares, firearms, dry goods, jewelry, more. Invaluable for dating, identifying vintage items. Also, copyright-free graphics for artists, designers. Co-published with Henry Ford Museum & Greenfield Village. 160pp. 8¼ x 11.   25780-0

HISTORIC COSTUME IN PICTURES, Braun & Schneider. Over 1,450 costumed figures in clearly detailed engravings–from dawn of civilization to end of 19th century. Captions. Many folk costumes. 256pp. 8⅜ x 11¾.   23150-X

LITTLE BOOK OF EARLY AMERICAN CRAFTS AND TRADES, Peter Stockham (ed.). 1807 children's book explains crafts and trades: baker, hatter, cooper, potter, and many others. 23 copperplate illustrations. 140pp. 4⅝ x 6.   23336-7

VICTORIAN FASHIONS AND COSTUMES FROM HARPER'S BAZAR, 1867–1898, Stella Blum (ed.). Day costumes, evening wear, sports clothes, shoes, hats, other accessories in over 1,000 detailed engravings. 320pp. 9⅜ x 12¼. 22990-4

GUSTAV STICKLEY, THE CRAFTSMAN, Mary Ann Smith. Superb study surveys broad scope of Stickley's achievement, especially in architecture. Design philosophy, rise and fall of the Craftsman empire, descriptions and floor plans for many Craftsman houses, more. 86 black-and-white halftones. 31 line illustrations. Introduction 208pp. 6½ x 9¼.   27210-9

THE LONG ISLAND RAIL ROAD IN EARLY PHOTOGRAPHS, Ron Ziel. Over 220 rare photos, informative text document origin (1844) and development of rail service on Long Island. Vintage views of early trains, locomotives, stations, passengers, crews, much more. Captions. 8⅞ x 11¾.   26301-0

VOYAGE OF THE LIBERDADE, Joshua Slocum. Great 19th-century mariner's thrilling, first-hand account of the wreck of his ship off South America, the 35-foot boat he built from the wreckage, and its remarkable voyage home. 128pp. 5⅜ x 8½.
40022-0

TEN BOOKS ON ARCHITECTURE, Vitruvius. The most important book ever written on architecture. Early Roman aesthetics, technology, classical orders, site selection, all other aspects. Morgan translation. 331pp. 5⅜ x 8½.   20645-9

THE HUMAN FIGURE IN MOTION, Eadweard Muybridge. More than 4,500 stopped-action photos, in action series, showing undraped men, women, children jumping, lying down, throwing, sitting, wrestling, carrying, etc. 390pp. 7⅞ x 10⅝.
20204-6 Clothbd.

TREES OF THE EASTERN AND CENTRAL UNITED STATES AND CANADA, William M. Harlow. Best one-volume guide to 140 trees. Full descriptions, woodlore, range, etc. Over 600 illustrations. Handy size. 288pp. 4½ x 6⅜.   20395-6

SONGS OF WESTERN BIRDS, Dr. Donald J. Borror. Complete song and call repertoire of 60 western species, including flycatchers, juncoes, cactus wrens, many more–includes fully illustrated booklet.   Cassette and manual 99913-0

GROWING AND USING HERBS AND SPICES, Milo Miloradovich. Versatile handbook provides all the information needed for cultivation and use of all the herbs and spices available in North America. 4 illustrations. Index. Glossary. 236pp. 5⅜ x 8½.
25058-X

BIG BOOK OF MAZES AND LABYRINTHS, Walter Shepherd. 50 mazes and labyrinths in all–classical, solid, ripple, and more–in one great volume. Perfect inexpensive puzzler for clever youngsters. Full solutions. 112pp. 8⅛ x 11.   22951-3

CATALOG OF DOVER BOOKS

PIANO TUNING, J. Cree Fischer. Clearest, best book for beginner, amateur. Simple repairs, raising dropped notes, tuning by easy method of flattened fifths. No previous skills needed. 4 illustrations. 201pp. 5⅜ x 8½. 23267-0

HINTS TO SINGERS, Lillian Nordica. Selecting the right teacher, developing confidence, overcoming stage fright, and many other important skills receive thoughtful discussion in this indispensible guide, written by a world-famous diva of four decades' experience. 96pp. 5⅜ x 8½. 40094-8

THE COMPLETE NONSENSE OF EDWARD LEAR, Edward Lear. All nonsense limericks, zany alphabets, Owl and Pussycat, songs, nonsense botany, etc., illustrated by Lear. Total of 320pp. 5⅜ x 8½. (Available in U.S. only.) 20167-8

VICTORIAN PARLOUR POETRY: An Annotated Anthology, Michael R. Turner. 117 gems by Longfellow, Tennyson, Browning, many lesser-known poets. "The Village Blacksmith," "Curfew Must Not Ring Tonight," "Only a Baby Small," dozens more, often difficult to find elsewhere. Index of poets, titles, first lines. xxiii + 325pp. 5⅜ x 8¼. 27044-0

DUBLINERS, James Joyce. Fifteen stories offer vivid, tightly focused observations of the lives of Dublin's poorer classes. At least one, "The Dead," is considered a masterpiece. Reprinted complete and unabridged from standard edition. 160pp. 5³⁄₁₆ x 8¼. 26870-5

GREAT WEIRD TALES: 14 Stories by Lovecraft, Blackwood, Machen and Others, S. T. Joshi (ed.). 14 spellbinding tales, including "The Sin Eater," by Fiona McLeod, "The Eye Above the Mantel," by Frank Belknap Long, as well as renowned works by R. H. Barlow, Lord Dunsany, Arthur Machen, W. C. Morrow and eight other masters of the genre. 256pp. 5⅜ x 8½. (Available in U.S. only.) 40436-6

THE BOOK OF THE SACRED MAGIC OF ABRAMELIN THE MAGE, translated by S. MacGregor Mathers. Medieval manuscript of ceremonial magic. Basic document in Aleister Crowley, Golden Dawn groups. 268pp. 5⅜ x 8½. 23211-5

NEW RUSSIAN-ENGLISH AND ENGLISH-RUSSIAN DICTIONARY, M. A. O'Brien. This is a remarkably handy Russian dictionary, containing a surprising amount of information, including over 70,000 entries. 366pp. 4½ x 6⅛. 20208-9

HISTORIC HOMES OF THE AMERICAN PRESIDENTS, Second, Revised Edition, Irvin Haas. A traveler's guide to American Presidential homes, most open to the public, depicting and describing homes occupied by every American President from George Washington to George Bush. With visiting hours, admission charges, travel routes. 175 photographs. Index. 160pp. 8¼ x 11. 26751-2

NEW YORK IN THE FORTIES, Andreas Feininger. 162 brilliant photographs by the well-known photographer, formerly with *Life* magazine. Commuters, shoppers, Times Square at night, much else from city at its peak. Captions by John von Hartz. 181pp. 9¼ x 10¾. 23585-8

INDIAN SIGN LANGUAGE, William Tomkins. Over 525 signs developed by Sioux and other tribes. Written instructions and diagrams. Also 290 pictographs. 111pp. 6⅛ x 9¼. 22029-X

CATALOG OF DOVER BOOKS

THE WIT AND HUMOR OF OSCAR WILDE, Alvin Redman (ed.). More than 1,000 ripostes, paradoxes, wisecracks: Work is the curse of the drinking classes; I can resist everything except temptation; etc. 258pp. 5⅜ x 8½.   20602-5

SHAKESPEARE LEXICON AND QUOTATION DICTIONARY, Alexander Schmidt. Full definitions, locations, shades of meaning in every word in plays and poems. More than 50,000 exact quotations. 1,485pp. 6½ x 9¼. 2-vol. set.
Vol. 1: 22726-X
Vol. 2: 22727-8

SELECTED POEMS, Emily Dickinson. Over 100 best-known, best-loved poems by one of America's foremost poets, reprinted from authoritative early editions. No comparable edition at this price. Index of first lines. 64pp. 5³⁄₁₆ x 8¼.   26466-1

THE INSIDIOUS DR. FU-MANCHU, Sax Rohmer. The first of the popular mystery series introduces a pair of English detectives to their archnemesis, the diabolical Dr. Fu-Manchu. Flavorful atmosphere, fast-paced action, and colorful characters enliven this classic of the genre. 208pp. 5³⁄₁₆ x 8¼.   29898-1

THE MALLEUS MALEFICARUM OF KRAMER AND SPRENGER, translated by Montague Summers. Full text of most important witchhunter's "bible," used by both Catholics and Protestants. 278pp. 6⅝ x 10.   22802-9

SPANISH STORIES/CUENTOS ESPAÑOLES: A Dual-Language Book, Angel Flores (ed.). Unique format offers 13 great stories in Spanish by Cervantes, Borges, others. Faithful English translations on facing pages. 352pp. 5⅜ x 8½.   25399-6

GARDEN CITY, LONG ISLAND, IN EARLY PHOTOGRAPHS, 1869–1919, Mildred H. Smith. Handsome treasury of 118 vintage pictures, accompanied by carefully researched captions, document the Garden City Hotel fire (1899), the Vanderbilt Cup Race (1908), the first airmail flight departing from the Nassau Boulevard Aerodrome (1911), and much more. 96pp. 8⅞ x 11¾.   40669-5

OLD QUEENS, N.Y., IN EARLY PHOTOGRAPHS, Vincent F. Seyfried and William Asadorian. Over 160 rare photographs of Maspeth, Jamaica, Jackson Heights, and other areas. Vintage views of DeWitt Clinton mansion, 1939 World's Fair and more. Captions. 192pp. 8⅞ x 11.   26358-4

CAPTURED BY THE INDIANS: 15 Firsthand Accounts, 1750-1870, Frederick Drimmer. Astounding true historical accounts of grisly torture, bloody conflicts, relentless pursuits, miraculous escapes and more, by people who lived to tell the tale. 384pp. 5⅜ x 8½.   24901-8

THE WORLD'S GREAT SPEECHES (Fourth Enlarged Edition), Lewis Copeland, Lawrence W. Lamm, and Stephen J. McKenna. Nearly 300 speeches provide public speakers with a wealth of updated quotes and inspiration–from Pericles' funeral oration and William Jennings Bryan's "Cross of Gold Speech" to Malcolm X's powerful words on the Black Revolution and Earl of Spenser's tribute to his sister, Diana, Princess of Wales. 944pp. 5⅜ x 8⅜.   40903-1

THE BOOK OF THE SWORD, Sir Richard F. Burton. Great Victorian scholar/adventurer's eloquent, erudite history of the "queen of weapons"–from prehistory to early Roman Empire. Evolution and development of early swords, variations (sabre, broadsword, cutlass, scimitar, etc.), much more. 336pp. 6⅛ x 9¼.
25434-8

CATALOG OF DOVER BOOKS

AUTOBIOGRAPHY: The Story of My Experiments with Truth, Mohandas K. Gandhi. Boyhood, legal studies, purification, the growth of the Satyagraha (nonviolent protest) movement. Critical, inspiring work of the man responsible for the freedom of India. 480pp. 5⅜ x 8½. (Available in U.S. only.) 24593-4

CELTIC MYTHS AND LEGENDS, T. W. Rolleston. Masterful retelling of Irish and Welsh stories and tales. Cuchulain, King Arthur, Deirdre, the Grail, many more. First paperback edition. 58 full-page illustrations. 512pp. 5⅜ x 8½. 26507-2

THE PRINCIPLES OF PSYCHOLOGY, William James. Famous long course complete, unabridged. Stream of thought, time perception, memory, experimental methods; great work decades ahead of its time. 94 figures. 1,391pp. 5⅜ x 8½. 2-vol. set.
Vol. I: 20381-6   Vol. II: 20382-4

THE WORLD AS WILL AND REPRESENTATION, Arthur Schopenhauer. Definitive English translation of Schopenhauer's life work, correcting more than 1,000 errors, omissions in earlier translations. Translated by E. F. J. Payne. Total of 1,269pp. 5⅜ x 8½. 2-vol. set.   Vol. 1: 21761-2   Vol. 2: 21762-0

MAGIC AND MYSTERY IN TIBET, Madame Alexandra David-Neel. Experiences among lamas, magicians, sages, sorcerers, Bonpa wizards. A true psychic discovery. 32 illustrations. 321pp. 5⅜ x 8½. (Available in U.S. only.) 22682-4

THE EGYPTIAN BOOK OF THE DEAD, E. A. Wallis Budge. Complete reproduction of Ani's papyrus, finest ever found. Full hieroglyphic text, interlinear transliteration, word-for-word translation, smooth translation. 533pp. 6½ x 9¼. 21866-X

MATHEMATICS FOR THE NONMATHEMATICIAN, Morris Kline. Detailed, college-level treatment of mathematics in cultural and historical context, with numerous exercises. Recommended Reading Lists. Tables. Numerous figures. 641pp. 5⅜ x 8½. 24823-2

PROBABILISTIC METHODS IN THE THEORY OF STRUCTURES, Isaac Elishakoff. Well-written introduction covers the elements of the theory of probability from two or more random variables, the reliability of such multivariable structures, the theory of random function, Monte Carlo methods of treating problems incapable of exact solution, and more. Examples. 502pp. 5⅜ x 8½. 40691-1

THE RIME OF THE ANCIENT MARINER, Gustave Doré, S. T. Coleridge. Doré's finest work; 34 plates capture moods, subtleties of poem. Flawless full-size reproductions printed on facing pages with authoritative text of poem. "Beautiful. Simply beautiful."–*Publisher's Weekly.* 77pp. 9¼ x 12. 22305-1

NORTH AMERICAN INDIAN DESIGNS FOR ARTISTS AND CRAFTSPEOPLE, Eva Wilson. Over 360 authentic copyright-free designs adapted from Navajo blankets, Hopi pottery, Sioux buffalo hides, more. Geometrics, symbolic figures, plant and animal motifs, etc. 128pp. 8⅜ x 11. (Not for sale in the United Kingdom.) 25341-4

SCULPTURE: Principles and Practice, Louis Slobodkin. Step-by-step approach to clay, plaster, metals, stone; classical and modern. 253 drawings, photos. 255pp. 8⅛ x 11. 22960-2

THE INFLUENCE OF SEA POWER UPON HISTORY, 1660–1783, A. T. Mahan. Influential classic of naval history and tactics still used as text in war colleges. First paperback edition. 4 maps. 24 battle plans. 640pp. 5⅜ x 8½. 25509-3

THE STORY OF THE TITANIC AS TOLD BY ITS SURVIVORS, Jack Winocour (ed.). What it was really like. Panic, despair, shocking inefficiency, and a little heroism. More thrilling than any fictional account. 26 illustrations. 320pp. 5⅜ x 8½. 20610-6

FAIRY AND FOLK TALES OF THE IRISH PEASANTRY, William Butler Yeats (ed.). Treasury of 64 tales from the twilight world of Celtic myth and legend: "The Soul Cages," "The Kildare Pooka," "King O'Toole and his Goose," many more. Introduction and Notes by W. B. Yeats. 352pp. 5⅜ x 8½. 26941-8

BUDDHIST MAHAYANA TEXTS, E. B. Cowell and others (eds.). Superb, accurate translations of basic documents in Mahayana Buddhism, highly important in history of religions. The Buddha-karita of Asvaghosha, Larger Sukhavativyuha, more. 448pp. 5⅜ x 8½. 25552-2

ONE TWO THREE . . . INFINITY: Facts and Speculations of Science, George Gamow. Great physicist's fascinating, readable overview of contemporary science: number theory, relativity, fourth dimension, entropy, genes, atomic structure, much more. 128 illustrations. Index. 352pp. 5⅜ x 8½. 25664-2

EXPERIMENTATION AND MEASUREMENT, W. J. Youden. Introductory manual explains laws of measurement in simple terms and offers tips for achieving accuracy and minimizing errors. Mathematics of measurement, use of instruments, experimenting with machines. 1994 edition. Foreword. Preface. Introduction. Epilogue. Selected Readings. Glossary. Index. Tables and figures. 128pp. 5⅜ x 8½. 40451-X

DALÍ ON MODERN ART: The Cuckolds of Antiquated Modern Art, Salvador Dalí. Influential painter skewers modern art and its practitioners. Outrageous evaluations of Picasso, Cézanne, Turner, more. 15 renderings of paintings discussed. 44 calligraphic decorations by Dalí. 96pp. 5⅜ x 8½. (Available in U.S. only.) 29220-7

ANTIQUE PLAYING CARDS: A Pictorial History, Henry René D'Allemagne. Over 900 elaborate, decorative images from rare playing cards (14th–20th centuries): Bacchus, death, dancing dogs, hunting scenes, royal coats of arms, players cheating, much more. 96pp. 9¼ x 12¼. 29265-7

MAKING FURNITURE MASTERPIECES: 30 Projects with Measured Drawings, Franklin H. Gottshall. Step-by-step instructions, illustrations for constructing handsome, useful pieces, among them a Sheraton desk, Chippendale chair, Spanish desk, Queen Anne table and a William and Mary dressing mirror. 224pp. 8⅛ x 11¼. 29338-6

THE FOSSIL BOOK: A Record of Prehistoric Life, Patricia V. Rich et al. Profusely illustrated definitive guide covers everything from single-celled organisms and dinosaurs to birds and mammals and the interplay between climate and man. Over 1,500 illustrations. 760pp. 7½ x 10⅛. 29371-8

Paperbound unless otherwise indicated. Available at your book dealer, online at **www.doverpublications.com**, or by writing to Dept. GI, Dover Publications, Inc., 31 East 2nd Street, Mineola, NY 11501. For current price information or for free catalogues (please indicate field of interest), write to Dover Publications or log on to **www.doverpublications.com** and see every Dover book in print. Dover publishes more than 500 books each year on science, elementary and advanced mathematics, biology, music, art, literary history, social sciences, and other areas.